Dance Music

A Feminist Account of an Ordinary Culture

Tami Gadir

BLOOMSBURY ACADEMIC
NEW YORK • LONDON • OXFORD • NEW DELHI • SYDNEY

BLOOMSBURY ACADEMIC
Bloomsbury Publishing Inc
1385 Broadway, New York, NY 10018, USA
50 Bedford Square, London, WC1B 3DP, UK
29 Earlsfort Terrace, Dublin 2, Ireland

BLOOMSBURY, BLOOMSBURY ACADEMIC and the Diana logo are
trademarks of Bloomsbury Publishing Plc

First published in the United States of America 2023

A catalog record for this book is available from the Library of Congress.

ISBN: HB: 978-1-5013-4641-5
          PB: 978-1-5013-4640-8
          ePDF: 978-1-5013-4643-9
          eBook: 978-1-5013-4642-2

Typeset by Integra Software Services Pvt. Ltd.

To find out more about our authors and books visit www.bloomsbury.com
and sign up for our newsletters.

Contents

Preface

I started the research for this book out of a love for dance music and DJ culture. After a life at the piano, genres like techno and house taught me release, escape, fun. And I was far from alone. In trying to make sense of my fondness, in wondering how this music and its culture achieved their effects, I discovered books and articles by others who were similarly gripped.

Coincidentally, this was also around the moment when the journal *Dancecult* was launched. The timing of those early issues exposed me to a community of researchers who were also gathering around a sense of intrigue with dance music. Like the decades of distributed studies that preceded the concentrated effort of *Dancecult*, much of what I encountered in the journal expressed a particular message. The sonic, kinetic, and collective dimensions of dance music were said to be exceptional in the ways they offered euphoric experiences and articulated progressive politics. Dance music was liberation.

But there was a problem. Outside my own initial experience, and beyond what I had read in dance music scholarship and journalism, I did not know many people who spoke about euphoria and progress on the dance floor. The people I knew were more likely to be uneasy about going to club nights, festivals, and free parties. The social dynamics deterred them. Most reservations were expressed by women.

The unease of these women was put into sharp relief when I started working as a DJ and conducting fieldwork. Venue staff repeatedly assumed I was someone's girlfriend, rather than a peer of the other DJs with whom I shared a club night residency. Clubbers (always men) would regard my technique and tell me I was pretty good—for a girl. Sometimes, I went to nightclubs alone to conduct fieldwork. Once, on the way to a small venue in Berlin, I was attacked,

restrained, assaulted, and robbed by two strangers. Disbelieving locals told me nothing like this ever happened there, that I was just unlucky. Others told me it must have been because I looked like a tourist. (You mustn't look like a tourist.)

As my research developed, men continued to harass me in venues, on dance floors, and on my way home from clubs—regardless of where I was in the world. But something else happened, too. As a clubber, DJ, and occasional event organizer who did everything from booking and promotion to taking cash and stamping wrists, I absorbed the regularities of distinction that define this and many other musical worlds. I developed prejudices about how people dressed, talked, and behaved. I could tell immediately which people would "ruin a vibe," who would "cause trouble," how a gathering of women for a bachelorette party or hen night would "miss the point." In short, I was part of the problem that I was learning to identify. I inhabited the fundamental tension at the heart of dance music culture—and at the core of this book.

In my interviews with people from most of the world's continents, and in ways consonant with dance music scholarship, there was a broad consensus about the euphoric and progressive potential of dance music culture. This was often expressed in terms of liberatory goals, capacities, and imaginaries. At the same time, for women and gender diverse interviewees especially, there were ways that dance music fell short of its ideals. These shortfalls ranged from relatively minor aggressions of distinction to more overt forms of exclusion, discrimination, and wrongdoing.

For example, in Edinburgh and Oslo, the two cities where I lived while researching this book, overt gender and sexuality nonconformity was rare to see, except for the few dedicated LGBTQI+ clubs. For years, I witnessed bouncers and promoters performing ethnic and age profiling at nightclub doors. I hardly ever saw people in wheelchairs or with mobility needs at such events, as venues typically had poor accessibility. For someone who treasured the social and musical life of clubs, these realities were dispiriting. I knew—from reading the literature and from various stories that some interviewees, mostly men, told me—that in clubs people not only gathered around a common love of music and dance, they also found spaces of inclusion, safety, and escape from the everyday. Nevertheless, it was also clear that the music did

not work as its ideology intended. All clubbers may have been equal. But some were more equal—more liberated—than others.

It is easy enough to come across accounts of extraordinary music and dance floors, such as New York, Detroit, Chicago, Berlin, London, Goa, and more. This book emerges from my love of scenes like those—dance music experiences that continue to influence dance music culture everywhere. The book equally is a product of research that took me by surprise, that showed me dance music must be understood in terms of euphoria and promise as well as disappointment and trauma. It reminded me that whatever extraordinary possibilities of liberation might exist in dance music will be formed in the realities of ordinary struggle.

So this book is written for my interviewees: from the DJs and fans of techno in Europe, to the psytrance parties in the forests of Taiwan and clubs in Argentina, to those who play for a living at Top 40 nightclubs, student union bars, cocktail bars, weddings, company Christmas parties, sports events, and fashion shows the world over. The people in these categories do not normally feature in dance music's liberatory literature, because the places and events they frequent are seen as unremarkable. But they, too, are part of dance music culture.

The book is also written for people whose maltreatment has damaged their love of the music. It is written for those from across classes, colors, and creeds who attend ordinary venues, in ordinary cities, with just one common purpose:

To let go, and have a good dance.

Introduction

Dance music is ordinary: that is where we must begin.[1] It is true that for some people, at some times, in some places, on some drugs, dance music can be a gateway to transformative, even transcendent experiences. With the help of skilled DJs delivering forceful sounds that range the audible frequency spectrum, using electronic instruments and playback equipment, dancers can reach euphoric trance states, discard their egos, and feel social barriers dissolve. Dance floors can be sites of openness, subversion, and even small-scale acts of political resistance. At a minimum, dance music lightens the burden of contemporary life. At its best, dance music offers glimpses of better worlds. Yet even where a dance music community is built on an explicit, symbolic resistance to a parent culture, has formed in a way that appears culturally self-contained, or provides an escape from mainstream life, it does not constitute a substantive politics of emancipation.

Dance music is not just a culture, but an industry, and not only a singular industry, but a set of industries—just as dance music culture is an amalgam of many cultures all over the world that have something in common. As an industry, dance music is concerned with its economic capacities as much as with the ideological or symbolic concerns of workers or participants, who, in industry

---

[1] I appropriate this concept and phrasing: see Raymond Williams, "Culture Is Ordinary [1958]," in *The Everyday Life Reader*, ed. Ben Highmore (London: Routledge, 2002), 92. The idea has also been discussed in other ways with reference to music; see, for example, Simon Frith, "The Popular Music Industry," in *The Cambridge Companion to Pop and Rock*, ed. Simon Frith, Will Straw, and John Street (Cambridge: Cambridge University Press, 2001), 26–7; Anahid Kassabian, *Ubiquitous Listening: Affect, Attention, and Distributed Subjectivity* (Berkeley: University of California Press, 2013); Tia DeNora, *Music in Everyday Life* (Cambridge: Cambridge University Press, 2000).

terms, are individual consumers of goods and services. This necessarily means a world with exploitative work practices and asymmetrical power relations that occur at all stages of the dance music event, from screening by security or door staff to precarious nocturnal journeys home. The exploitative work practices are bolstered materially by people's needs to survive a financially punishing system and reinforced culturally by the belief in meritocracy and competition.[2] Asymmetrical power relations are an enactment of the social prejudices and oppressions of the rest of society. One of the ways this plays out most visibly in dance music is through gender. For example, some DJs, especially men, accuse other DJs, especially women, of lacking musical and technological skill. Some clubbers, usually men, grope other clubbers on dance floors, usually women, without their consent. Managers, usually men, tell DJs, especially women, what to wear while they are DJing and how they should photograph themselves for promotion. Clubbers, especially women, cannot easily travel safely to and from venues. The above observations constitute the key case studies of this book as they come from first-hand encounters I had with them during research.[3] There are, clearly, parallels with the world off the dance floor.[4]

Methods and Background

This book is based on two related but distinct periods of research, each approximately four years in length. The first was motivated by the question of what makes people dance and included participant observation and interviews together with some musical analysis. It took place mostly in the

---

[2]Angela McRobbie, *Be Creative: Making a Living in the New Culture Industries* (Cambridge: Polity Press, 2016); Sally Anne Gross and George Musgrave, *Can Music Make You Sick? Measuring the Price of Musical Ambition* (London: University of Westminster Press, 2020); Tami Gadir, "Forty-Seven DJs, Four Women: Meritocracy, Talent and Postfeminist Politics," *Dancecult* 9, no. 1 (November, 2017): 50–72.

[3]This book does not deal with the underpaid and dangerous labor of making and assembling electronics which enables anyone who makes music with computers to do their work; see, for example, Lucie Vágnerová, "Nimble Fingers in Electronic Music: Rethinking Sound Through Neo-Colonial Labour," *Organised Sound* 22, no. 2 (July 2017): 250–8. This would require additional research.

[4]While not every detail of dance music culture in this book is about gender, feminism, especially anticapitalist feminism, is the broad framework with which all the social issues that are raised about dance music are connected.

UK in the years 2010–13. The majority of fieldwork during that period was conducted in Edinburgh, with the remainder in Glasgow, London, Tel Aviv, Zurich, and Sydney. The second period of research was from 2015 to 2018. It was primarily interview-based and was focused on gender issues in dance music culture. Specifically, the goal was to examine how gender prejudices affect women, gender nonbinary, and transgender DJs from all over the world. The number of interviews from those two periods together amounted to around eighty, while the countries that they came from included Argentina, Australia, Belgium, Brazil, Canada, Germany, Iceland, India, Israel-Palestine, Japan, the Netherlands, Norway, South Africa, Sweden, Switzerland, Taiwan, Thailand, the United Arab Emirates, the UK, and the United States. While some interviewees are quoted directly, all collectively helped to shape the understanding of dance music culture that makes up this book.[5]

Most interviewees who feature in this book talk about clubbing, DJing, or producing as a central component of their lives. Dance music comprises one of many cultural activities that some people do in their leisure time, others do as a job (some very successfully), and still others participate in as unpaid or low-paid creative labor.[6] Club, rave, and festival DJs view DJing as an essential aspect of their identity, regardless of whether they make a living from the activity. For all interviewees, social connection and music are the most important. Genre or scene loyalty matters too. For a smaller number of interviewees, politics are central to their participation. And for an even smaller number, mystical, transformative, or transcendent experiences are their means of engagement with their favorite genre and the community that surrounds it. Those who identify the spiritual dimensions of dance music are often the same people who participate in ways that extend beyond clubbing or dancing alone: whether as DJs who make a partial or whole living from gigs, as event organizers, or through their personal relationships to DJs and event organizers.

---

[5] All names of venues and interviewees and other identifying information from primary research in this book are pseudonyms, with the exception of those who expressly asked for their real names to be included.

[6] Rosa Reitsamer, "The DIY Careers of Techno and Drum 'n' Bass DJs in Vienna," *Dancecult* 3, no. 1 (June, 2011): 36–9; see also Gross and Musgrave, *Can Music Make You Sick*, 44–6; McRobbie, *Be Creative*, 43–6.

The cultural histories of dance music tend to center around certain dance floors, focus on specific technologies, and take place within broader histories of electronic music spanning the avant-garde and the popular. The overview of such histories provided in Chapter One may therefore be familiar to both readers who have read any dance music writing before, and to fans of some of dance music's key people, places, and things. While connecting these stories, the chapter also teases out dance music settings that show the direct line from subculture (in the Global North and West) to capital and exploitation (in the Global South and East). For example, "checking out" of modern life in the West through participation in subcultural activities in "exotic" locations exposes the contradictions that are more subtly present within the very idea that dance music culture is an alternative haven. The overarching purpose of this account is a historiographic critique of a particular consensus paradigm and ritual of agreement that defines dance music scholarship and writing.

The same rituals of agreement can be found in expressions of fandom within dance music cultures themselves. Some people see themselves as part of something holistic that includes aesthetics, politics, and ways of life, such as in the genre of psytrance. Drum 'n' bass, house, and techno, to name a few other genres, also have their passionate fans, even if the scenes attached to these genres do not share the same degree of visible "alternative" sensibilities and aesthetics. The energies of these fans may be focused on dance music events and music listening rather than encompassing a total lifestyle. Across genres, it is often necessary to accept that working in insurance, banking, or civil service is not an incursion on fandom and scene loyalty. This is as true for DJs and producers as it is for clubbers. Without a large financial buffer or backup, it is rare that DJ and production work can comprise the equivalent of a living wage. There is an entirely different category of DJs who make most of their income from other kinds of events, such as corporate parties. One interviewee's most regular gig was to play music for a local roller derby event. Another made a substantial proportion of her income from fashion shows and corporate brand events, though she also played at nightclubs and bars. Such DJs are less likely to be invested in the idea of a particular kind of music or scene, seeing themselves as specialist technical workers whose job is to keep people entertained. Dance music studies—as this book will henceforth

refer to the amalgam of scholarship that examines dance music—tends not to include these DJs in the world of dance music culture. Instead, and as Chapter Two will show, the focus of this work is on the kinds of communities that behave more like subcultures, and whose music receives neither radio play nor algorithmic boosts on YouTube. Dance music studies tends to argue that some dance music cultures meet this goal more effectively than others because of factors such as spatial surroundings, preferred drugs, cultural geography, or musical aesthetics.[7] In this sense, dance music studies shares the genre and scene allegiances of fans.

Genre and scene allegiances vary not only by music but in large part by location. Several of the factors that shape the local character of a musical community include the physical and cultural geographic attributes of a locality, the way it is governed (including how strictly its laws are administered), its population density, its history, and its economy. Chapter Three addresses these factors because they are common preoccupations of dance music fans and they frame how dance music cultures are understood. It is logical, given that one of the core elements of clubbing is a regular co-presence with other clubbers on physical dance floors, that fans should be concerned with the ways that their dance music communities relate to their local communities more generally. Many of the local variations also affect people's experiences of safety and danger, which are central concerns of many participants, given that dance music culture is a mostly nocturnal culture. Those who are as attracted to the social aspects of dance music as they are the sonic tend to be willing to pursue such pleasures despite some of the dangers that participation can involve in their local settings. As Chapter Three shows, dangers can result from harsh government policies on nightlife, policing, and surveillance, which, paradoxically, are promoted as the very means to protect people from danger. Dangers also arise from commonplace social prejudices such as sexism, homophobia, and transphobia. In addition, nightlife becomes more dangerous for the poorest and most marginalized people in society, due to such material pressures as gentrification.

---

[7]Graham St. John, "Liminal Being: Electronic Dance Music Cultures, Ritualization and the Case of Psytrance," in *The Sage Handbook of Popular Music*, ed. Andy Bennett and Steve Waksman (London: Sage, 2015), 252–3, 256; Melville, *It's a London Thing*, 157.

Wealth, political influence, and the powers of the state are all used to actively suppress the social and cultural nocturnal life of a city, making it ultimately less safe to pursue the pleasures of activities such as dance music.

It is precisely these pleasures of dance music that people will go to the greatest lengths to pursue. At their heights, such pleasures can manifest as transcendent experiences, the theme of Chapter Four. Transcendent experiences are the results of the affective stimuli typically encountered at dance music events, such as the sensation of bodily movement to loud, bass sounds, on drugs. Some participants who describe how sounds work in this way make connections between their own experiences and the notion of a collective, higher consciousness. This, in turn, is reflected in the consensus paradigm of dance music studies: that certain dance floors in certain places fulfill subversive social and political functions. The implication is that the right kinds of dance floors constitute radical political happenings and that people on dance floors who have such experiences can collectively transcend "outside world" social divisions such as race, or material divisions such as class.[8] Together, resistance to authority and rules through occupation of unlicensed spaces (in particular, those places that become incorporated into the dance music geography mythology), use of empathy-inducing illicit drugs, and subversion of the accepted rhythms of work, leisure, and sleep are taken as radical acts of resistance. Accounts that sound like this within dance music studies, popular writing, and other kinds of media enter the consciousness of fans and DJs, who pass them around verbally and take them on as their own. Yet, as this chapter shows, there are some bleak realities that disrupt, undermine, or prevent transcendent experiences for those who want them. Finally, the relationship of the transcendent experience to the wider politics of dance music has a historic relationship with parts of the 1960s counterculture, which Chapter Four will also address.

---

[8]Melville, *It's a London Thing*, 7, 102, 180, 230–41. Melville's evaluation of the "post-racial communalism" in London dance music cultures is ambivalent, especially in light of capital's degradation of the lives of anyone in the city who is not wealthy. Yet despite a quite dystopian description of contemporary life in London since the early 2000s, Melville never abandons his faith in the scene's expression of "alternative ideas about how to build a good society and [its capacity to] unleash new spatial imaginaries" and ultimately pins his hopes on the proliferation of new "hybrid" genres that continue to be simultaneously uniquely black *and* multicultural in their expression.

A common way that some of the aforementioned realities stand in the way of transcendent experiences is through gender prejudice and discrimination. This issue, while threaded all the way through the book as part of the critique of dance music utopianism, is brought into focus in Chapters Five and Six. Chapter Five analyzes many examples of DJs and clubbers whose participation is hindered by the attitudes that people have toward gender in relation to sounds, electronic music technologies, dance, and appearance. Class prejudices overlap with gender prejudices and often work together to undermine participants' subcultural credibility.[9] All of this can be understood in the context of the dramatic shifts in mainstream discourse that took place during the research on gender, for which Chapter Six provides a zoomed in, geographically specific case study. The case study, which takes the form of a gender-related media controversy in a dance music community in Oslo, illustrates how such shifts in mainstream discourse can themselves take on a social life that includes a re-establishment of reactionary ideas. In this instance, the pushback about gender takes place through the employment of the neoliberal concepts of merit and talent. Such ideas are examples of the limitless malleability of capitalist doctrine, which are transplanted onto idealizations of artistic quality through fair competition, and which privilege the individual realization of postfeminist empowerment. As this chapter argues, the effects of these ideologies are ultimately to rationalize the status quo and quash the struggle for equality.

Overall, this book is informed by an anticapitalist and feminist political lens through which observations and conversations took place.[10] Through that

---

[9]See Sarah Thornton, *Club Cultures: Music, Media and Subcultural Capital* (Cambridge: Polity Press, 1995).

[10]Given the total lifespan of the research, the speed at which social conditions change, and the fact that at the time of writing this book I no longer live in either of the cities where I undertook most of the research, there is an unavoidable way in which this book is already about dance music cultures of the past, and thus out of date at the time of its completion. I am unqualified to account for any significant shifts in the circumstances of either city or its dance music nightlife. This is especially true for Edinburgh, where the research began thirteen years ago. Regardless, I maintain a present tense when describing fieldwork and excerpting interviews with few exceptions, as the data were contemporary at the time that I documented them. One of the bigger changes that have taken place concerns how society and culture treats gender issues, and in turn, how dance music culture treats gender issues. The changes, by and large, are positive. Nevertheless, awareness does not immediately transform into widespread and long-term change, so many of the issues that I documented are still relevant today, and are likely to be for some time.

lens, it is possible to see the ways that participants and organizers can, and sometimes do, harness dance music sounds, spaces, and technologies to protest and act in response to social and political injustices. But it is only by confronting the decidedly ordinary realities of many dance floors, understanding the envelopment of dance music cultures in global capitalism—and by extension the social inequalities that dance music reproduces—and acknowledging that even exceptional spaces can be host to ordinary problems, that it may become possible to make space for something better.

1

Dance Music Histories

Dance music, as it is used here, refers to electronically produced music normally with a repetitive, looping form in a regular four-four or duple meter, played loudly by DJs at social events dedicated mostly to dancing, which take place usually at night. Drinking and taking drugs are also a common practice. As the name "dance music" suggests, dancing is the main point, but many people listen to dance music at home as part of their eclectic, genre-diverse music collections. It forms the auditory atmosphere at bars, restaurants, and hotel lobbies, and is a frequent choice for a wide range of advertising. For as long as recorded music has been a mass-consumer market, people have been listening to dance tunes at home, including to get into the mood before they go out and when they come home.[1] The venues that host dance music events include nightclubs, bars, sports stadiums, beaches, forests, fields, farms, mountains, deserts, squat houses, corporate venues, private homes, and abandoned buildings such as former warehouses, factories, or castles. Dance music at night clubs takes place at night in cities around the world, though there are some cities where clubs are open and active around the clock. Festivals operate with a schedule more affected by local government licensing rules and noise regulation, as they tend to be outdoors or at large venues that are neither sound-proofed nor

---

[1]See James Nott, "Getting Together to 'Get Down:' Social Dancing from Dance Hall to Rave," in *Musicking in Twentieth-Century Europe: A Handbook*, ed. Klaus Nathaus and Martin Rempe (Oldenburgh: De Gruyter, 2020), 263.

dedicated exclusively to music. For example, daytime festivals are common in cities or towns where licensing does not permit them to run late because of the proximity of residents or laws that exclude loud music as part of their definitions of public order. Contrastingly, illicit or unlicensed events can, by their nature, take place at any time of the day or night. Their schedule depends on factors such as where they are, who organizes them, and their tactics for evading law enforcement.

Clubbers, DJs, producers, and people who organize parties have a shared language and set of experiences that make them part of a global web of electronic dance music culture. Electronic dance music parties of various genres take place all over the world across cultures, languages, and nations that differ enormously. In addition, dance music fans everywhere tend to be fans in conspicuously similar ways. Such similarities include the informal way that people normally learn how to DJ or ask someone to show them how, the attachment to particular technologies, the common experience of women and gender diverse DJs around the world of discrimination and harassment, and the passionate, sometimes obsessive allegiance to a genre or scene, as described in the introduction.

The stories compiled in this chapter and the next come from writers who have had access to key figures, been to key places and venues, or done extensive archival, oral, and cultural historical research. If the accounts of places, figures, technologies, and cultures appear nonlinear, even messy, it is because they are. There are several strands of dance music cultural history to trace, and each has its own routes with key figures, places, and people, depending on the combination of technologies, geographies, social dance practices, venues, and cultures one wishes to follow. Many of the books cited here have become absorbed into a core, informal canon of global electronic dance music history that many participants have either read or tacitly learned from media or other fans. Some have even been included in university reading lists. While all such histories tend to focus on culture and "happenings" on dance floors themselves, a few are more concerned with formal musical elements or technologies. That is the broad division used in what follows.

DJ Dance Floors

The phenomenon of social dancing may be as old as human culture itself and the kinds of dance that take place in dedicated dancing spaces, normally as part of nocturnal social activities, are also older than what is covered here.[2] What the dance music cultures in this book do share, however, is a recognizable set of social, cultural, technological, and musical characteristics that result from a hybrid of dance cultures ranging from Jamaica in the 1960s to New York in the 1970s, Chicago and Detroit in the 1980s to the UK, Berlin, Belgium, the Netherlands, South Africa, Goa, Australia, and others, from the 1990s. Most cultural histories tell us that in the globalized, US-American and Anglo-European popular music worlds, bands and musicians started to produce dance music and pop music electronically in the 1970s and 1980s. There are several overlaps with people, styles, techniques, and technologies from hip hop culture, which emerged from the Bronx in the 1970s, but such histories tend to highlight hip hop's distinct musical, cultural, and technical characteristics, such as the practices of turntablism and DJ battles, neither of which features as prominently in the kinds of dance music culture addressed here.[3]

Dance music culture histories tend to foreground the emergence of LGBTQI+ (henceforth referred to in the shorthand, "queer"), Black, and Latino voices out of urban, diverse hubs such as New York City from a white, heterosexual mainstream.[4] Against this backdrop, dance clubs in early-1970s New York City were spaces of entertainment and cultural and physical refuges

---

[2]For example, Julie Malnig, ed. *Ballroom, Boogie, Shimmy Sham, Shake: A Social and Popular Dance Reader* (Chicago: University of Illinois Press, 2009); and James Nott, *Going to the Palais: A Social and Cultural History of Dancing and Dance Halls in Britain, 1918–1960* (Oxford: Oxford University Press, 2015).

[3]Mark Katz, *Capturing Sound: How Technology Has Changed Music* (Berkeley: University of California Press, 2010), 116–20; Tricia Rose, *Black Noise: Rap Music and Black Culture in Contemporary America* (Hanover, NH: Wesleyan University Press, 1994).

[4]Bill Brewster and Frank Broughton, *Last Night a DJ Saved My Life: The History of the Disc Jockey* (London: Headline, 2006), 136–7; Kai Fikentscher, *You Better Work! A Study of Underground Dance Music in New York City* (Hanover: Wesleyan University Press, 2000); Simon Reynolds, *Energy Flash: A Journey Through Dance Music and Rave Culture* (London: Picador, 2008), 14–24; Dan Sicko, *Techno Rebels: The Renegades of Electronic Funk* (New York: Billboard, 1999).

for queer people. Rather than any one musical style, DJs played a mix of genres. It was the venues and events rather than the sounds that were the starting point for what later became known as disco. Other spaces where DJ-oriented dance floors developed and influenced the rest of the world included Chicago (house) and Detroit (techno). Like hip hop, both were black dance music cultures led by the music of black DJs and producers who influenced each other. Jeremiah McAllister, a keyboard player and producer, refers to disco as a trend of "Africanization" that began with an addition of rhythms such as the bossa nova in the 1960s.[5] Frankie Knuckles had started out playing regularly with Larry Levan at the club, Continental Baths, in New York, in 1971. The Baths are described by Tim Lawrence as "America's first gay male discotheque," and by Brewster and Broughton as an "opulent gay bath-house with steam rooms, swimming pool, private apartments, restaurant and disco." Frankie Knuckles later moved to Chicago and became most well-known in association with the Warehouse, the venue after which the genre "house" is named, taking with him the mixing techniques that were used on New York dance floors.[6] At some point, music communities in Europe (and those influenced by them) started to embrace house from Chicago, techno from Detroit, and various alternative rave cultures in the United States, including in states that are less documented in the literature, such as Ohio, Indiana, and Minnesota.[7]

After DJ-driven dance music culture became more established across Europe, people in other countries also embraced it. Psychedelic trance, or psytrance, emerged from communities of hippies, mostly westerners, living in

---

[5]Jeremiah McAllister, interview by Jason Myles, Pascal Robert, and Marcus of the Left Flank Vets, *This Is Revolution Podcast*, March 31, 2022, https://youtu.be/HGWSYIzyjTM?t=1539. Interviewer Pascal Robert's interpretation of this analysis relates to his overall critiques of the "fifty-year counterrevolution," that began in the 1960s and de-radicalized black politics: "disco is a product of the cultural nationalist turn in Black politics starting in the late sixties."

[6]Brewster and Broughton, *Last Night a DJ Saved My Life*, 165–7, 312–18. For a detailed account of the history of the Continental Baths, including its troubled interactions with the city and oppressive policing, see Tim Lawrence, *Love Saves the Day: A History of American Dance Music Culture, 1970–70* (Durham and London: Duke University Press, 2003), 42–7.

[7]The Blessed Madonna (DJ and producer), in discussion with the author, February 2015; Shayna (DJ and producer), in discussion with the author, April 2015; Dani (DJ and producer), in discussion with the author, October 2016.

Goa since the 1970s. A cult DJ figure, Goa Gil, would play a mix of music at beach parties for "an outlandish collection of hippies, punks, junkies, globe-trotters, artists, Rastafarians, and 'Osho people' (devotees of the infamous Rajneesh in Poona …)."[8] This influenced the music and practices of people who spent time there as tourists and returned home, who then continued to listen to it and make their own versions in countries such as Israel, Australia, the UK, the United States, Germany, the Netherlands, and Japan.[9] Psytrance cultures were exported to Europe and European-adjacent nations, as well as to tourist party scenes across Asia, especially South-East Asia. The latter geographical region had burgeoning party cultures that catered primarily to young travelers from the West. One such location is the island and tourist haven Kho Phangan in Thailand. Westerners in Thailand, like those in Goa, adopt hippy-like lifestyles as a "rite of passage." However, in the words of Arun Saldanha, "a passage to where? … their intention seems … nihilistic, to remain 'in passage' for as long as possible."[10] Like Goa, DJs in Ko Phangan started out by playing music that is already in circulation in the "global" music cultures of Europe, but unlike Goa, it remained that way. As an event with overtly commercial interests, the Thai tourist party culture followed in the footsteps of western dance music culture trends, rather than being particularly concerned with newness or difference. The now infamous Full Moon Party takes place on Haad Rin, a beach that only thirty years ago had no road access or electricity. By the 2010s, the event had become one of the centers of gravity for an enormous international tourist industry—an industry rife with tensions between commercial interests, the devastating environmental effects of unfettered consumption and waste on the

---

[8]Arun Saldanha, *Psychedelic White: Goa Trance and the Viscosity of Race* (Minneapolis: University of Minnesota Press, 2007), 37–8. The Rajneesh followers to which Saldanha refers include two of my interviewees, Gordon and Danielle, who came of age during the hippy period and attributed their ability to appreciate the trance-like state they could reach with techno to the experiences meditating with thousands of others through physical movement at Rajneesh events.
[9]Hillegonda Rietveld, "Infinite Noise Spirals: The Musical Cosmopolitanism of Psytrance," in *The Local Scenes and Global Cultures of Psytrance*, ed. Graham St. John (New York: Routledge, 2010), 69–88; Joshua I. Schmidt, "(En)Countering the Beat: Paradox in Israeli Psytrance," in *The Local Scenes and Global Cultures of Psytrance*, ed. Graham St. John (New York: Routledge, 2010), 131–48; Graham St. John, *Global Tribe: Technology, Spirituality and Psytrance* (Sheffield: Equinox, 2012), 233–63.
[10]Arun Saldanha, "The Ghost of Goa Trance: A Retrospective," in *The Local Scenes and Global Cultures of Psytrance*, ed. Graham St. John (New York: Routledge, 2010), 59.

region, and heavy-handed government policies to attempt to control some of the social fallout.[11]

DJ-focused histories also focus on venues, so it is common to see names of well-known clubs or spaces recur across them, such as the Warehouse in Chicago, the Hacienda in Manchester, the Paradise Garage or the Loft in New York, and others. Such an interest in venues is due in part to the long-term association that DJs form with them. By way of a current and proximate example, a DJ in Melbourne, "Cory"—also a booking agent—has been a resident DJ at the same venue for a weekly club night for twelve years. One of Cory's colleagues has played at the club every week since 1997. Cory refers to him as "part of the furniture." DJ and dance floor histories focus on venues among other aspects of space and place because of their critical role in the cultural geography of dance music communities and the formation of microcultures that form around their spatial, physical, and cultural qualities.

Technologies

Music technologies play a central role in dance music sound and culture, including on the dance floor histories accounted above. For instance, there are various figures who claim to be the first to beat match or beat mix two or more records for dance floors.[12] Such stories vary in turn from those that come out of hip hop, which are about the first people to scratch, backspin, and loop.[13] In club cultural histories, Terry Noel, a DJ from Brooklyn, describes methods that

---

[11]Klaus Westerhausen, *Beyond the Beach: An Ethnography of Modern Travellers in Asia* (Bangkok: White Lotus Press, 2002); "The History of the Full Moon Party with Manop," Phanganist, November 30, 2017, https://phanganist.com/somewhere-phangan-full-moon-party-culture-article/history-full-moon-party-manop; "Full Moon Party Ko Phangan," Phanganist, 2018, last updated 2022, https://phanganist.com/full-moon-party-koh-phangan; Kyle Hulme, "How Thailand's Full Moon Parties Became an International Phenomenon," Culture Trip, March 19, 2019, https://theculturetrip.com/asia/thailand/articles/how-thailands-full-moon-party-went-from-small-gathering-to-international-phenomenon/; "The Original Full Moon Party, Thailand," Full Moon Party, last updated 2021, https://fullmoonparty-thailand.com/.

[12]Beat matching is a technique that merges and synchronizes the kick drum down beats of an incoming track with those of an outgoing track, to create an unbroken flow of music for dancing. In most electronic dance music played today, beat matching involves the maintenance of a uniform, or nearly uniform tempo. More detail on such techniques, along with others, can be found in Butler, *Unlocking the Groove*, 53–5, 242.

[13]Katz, *Capturing Sound*, 116.

he used in the 1960s that suggests he was doing this before the 1970s DJs in New York started to incorporate it.[14] In addition, Francis Grasso, one such DJ, is frequently credited with the first use of beat matching as a means to maintain continuous, all-night dancing in a way that "completely changed the relationship between the DJ and [their] audience."[15] Many of the analog, electronic instruments used in early dance music production had been initially designed to stand in for people playing instruments, to which there was understandable resistance from the unions that represented them. However, when it came to dance music, the DIY affordances of such instruments led to their creative use in new places.[16] In one sense, the uptake of these electronic instruments was economic. While the initial costs of purchasing such instruments was high, it took one person to make the music electronically, using instruments such as the Roland TR-808 drum machine, while a band took several capable people to play. Yet even this narrative requires its qualifications. McAllister points out in an interview that the affordability of such instruments was a relative concept:

> I think that it was not cheap. You know, it's a funny thing, I remember the 808 and I remember … my brother got my mother to buy him an 808, and I remember that it cost, like, about 800 [USD], and I remember that, because it was, like, the 808, and it was 800, you know. But … probably for a lot of black folks … you could not afford that at the time. You know, I mean, my mother had a pretty good job, you know … we were pretty much in the middle … lower-middle class, so we had a little extra money at the time and so she could afford to do that for us for Christmas, you know. But … a lot of us pooled our music … our instruments together, you know … my brother had the 808 and another friend of my brother's who bought a four-track recording machine and we could all kind of get together and work together to put, you know, the music together to do our demos, basically.[17]

---

[14]Bill Brewster, "Interview with Terry Noel," *DJhistory.com*, October 30, 1998, Accessed February 16, 2011, http://www.djhistory.com/interviews/terry-noel.

[15]Brewster and Broughton, *Last Night a DJ Saved My Life*, 139.

[16]Trevor Pinch and Frank Trocco, *Analog Days: The Invention and Impact of the Moog Synthesizer* (Cambridge, MA: Harvard University Press, 2002), 307, 322–3; see also Paul Harkins, *Digital Sampling: The Decline and Use of Music Technologies* (New York: Routledge, 2020), 30, 45.

[17]McAllister, interview, *This Is Revolution Podcast*, March 31, 2022, https://youtu.be/HGWSYIzyjTM?t=3406.

Another instrument considered foundational for electronic dance music is the Roland TB-303 Bass Line. The 303 is most famous for its "squelchy" sound and its use in acid house.[18] The success of the 303 is often described in terms of its early failures, including how far it is from the sound profile of acoustic and electric bass guitars and its user-unfriendly design. Due to the early failures of the 303, it entered the second-hand market, which naturally led people with less money to buy it.[19] The instruments were adopted for experimentation by bands and musicians who liked how they sounded and how they could be manipulated or modified to help create new "pop aesthetics."[20] Mythologies of certain dance music instruments formed from accounts of the latter kind of use. The German band Kraftwerk and the Detroit techno producer Derrick May were among those to recognize and exploit the unique (and unreal) qualities that some electronic instruments generated.[21] The cult-level reverence that surrounds the instruments lies partly in their prominence within the music they have come to define, and the extent to which their uses depart from the Roland Corporation's intentions for them.[22]

The 808 and 303 are both objects of nostalgia and imitation today, as dance music is mostly made by computer software containing "sound banks" of all kinds of instruments and sounds from acoustic to synthesized. It is possible to choose from countless samples of beats, loops, and riffs, all of which producers

---

[18]Mark J. Butler, *Unlocking the Groove: Rhythm, Meter, and Musical Design in Electronic Dance Music* (Bloomington: Indiana University Press, 2006), 69.

[19]Paul Harkins and Nick Prior, "Dislocating Democratization: Music Technologies in Practice," *Popular Music and Society* 45, no. 1 (2022): 91–2.

[20]Paul Théberge, "'Plugged In': Technology and Popular Music," in *The Cambridge Companion to Pop and Rock*, ed. Simon Frith, Will Straw, and John Street (Cambridge: Cambridge University Press, 2001), 14. In the context of the contemporary, digital reincarnations of such instruments, the capacities for manipulation and modification are increased. See Mark J. Butler, *Playing with Something that Runs: Technology, Improvisation, and Composition in DJ and Laptop Performance* (Oxford: Oxford University Press, 2014), 43–6.

[21]Simon Reynolds, "Kosmik Dance: Krautrock and Its Legacy," in *Modulations: A History of Electronic Music: Throbbing Words on Sound*, ed. Peter Shapiro (New York: Capirinha Productions, 2000), 33–4; Sicko, *Techno Rebels*, 23–6, 79–80.

[22]Butler, *Unlocking the Groove*, 64–70; Harkins and Prior, "(Dis)locating Democratization: Music Technologies in Practice," 94–5; Kodwo Eshun, "House: The Reinvention of House," in *Modulations: A History of Electronic Music: Throbbing Words on Sound*, ed. Peter Shapiro (New York: Capirinha Productions, 2000), 76–7; Sicko, *Techno Rebels*, 47.

can sequence to build a danceable track, which DJs, in turn, can play as part of a DJ set. The fact that the music is (usually) made by computer software does not distinguish it from most other contemporary popular music, since it is entirely standard that such electronic music production is integrated into pop. The musical form (over time) may be a greater point of difference. The verse-chorus structure is supplanted by so-called build-ups, main sections, breakdowns, and outros of dance music expressly made for dance floors. Speaking in general terms, the presence (and centering) of a human singer in pop music also distinguishes it from dance music. In the case of pop stars, the song is "by" the singer, even when the songwriting process and production of records involves a team of people. By contrast, the "authors" of dance music are the producers and where human singers are part of a record, they are merely "featured" after producers' names. In dance music, sampled vocal lines are common as a replacement for a human singer. When vocal samples are used, they often function as texture rather than as a purveyor of meaning. Depending on the genre, vocal sounds can be equal in importance to any other sound in the mix. In addition to the voice, some genres commonly use samples of acoustic instruments such as the piano to simulate, pay respects to, or sometimes even make light of, older musical genres such as jazz.[23]

Many of the technologies at the center of dance music's social life also bind it to other forms of electronic music, including experimental and other forms of art music. In the following section, dance music is placed within a broader musical context, which, in turn, places it in the broader context of dance cultures.

Other Music and Dance Histories

Electronic dance music blurs the divisions between art and popular, especially if it is understood as part of the larger history of electronic music. Early electronic music technologies such as the theremin can be viewed as precursors to instruments such as sequencers, synthesizers, and drum machines.

---

[23]For example, Guido Nemola, "Come Out," *Freakin' EP*, Recycle Records, 2012; Billie Holiday, "Don't Explain [dZihan and Kamien Remix]," *Verve Remixed*, Verve Records, 2002.

Similarly, performers such as Clara Rockmore make up the beginnings of a tradition of electronic music players, composers, and instrument makers or tinkerers, such as Pauline Oliveros, Wendy Carlos, and Robert Moog. Such histories bring together the importance of music associated with early- to mid-twentieth-century art and philosophical movements—Italian futurism, *musique concrete*, minimalism, Afrofuturism. The music of figures like Kraftwerk, Sun Ra, Afrika Bambaata, and the techno pioneers from Detroit in the early 1980s becomes aesthetic articulations of these movements. All of these figures, movements, and technological developments are seen as forming the backdrop of dance music culture, which is now culturally and musically ubiquitous and constitutes a significant component of global mass music industries.[24]

Given that cultures do not develop through linear, neatly traceable histories, and given that human migration and cultural interchange are as old as humanity itself, dance music culture is best viewed not as a monolith that has grown out of roots here or there.[25] Instead, like all phenomena that come to be called "culture," dance music culture is a convergence of ideas, activities, customs, and rituals that have become recognizable. Viewed in such a way, other tangential histories could be added to the list described earlier, of Jamaican dub, New York disco, Chicago house, and Detroit techno. Large-scale public dancing took place in nineteenth-century Europe, as well as unseated musical concerts. The London promenades of the 1830s shared features with the spectacle of the twenty-first-century rock or dance music festival, as the "grass or floor in front of the orchestra was always an open space; people could walk, talk, and take refreshments during the performance; and flashing colored lights or fireworks added a psychedelic air."[26] That said, most events

[24]Tara Rodgers, *Pink Noises: Women on Electronic Music and Sound* (Durham: Duke University Press, 2010); Peter Shapiro, ed., *Modulations: A History of Electronic Music: Throbbing Words on Sound* (New York: Capirinha Productions, 2000), 4–7.

[25]Carlos D. Bustamante and Brenna M. Henn, "Shadows of Early Migrations," *Nature* 486 (December 2010): 1044–5; Katerina Harvati, et al., "Apidima Cave Fossils Provide Earliest Evidence of *Homo Sapiens* in Eurasia," *Nature* 571 (July 2019): 500–4; Wu Liu, et al., "Human Remains from Zhirendong, South China, and Modern Human Emergence in East Asia," *Proceedings of the National Academy of Sciences of the United States of America* 107, no. 45 (November 2010): 19201–6.

[26]William Weber, "Mass Culture and the Reshaping of European Musical Taste, 1770–1870," *International Review of the Aesthetics and Sociology of Music* 8, no. 1 (June 1977), 13.

for public dancing such as in ballrooms and salons in the nineteenth century were for people with wealth and status. It was only from the 1910s that public venues became regularly used for social dancing by the working classes. From this point onward in the twentieth century, there was always a so-called dance craze with mass appeal across US-American and European dance floors. The dance halls in Britain after the First World War, the dance pavilions and rent parties of Chicago and Harlem in the 1920s, 1930s, and 1940s, and the swing dance halls in Los Angeles during the Second World War, all shared features of social dance that could be (and have been) interpreted by observers or participants as emancipatory or politically potent.[27]

The brief history provided here matters because dance music cultures are framed and understood with reference to specific origin stories. Most dance music and club cultures look and sound like they are descendent, aesthetically, of such genres as Chicago house, Detroit or Berlin techno, Goa trance, and so on. As such, contemporary dance music culture is experienced and understood as part of a historical continuum with these places and genres. This framing appears to be unaffected by the fact that dance music is a global phenomenon today, with geographically widespread, and musically and culturally diverse manifestations, each of which arises from its own local conditions. Having provided this background, the next chapter (which readers already familiar with dance music's intellectual history may wish to skip) situates and examines the interdisciplinary field of dance music studies that addresses such origin stories, as well as the larger intellectual contexts from which such studies emerge.

---

[27]Paul G. Cressey, *The Taxi-Dance Hall: A Sociological Study of Commercialized Recreation and City Life* (New York: Greenwood Press, 1968/Chicago: University of Chicago Press, 1932), 22.; Nott, "Getting Together to 'Get Down,'" 258–9; Sherrie Tucker, *Dance Floor Democracy: The Social Geography of Memory at the Hollywood Canteen* (Durham and London: Duke University Press, 2014).

2

Dance Music Studies

This chapter looks, first, at some of the academic approaches that have informed the field of dance music studies, followed by an analysis of some key contributions to it. Rather than dividing them by their research objects, I divide them thematically by their overarching arguments about dance music culture. An overview like this necessarily means being reductive but it also allows a broader arc of ideas that influence such a diverse field to be traced.

Popular music studies, a multidisciplinary field, is where dance music studies, as I have encountered it, is often nested. As such, it is an important starting point for understanding dance music studies overall. It would be quite a project to address all sources of the theories and methods of popular music studies. Instead, I first address popular music studies itself, then the sources of some of the intellectual influences on it and approaches to it that are shared with dance music studies. The first of these sources is subcultural studies, with its origins in the Birmingham Centre for Contemporary Cultural Studies (CCCS), the second is sociological research on popular music and dance cultures, and the third is analysis of music. Other theories and methods in dance music studies come from disciplines like anthropology and ethnomusicology. While this chapter acknowledges the work of some scholars from these two disciplines within the section on dance music studies, a detailed examination of them is outside the scope of this chapter. Furthermore, the research in this book has, over the years, found a scholarly home within studies of both art and popular musics, while it has also been in dialogue with music cognition, psychology, neuroscience, and even business studies. These are also outside the scope of this chapter. Lastly, dance music studies overlaps with

music journalism and music criticism in many ways. Dance music scholars, journalists, and critics are all typically fans, sometimes participants in other capacities.[1] It is unsurprising, then, that they share many similar ideas. There are some differences that characterize each way of approaching dance music writing, such as that many journalists and music critics have closer access to figures who tell their stories and give them inside scoops.[2] In the end, though, the core perspectives and interests of dance music scholarly writing are not clearly distinguishable from those in the dance music journalism. Therefore, rather than attempting to examine popular or journalistic writing in any kind of detail, this chapter is limited to a history of scholarly dance music studies.

Popular Music Studies

Popular music studies—to the extent that it is possible to call it one thing—positions itself in opposition to conservative beliefs in the aesthetic superiority of high art or culture. It is opposed to the notion that music that is sanctioned, institutionalized, or patronized is the only kind of music that should be taken seriously. A large part of it emerges historically from a populist, leftist intellectual politics—specifically, a New Leftist politics, where culture becomes the explanation for the complicity of the working classes in their own continued repression (while still holding Marx's understanding of class struggle to be true).[3]

---

[1]Hans Weisethaunet and Ulf Lindberg, "Authenticity Revisited: The Rock Critic and the Changing Real," *Popular Music and Society* 33, no. 4 (August 2010): 467; Frith, "Remembrance of Things Past," 148. Examples of journalists (or music critics) who became scholars who write about dance music (and popular music in general) include Dave Laing, Simon Frith, Gina Arnold, Caspar Melville, and Simon A. Morrison.

[2]For example, Sicko, *Techno Rebels*, Brewster and Broughton, *Last Night a DJ Saved My Life*, Reynolds, *Energy Flash*, Matos, *The Underground Is Massive*; Haslam, *Life After Dark*; Tobias Rapp, *Lost and Sound: Berlin, Techno and the Easyjet Set*, trans. Paul Sabin (Frankfurt: Inversions, 2010).
Exceptions include Tim Lawrence's meticulous accounts of New York dance music culture and Arun Saldanha's intimate, years-long ethnography of psychedelic trance in Anjuna, Goa. See Lawrence, *Love Saves the Day*; Tim Lawrence, *Life and Death on the New York Dance Floor 1980–1983* (Durham: Duke University Press) 2016; and Saldanha, *Psychedelic White*.

[3]Vivek Chibber, *The Class Matrix: Social Theory After the Cultural Turn* (Cambridge, MA: Harvard University Press, 2022), 81–5.

Paradoxically, the politics of the high-low art ideals against which popular music studies emerged—the idea that (high) art music is superior to (low) popular music—were also made in the service of allegedly Marxist arguments. Critical theorists such as Theodor W. Adorno is the most famous of these in popular music studies, from whom it is possible to trace the idea of something called a culture industry, an object of continued interest for popular music scholars. (It is striking that this culture industry concept, which was critical in its conception, has a contemporary variation called "creative industries," a way for neoliberal governments to celebrate the outsourcing of the arts to enterprise and market competition.) Adorno is known for combining an antitotalitarian discourse with a psychoanalysis-driven hermeneutics. The general understanding within popular music studies of one of his contentions is that he denigrated mass music—jazz, at the time—for being escapist rather than oppositional and as a tainted product of market forces that could "expose" underlying deviancies of the individual ego, unlike "autonomous art."[4] This oversimplification of Adorno's argument (which I am replicating here, for brevity) is framed as the original sin against which popular music studies positions itself. At the same time, Adorno's theories of culture and beliefs in what music can do are a continuing influence in popular music studies, beyond the culture industry idea. Adorno gave musical form a great deal of weight, and although his psychoanalytic, Marxist-informed hermeneutics continue to raise eyebrows, they are also a familiar genre to anyone who has read the strand of popular music studies influenced by "New Musicology" from the 1990s, which analyzes popular music as "texts" in "context."

The conviction that musical features and musical cultures, taken together, echo bigger cultural truths and shape "social consciousness" also reveals itself through how scholars evaluate dance music.[5] Take the example of *Dancecult*, an academic journal dedicated exclusively to the study of electronic dance music culture. While not being the only place of publication for dance music studies, the journal is nevertheless a hub for such scholarship, in part because

---

[4]Theodore W. Adorno, "On Jazz," trans. Jamie Owen Daniel, *Discourse* 12, no. 1 (Fall–Winter, 1989–90): 45–69. Adorno did not like all art or classical music, some of it also fell short of his understanding of worthy autonomous art.

[5]See DeNora, *Music in Everyday Life*, 1–3.

it is interdisciplinary. Music psychology, the social sciences, philosophy, critical theory, ethnomusicology, anthropology, popular music studies, cultural studies, gender studies, cultural geography, and more, all come together in a wide scholarly community focused on one thing: electronic dance music culture. The lines of musical style, practice, genre, scene, culture, industry, sound, happening, or any number of other categories that may be used to define dance music are abandoned in *Dancecult*. It publishes a diverse range of knowledge from a large spread of dance music cultures and includes multimedia and experimental forms of writing. In all these senses, it embodies the spirit of openness that dance music culture aspires to. Some contributions in the journal reflect the studies of the extraordinary dance floors described earlier, in that they treat the positive value of dance music's aesthetics, sociocultural dynamics, politics, or psychological effects either as the starting point for a more specific argument about a given scene or dance floor, or as their primary argument.[6] Those more ambivalent or critical about it usually, and unsurprisingly, incorporate feminist or gender critiques, critical race studies, critiques of Eurocentrism, studies of ageing, and capitalist critiques.[7] Whatever their arguments or conclusions in

---

[6]For example, Ramzy Alwakeel, "The Aesthetics of Protest in UK Rave," *Dancecult* 1, no. 2. (July 2010): 50–62; Chris Christodoulou, "Rumble in the Jungle: City, Place and Uncanny Bass," *Dancecult* 3, no. 1 (June 2011): 44–63; Alessio Kolioulis, "Borderlands: Dub Techno's Hauntological Politics of Acoustic Ecology," *Dancecult* 7, no. 2 (November 2015): 64–85; Alice O'Grady, "Dancing Outdoors: DIY Ethics and Democratised Practices of Well-Being on the UK Alternative Festival Circuit," *Dancecult* 7, no. 1 (June 2015): 76–96; Matthew T. Phillips, "Dancing with Dumont: Individualism at an Early Morning Melbourne Rave," *Dancecult* 13, no. 1 (December 2021): 88–100; Richard Pope, "Hooked on Affect: Detroit Techno and Dystopian Digital Culture," *Dancecult* 2, no. 1 (March 2011): 24–44; Hillegonda C. Rietveld, "Disco's Revenge: House Music's Nomadic Memory," *Dancecult* 2, no. 1 (March, 2011): 4–23; Graham St. John, "The Vibe of the Exiles: Aliens, Afropsychedelia and Psyculture," *Dancecult* 5, no. 2 (November 2013): 56–87; tobias c. van Veen, "Vessels of Transfer: Allegories of Afrofuturism in Jeff Mills and Janelle Monae," *Dancecult* 5, no. 2 (November 2013): 7–41.

[7]For example, Gay Jennifer Breyley, "Raving Iran (Review)," *Dancecult* 11, no. 1 (November 2019): 97–100; Rebekah Farrugia and Magdalena Olszanowski, "Introduction to Women and Electronic Dance Music Culture," *Dancecult* 9, no. 1 (November 2017): 1–8; Rebekah Farrugia, "'Let's Have At It!': Conversations With EDM Producers Kate Simko and DJ Denise," *Dancecult* 1, no. 2 (July 2010): 87–93; Tim Lawrence, "Life and Death on the Pulse Dance Floor: Transglocal Politics and the Erasure of the Latinx in the History of Queer Dance," *Dancecult* 8, no. 1 (November 2016): 1–25; Alice O'Grady and Anna Madill, "Being and Performing 'Older' Woman in Electronic Dance Movement Culture," *Dancecult* 11, no. 1 (November 2019): 7–29; Katherina Pawel, "Black Feminism and the Violence of Disco," *Dancecult* 13, no. 1 (December 2021): 22–35; Reitsamer "The DIY Careers of Techno and Drum 'n' Bass DJs in Vienna," 28–43; Bryan Schmidt, "Boutiquing at the Raindance Campout: Relational Aesthetics as Festival Technology," *Dancecult* 7, no. 1 (June 2015): 35–54.

this regard, it is still possible to see traces of the Adorno effect in most of the big-picture questions being addressed. What ideal "social character" do specific musical qualities or aesthetics of dance music and/or dance music culture symbolize or enable? What radical or affirming "schemes of social behavior" do they establish?[8] What are the emancipatory politics of participation in dance music culture, broadly defined? Adorno's hate-listening (to use today's parlance) of popular music may be a permanent source of disagreement at the heart of popular music studies. But his analytical methods and faith in the significance of music to culture and politics remain at the center of studies of dance music.

In sum, just as the fear of mass or popular music came from offshoots of Marxist thought, so too did the dismissal of the high-low art dichotomy by journalists and popular music scholars later in the century. The idea (also from Adorno) that the jazz orchestra's comparable features to military bands could bring it dangerously close to totalitarianism could not be more in conflict with the populist idea that the proletariat can use music to join forces, across lines of vested interest and internal conflict to fight for their own emancipation.[9] The ethos that made its way into popular music scholarship was that taking popular music seriously meant taking the lives and tastes of the working classes seriously, and asking to what extent such music could be a force for solidarity and anticapitalist politics. Subcultural studies, as I will show below, took up this purpose in its own way.

Subcultural Studies

The formation of the Birmingham Centre for Contemporary Cultural Studies, led by Stuart Hall and, for a short time, Richard Hoggart, has been perhaps the greatest single influence on the cultural studies of dance music most prevalent in publications such as *Dancecult*. The Birmingham School takes care of one of the goals of popular music studies, which is to take mass

---

[8]Adorno, "On Jazz," 67; Theodore W. Adorno, *Prisms*, trans. Samuel and Shierry Weber (Cambridge, MA: The MIT Press, 1967), 126.

[9]Adorno, "On Jazz," 61; Karl Marx and Friedrich Engels, *The Communist Manifesto* (Milton Keynes: Penguin Random House UK, 2015), 15–16.

culture, both mainstream and fringe/subculture, seriously and treat the people who engage with it (youth, and working class youth in particular) as if they matter. More than this, the early subcultural scholarship within the School, led by scholars such as Dick Hebdige, treats subculture as a potential form of symbolic resistance.[10] It also treats the people who participate in it as active political agents. At the same time, Hebdige points out that those involved in subcultures may not share the scholarly "readings" of their roles, arguing that "it is highly unlikely … that the members of any of the subcultures described in this book would recognize themselves reflected here. They are still less likely to welcome any efforts on our part to understand them."[11]

Both the contributions and pitfalls of the Birmingham School have been addressed many times by dance music studies and popular music studies. While it has been influential, it is simultaneously dismissed by many scholars as overly simplistic, naïve, lacking in nuance, myopic (in terms of the identities of subcultural subjects), and in many cases has been replaced by updated concepts such as scenes and neotribes.[12] Subcultural studies have been the object of critique for decades now, to the point that such critiques are almost as commonplace as the rejection of Adorno as the starting point for popular music studies. Yet despite the idea that it is important to get beyond subcultural studies, the overarching CCCS framework continues to underpin a lot of popular music writing. Within this, dance music studies stands out in its strident continuation of the idea that there is (or was) an oppositional politics on dance floors. In a way that mirrors many of the interests in popular

---

[10]For example, John Clarke, Stuart Hall, Tony Jefferson, and Brian Roberts, "Subcultures, Cultures and Class," in *Resistance Through Rituals: Youth Subcultures in Post-War Britain*, ed. Stuart Hall and Tony Jefferson (Birmingham: The Centre for Contemporary Cultural Studies, 1976), 9–74; Dick Hebdige, *Subculture: The Meaning of Style* (London: Routledge, 1979), 132–3; Klaus Nathaus, "Why 'Pop' Changed and Why It Mattered (Part I): Sociological Perspectives on Twentieth-Century Popular Culture in the West," *Soziopolis*, August 1, 2018, https://www.soziopolis.de/why-pop-changed-and-how-it-mattered-part-i.html#_ftn6.

[11]Hebdige, *Subculture: The Meaning of Style*, 139.

[12]For example, Will Straw, "Systems of Articulation, Logics of Change: Communities and Scenes in Popular Music," *Cultural Studies* 5, no. 3 (1991): 368–88; Andy Bennett, "Subcultures or Neo-Tribes? Rethinking the Relationship Between Youth, Style and Musical Taste," *Sociology* 33, no. 3 (August 1999): 599–617; Andy Bennett, "Consolidating the Music Scenes Perspective," *Poetics* 32, no. 3–4 (June–August 2004): 223–34.

music studies, the dance floors that receive the most attention are those that have an overtly subversive or alternative sensibility. "Electronic dance music culture" does not often refer, in dance music studies, to most people who participate in such a culture as part of their weekend entertainment and social lives, as part of the mainstream nighttime economies of cities around the world.[13] What is more, the politics described are not about organizing, mobilizing, or pressuring establishments for material redistribution or transformation of the political and economic systems that administrate everyone's lives. What is referred to as politics in dance music is not always defined clearly, nor even named as politics. It is not that there are no political attitudes, but rather that their expression is packaged in idealistic, sometimes oblique terms—a tactic that is itself a part of the politics. In this sense, it is a continuation of subcultural studies. It can, though, be characterized in some concrete terms: resistance within the act of gathering *en masse* regardless of licensing or permission; the freedom to consume recreational drugs, whether legal or illegal; and in some cases, the practice of participating in socially unsanctioned activities such as public expressions of non-normative sexuality or gender.[14] It can also include a support for alternative lifestyles that center on ecological consciousness and activism, interpretations of indigenous practice and symbolism, use of computing and other new technologies, and opting out of normative work-life temporalities and trajectories. Or, as St. John offers, "open source commitments, spiritual revitalization, anarcho-capitalism, pleasure without guilt" and later, "acts of freedom."[15] In short, this view holds that cultural practices and symbols constitute politics.

While the conclusions to such ideas may be different, acknowledging the roles of cultural practices and symbols in people's lives is not unique to

---

[13]For an exception, see Ed Montano, "DJ Culture in the Commercial Sydney Dance Music Scene," *Dancecult* 1, no. 1 (September 2009): 81–93.

[14]Luis-Manuel Garcia, "An Alternative History of Sexuality in Club Culture," *Resident Advisor*, January 28, 2014, http://www.residentadvisor.net/feature.aspx?1927; Luis-Manuel Garcia, "Whose Refuge, This House? The Estrangement of Queers of Color in Electronic Dance Music," in *The Oxford Handbook of Music and Queerness* ed. Fred Everett Maus and Sheila Whiteley (Oxford: Oxford University Press, 2022).

[15]Graham St. John, *Technomad: Global Raving Countercultures* (London: Equinox, 2009), 17–18.

subcultural studies. It has been a part of sociological work on music, dance, and culture more broadly, since the early twentieth century. Such sociologies are the focus of the section that follows.

Sociology

Sociology contributes to the bigger intellectual history of dance music studies in its studies of urban life, social dance, and vernacular cultures. It is possible to find, in early sociologies, versions of what scholars might recognize today as participant observation and ethnography, together with matter-of-fact commentary on mass or popular entertainment. However, "matters of fact" are themselves historical. Observational writing can be found on dance in the United States since the nineteenth century (and into the 1920s), from what would be viewed today as extreme—religious-moral and racial eugenic—points of view, all of which influenced the kinds of research undertaken by punitive government authorities such as the Juvenile Protective Association.[16] Although those calling themselves sociologists in the early twentieth century began to immerse themselves directly in urban social lives and cultures of people they were proximate to, such studies were facilitated and steered by funding from governments. Framed favorably, they often sought to learn more about the social lives of "ordinary people" within a broader institutional agenda of pursuing public good. Formal studies revealed how important popular music and dance, of the kind that such ordinary people enjoyed, were to social life. Such sociological studies also did their part in perpetuating ideological divisions between high art music and low popular or dancing music, in that they had distinctly class and race overtones, rife with all of the usual moralistic judgements that came along with them. A primary concern for early government-funded sociological research was to understand the "commercialisation of urban working-class leisure," of which social, popular

---

[16]T. A. Faulkner, *From the Ball-Room to Hell* (Chicago: The Henry Publishing Co., 1892); T. A. Faulkner, *The Lure of the Dance* (Los Angeles, 1916); W. C. Wilkinson, *The Dance of Modern Society* (New York: Oakley, Mason & Co., 1869); R. A. Adams, *The Social Dance* (Kansas, 1921); Louise De Koven Bowen, *The Public Dance Halls of Chicago* (The Juvenile Protective Association of Chicago, 1917).

dance was seen as a negative symptom.[17] In this paradigm, ordinary people gathering to dance in a way that is not formally endorsed by institutions was a moral and societal problem.

Sociological evaluations of popular dance cultures that no longer portrayed them first and foremost as morally debased, tended toward neutrality (by the standards of their times), and even veered toward acknowledgement of the positive value of social dance to participants, started to concurrently emerge in the early twentieth century. The friendlier approach may have come from the overall reformist roots of the field of American sociology itself. According to Zine Magubane, the Chicago School grew from the need to address unrest in a post-slavery society. As Magubane notes, before Robert E. Park joined the University of Chicago, he worked at the American Congo Reform Association and became a coauthor and researcher (as well as ghostwriter) for the educator and former slave Booker T. Washington.[18] The building tensions between white elites and black workers were to be addressed, according to Washington, not by demanding better conditions, but by means of education and cooperation. These constitute examples of the preference by institutions, including sociologists and other scholars, for respectability and reform over discord and revolution.

This early sociology has informed dance music cultural research through both substance and method. The work of Klaus Nathaus on popular dance is helpful here. In his discussion of Paul Cressey's sociological study of taxi-dance halls in 1930s Chicago, Nathaus notes the Chicago School ethos in Cressey's "close observation of people's interactions and the situational context in which they unfold." While the study, which was "commissioned by Chicago's Juvenile Protective Association … shows traces of a reformist agenda," it nevertheless explores the particularities of the taxi-dance hall and the "practices and motives of both the providers and consumers."[19] Cressey's framing betrays the

---

[17]Nathaus, "Why Pop Changed and How It Mattered (Part I)," https://soziopolis.de/beobachten/kultur/artikel/why-pop-changed-and-how-it-mattered-part-i/#_ftnref22.

[18]Zine Magubane, "Science, Reform, and the 'Science of Reform': Booker T. Washington, Robert Park, and the Making of a 'Science of Society,'" *Current Sociology* 62, no. 4 (July 2014): 568–83.

[19]Nathaus, "Why Pop Changed and How It Mattered (Part I)," https://soziopolis.de/beobachten/kultur/artikel/why-pop-changed-and-how-it-mattered-part-i/#_ftnref22.

limited view of morality consistent with the prevailing view of 1930s white America. He refers to the longer-term intimate relationships that white, young women dancers developed with the Filipino, Greek, and Mexican migrant men who paid them as a process of "demoralization." Cressey's report examines the individual motivations and circumstances of all the people at taxi-dances, including the dancers. There is a sense that, in the tradition of sociology, Cressey describes the understandings of morality as they are observable to him in the field, rather than subscribing to them himself.[20]

By the mid-twentieth century, sociologists were engaging more intimately with their research environments. One example of this is Howard Becker's 1951 article, "The Professional Dance Musician and His Audience," adapted from a part of the author's M. A. thesis, which uses an "insider-outsider" or "insider/ outsider" perspective. This approach has long been the object of contention and debate in the social sciences, particularly fields that use ethnographic methods, such as anthropology.[21] Many aspects of Becker's approach are common in popular music studies today, such as gaining access to, and trust of, participants. They speak freely and casually with Becker due to the rapport he already has with them, using the language they would ordinarily use. He can also translate terms for readers who are outsiders.

This kind of familiarity—the kind that is only possible for people who are or have been insiders—is also present across most of the scholarly work on electronic dance music culture. One point of difference is the way that the sociological tradition, exemplified in the work of Becker, uses insider knowledge. Becker distances himself from his own milieu by treating the attitudes and discourses of participants as novel—as *if* he were an outsider. There is a serious attempt at separating his understanding of his research world from the ways that he already understands it from having participated

---

[20]Cressey, *The Taxi-Dance Hall*, 237–61. See also Fabian Holt, *Everyone Loves Live Music: A Theory of Performance Institutions* (Chicago: The University of Chicago Press, 2020), 66.
[21]Howard Becker, "The Professional Dance Musician and His Audience," *American Journal of Sociology* 57, no. 2 (September 1951): 136–44. For a relatively recent example of the insider/outsider debates and how they pertain to the notion of "decolonizing knowledge," see Gustavo Lins Ribeiro, "Outsiders and Insiders in the Making of Anthropological Knowledge," *American Anthropologist* 118, no. 3 (September 2016): 628–9.

in it. Rather than writing as an insider, he takes insider knowledge as a means of access and then sets it aside so that he can learn something new. Such a separation includes the ability to understand the agendas, beliefs, and perspectives of insiders, without adopting or valorizing them, or occupying them as one's own. In this respect, Pierre Bourdieu's articulation of the complicated position of researcher to what they are researching is also helpful:

> It seems to me that one of the main causes of error in sociology lies in an unexamined relationship to the object—or, more precisely, in ignorance of all that the view of the object owes to the point of view, that is, to the viewer's *position* in the social space and the scientific field.[22]

Contemporary cultural sociologists looking at music and dance thus acknowledge the impossibility of actual neutrality, of the inevitability of bias, of the ways that colonial, patriarchal, and paternalistic practices have informed their field, and of the temporal and other constraints that mean all research is necessarily incomplete.

Where does the ability of the insider to take on the critical distance of an outsider come into this? Returning to Magubane's analysis of the early histories of sociology may help. Park believed that it was important to establish so-called natural laws by which the conditions of society after slavery could be understood. Thus, the history of sociology and the Chicago School's growing interest in qualitative and empirical research approaches were coupled with an idea that society was a big scale "laboratory" that could be observed and made sense of systematically.[23] If this is to be believed, this would appear to resolve the problem of bias, but of course, it does not. Rather than focusing on a defense of sociology as a "science," the contribution of such a defense to the notion of radical doubt is where this legacy is most useful:[24]

> The construction of a scientific object requires first and foremost a break with common sense, that is, with the representations shared by all, whether they be the mere commonplaces of ordinary existence or official

---

[22]Pierre Bourdieu, *Sociology in Question*, trans. Richard Nice (London: Sage, 1993), 10.

[23]Magubane, "Science, Reform, and the 'Science of Reform,'" 573.

[24]Bourdieu, "A Science that Makes Trouble," 8–9.

representations, often inscribed in institutions and thus present both in the objectivity of social organizations and in the minds of their participants. *The preconstructed is everywhere.* The sociologist is literally beleaguered by it, as everybody else is. The sociologist is thus saddled with the task of knowing an object—the social world—of which he is the product, in a way such that the problems that he raises about it and the concepts he uses have every chance of being the product of this object itself.[25]

Such radical doubt here is not meant to be what Eve Kosofsky Sedgwick would call a paranoid reading: a takedown for the sheer sport of it—a hermeneutics of suspicion, an uncovering of truths that hide under the surface of participants' delusions, a desire to prove flaws in other scholarly work.[26] On the contrary: it comes from an enthusiastic fan whose original goal was to look for what leads others to love dance music equally or more. The resulting evaluation is based on observations of unexpected things and on having received unexpected answers to questions. Anyone willing to similarly document what they observe is capable of reaching similar conclusions.

Analyzing Music

This section deals mainly with an approach to studying dance music rather than a particular field or discipline that uses such an approach. Analyzing music can mean analyzing sound, attending to the formal structures of music, and linking musical features to cultural phenomena. Scholars such as Mark J. Butler have looked particularly at dance music's sound and formal compositional attributes, while also incorporating "on the ground" research approaches such as interviews and fieldwork. Rhythm and meter are among the formal, sonically defining musical features that he centers, using classical notation and graphic depictions of formal musical structures. Both this and

---

[25]Pierre Bourdieu, "The Practice of Reflexive Sociology (The Paris Workshop)," in *An Invitation to Reflexive Sociology,* ed. Pierre Bourdieu and Loïc J. D. Wacquant (Chicago: The University of Chicago Press, 1992), 235.

[26]Eve Kosofsky Sedgwick, "Paranoid Reading and Reparative Reading; or, You're So Paranoid, You Probably Think This Introduction Is about You," in *Novel Gazing: Queer Readings in Fiction,* ed. Eve Kosofsky Sedgwick (Durham: Duke University Press, 1997), 17–19; William Cheng, *Just Vibrations: The Purpose of Sounding Good* (Ann Arbor: University of Michigan Press, 2016), 37–53.

his later work undertake the kind of research and analysis that legitimates it, granting it institutional recognition within a field that has historically privileged classical music, then jazz, and later, rock, punk, and other forms of guitar-based popular music. Butler distances himself from the utopianism of cultural dance music studies, though evaluations of the "experiential and interpretive possibility" that dance music affords hint at a positive attitude toward it. In more recent work, which is informed not only by music theory but by sound studies, media studies, and other fields, Butler reiterates the critique of utopian arguments, stating that he does not subscribe to analysis for the sake of defending the music style/form, calling it an "ideologically suspect maneuver." There remains, though, a gesture toward the distinctiveness of certain scenes, for example, in the choice to focus on Berlin "as a site for field research because of its exceptional concentration of world-class musicians … [and] because … its nightlife proved to be without parallel in terms of both the quantity and quality of performances on offer."[27]

Some scholars conduct analysis of musical features as part of the broader project of understanding the social and cultural dynamics of dance music. Hillegonda C. Rietveld, for example, has attributed 1980s house to specific, positive cultural meanings:

> As house music has a trance inducing beat, which seems to induce a sensual celebration of community and which (in African-American gospel influenced productions) deals with a sense of religious bliss, its prominent intertextuality adds to the effect of ecstasy. By never quite locking the meaning of the text into place, a desire to acquire a totality, an Imaginary, is created. Perhaps it is this desire which makes people dance all night and urges them to come back for more. However, the (intoxicated) dancer also may want to 'let go' of all desire to acquire a sense of totality. In that case, the untying of the subject occurs in a state of complete jouissance, in a loss of its construction in language.[28]

---

[27]Butler, *Playing with Something that Runs*, 15–20; Butler, *Unlocking the Groove*, 18, 257. For more on this discussion, see Tami Gadir, "Understanding Agency from the Decks to the Dance Floor," *Music Theory Online* 24, no. 3 (September 2018).

[28]Hillegonda C. Rietveld, *This Is Our House: House Music, Cultural Spaces and Technologies* (London: Ashgate, 1998), 147–8.

In this reading, house music can cause "awareness of an outside world to disappear ... [a] dream world is generated which does not exist outside of it." It is a gathering that Rietveld describes as "a kind of night-time 'church,' where an experience can be achieved of a self-effacing identity which becomes part of a community." House "at English and Dutch raves between 1988 and 1990" rendered social class, gender, and race "less important" where people "celebrat[ed] the body rather than the mind." Rietveld notes the mystical tone of the theories that inform her interpretation of house music participation. While she sees house music as a space that can facilitate loss of subjective senses of self or ego, she also acknowledges that such experiences can be "contained and controlled in a particular space and time in order to accommodate a hegemonic status quo." Ultimately, though, Rietveld argues that house serves a "secular longing to make sense of the rhythms of urban life in the late twentieth century." The power of dance music here is in its affect, and perhaps also in the same spirit as José Esteban Muñoz' queer alternative present, where "majoritarian belonging, normative tastes, and 'rational' expectations" are not the goal, but "unrealized potential" and "political imaginary" are.[29]

For tobias c. van Veen, the unrealizable nature of the utopia—the fact that it is an imaginary and cannot be pinned down—is precisely the point, along the lines of speculative philosophies such as Afrofuturism. From such a perspective, seeking the "outcome" from rave culture is misguided. When thinking through the implications of the radical proposal that "rave culture has interrogated ... embodied and technological practices" as well as having produced "ecstatic and collective subjectivities" and "complicated the very question of the political, the communal and the ethical," van Veen is suggesting to look beyond political action as it is normally defined. It is implicit that dance music is so radical that it supersedes the limits of big P politics. Do not bother trying to substantiate; instead, accept and embrace the impossible as a radical imperative.[30] This argument is a preview of some of the scholarship addressed in what follows, which asserts dance music's utopian attributes most enthusiastically.

---

[29]José Esteban Muñoz, *Cruising Utopia: The Then and There of Queer Futurity* (New York: New York University Press, 2009), 27–8, 189; Rietveld, *This Is Our House*, 192–205.
[30]tobias c. van Veen, "Technics, Precarity and Exodus in Rave Culture," *Dancecult* 1, no. 2 (2010): 31, 44–5.

Celebratory Dance Music Studies

Celebratory studies of dance focus on specific, local communities, even as there is a collective consciousness of a coherent global dance music and DJ culture. The specific dance music cultures under examination are aesthetically and culturally (and, as some argue, therefore politically) exceptional and are motivated by a common goal of advocacy. Graham St. John refers to this common goal in matter-of-fact terms: such a consensus is "representative of commitments among scholars of EDMCs [electronic dance music cultures] for whom the dance music experience is held to be efficacious, and where dance cultures are recognized [*sic*] as experimental, transcendent and transformative."[31] Two implications follow from such an assertion. The first is that all dance music cultures ought to aspire to be like the exceptional ones, since they are dance music in its purest, unadulterated state. All dance music cultures could be Good if they pursued the same ideals from dance music in its "original" forms. The second is that the circumstances that brought such scenes about are entirely unique, and because they arise from specific historical, geographical circumstances, they are irreplicable. If you want to experience Good dance music culture, and you are not in Berlin (preferably in the late 1990s), New York in the 1970s or 1980s, Detroit in the 1980s, the UK in 1989–91, or Goa in the 1990s, then too bad: you have missed out.

Both implications, contrasting though they are, assume that the qualities attributed to the scenes are themselves worth pursuing. Some scholars argue explicitly that this is the case. In his second book-length history of New York City's dance music culture, Lawrence contextualizes early 1980s dance floor politics within contemporary intellectual shifts that influenced arts scenes. He notes that under the influence of French critical theory, there was a move away from "authoritarian" Marxist ideologies to "neo-Marxism," with revised meanings of labor and an embrace of "decentralized, fluid, pluralistic" ways of being. These ways of being are framed as desirable, meeting the needs of a culture "born out of hardship, resistance, and desire for communal pleasure." For Lawrence, New York underwent "a period of boundless action

---

[31]St. John, "Liminal Being," 249.

or, in philosopher Hannah Arendt's terms, freedom and plurality" which "engendered a cornucopia of creative ventures"; and New York City's "writhing, coiling personality" led to the social circumstances that characterized its dance music scenes in this historical moment.[32]

The bigger picture argument is historically and geographically transferrable beyond New York. Speaking in general and global terms about rave culture, van Veen similarly sees a "deconstruction of the material and social categories of labour and leisure" as one of many ways that rave leads to "de-scripted subjectivities." The multitude supplants the unified and noncompliance replaces conformity. That is to say, the blurring of labor and leisure is not a problem, as Angela McRobbie sees it, but the beginning of something politically more imaginative:[33]

> That there is no return to politics-as-usual signals not a failure in the particular, but a caesura in "the modes of subjectification" from which politics arrives in its antagonism ... Rave's micro-economies of sharing produce what Negri and Hardt would call the "experience of the common" that breaks the impasse of the universal to the particular through love ... Precarious workplay itself is a labour of love inasmuch as it is love's corruption. It is this plurality or hybridity that reflects the energy of the multitude.[34]

The celebration of descripted subjectivities includes the belief that dance music cultures allow people to challenge restrictive societal norms. One strand of this argument is that the spatial and social aspects of the dance floor can facilitate freedom for women from repressive gender dynamics. Maria Pini argues, with the help of her interviewees, that the subcultural rave dance floor is more conducive to challenging gender norms than commercial clubs, pubs, or bars. She focuses on participant accounts that emphasize the "adventure narrative" of rave dancing:

> What raving appears to offer these women are the conditions of possibility for experiences of adventure, exploration, and discovery: experiences which

---

[32]Lawrence, *Life and Death on the New York Dance Floor*, 457–77.

[33]Angela McRobbie, "Clubs to Companies: Notes on the Decline of Political Culture in Speeded Up Worlds," *Cultural Studies* 16, no. 4 (2002): 516–31.

[34]van Veen, "Technics, Precarity and Exodus in Rave Culture," 34–6.

are often denied them within other spheres of their lives … The 'elsewheres' or 'other worlds' opened up through raving are, I want to argue, particularly significant sites for expressing and exploring what can be thought of as a collapse of femininity's traditional landmarks.[35]

Pini takes this further, arguing that rave dancing's potential as a feminist space can be theorized as the "political fictions" of Rosi Braidotti's "nomad" and Donna Haraway's "cyborg":

> [D]rawing a flow of connections between the raver, the cyborg and the nomad, is not about appropriating the raver into the arms of high theory as if suggesting that she were actually, or that she were somehow the same as, Haraway's Cyborg or Braidotti's nomad. Instead, and in Braidotti's words, it is about drawing an otherwise unlikely flow of connections intended to make manifest something about contemporary cultural visions and contemporary cultural fantasies about both the present and the future. Here, the female raver, like the Cyborg and the nomad is considered to be involved in a wider staking-out of new possibilities for being-in-culture.[36]

For Haraway, the culture with such new possibilities is a reconfigured one. The fantasy future culture is not only post-gender, it is "oppositional, utopian, and completely without innocence." Pini's overall account, in turn, ascribes a freer sexual politics to dance music cultures that removes the heteronormative, courtship dynamics of other nighttime entertainment spaces. While interview accounts show the clear limits of such empowerment, they are also presented as an intervention against what Pini sees as the masculine orientations of subcultural studies. Overall, her contention is that because of how they are configured, rave dance floors encourage acts of symbolic resistance with respect to gender, in ways that other nightlife spaces are less likely to.[37]

---

[35]Maria Pini, *Club Cultures and Female Subjectivity: The Move from Home to House* (Basingstoke: Palgrave, 2001), 13–14. See also Angela McRobbie, *Postmodernism and Popular Culture* (London: Routledge, 1994), 155–76.

[36]Pini, *Club Cultures and Female Subjectivity*, 155–7.

[37]Donna Haraway, *Simians, Cyborgs, and Women: The Reinvention of Nature* (London: Free Association Books, 1991), 150–1; Pini, *Club Cultures and Female Subjectivity*, 189–92.

Variations of symbolic resistance are a central theme even in the studies that set themselves apart from the CCCS, such as Ben Malbon's analysis of clubbing scenes in London. Malbon notes the limitations of "cool" clubbing practices by accounting for their exclusionary nature and noting the self-monitoring required for successful participation in them. He frames clubbing as an expression of consumption more than of resistance *per se*. At the same time, he employs the notions of "playful vitality," "flow," and *"communitas,"* among others, influenced by the theories of Michel Maffesoli, Mihalyi Csikszentmihlayi, and Victor Turner. His theory of clubbing is about this combination of symbolic acts: expressing identity through consumption, belonging, and "playful resistance"—where clubbers self-direct ecstatic (or what he calls "oceanic") experiences through music, dance, drugs, "reflective exploration of the self" and "collective unshackling of identity." In the end, the analysis does not stray far from the subcultural resistance from which he seeks to distinguish himself. Kai Fikentscher's comprehensive ethnography of dance music in New York does similar theoretical work. Fikentscher adopts the term "vibe" (used by participants) to theorize the connection between dancers and DJs. This is a helpful concept for understanding the ephemeral and imprecise nature of dance floor experience. Beyond this, a core argument is that the dance floors he has studied are safe havens for marginalized people to fully express themselves in the context of an unsafe wider culture. While it is very possible that this is an accurate representation of these dance floors at this historical moment, the conclusions are nevertheless part of a readymade utopian narrative, where participants' own definitions of "underground" are subsumed into the book's core thesis.[38]

Such ideas underlie most celebratory dance music studies in one form or another, which tend to accept and incorporate the terms of their participants without also seeking dissonance or radical doubt. Together, such works represent a belief in the tenet that Fred Turner refers to as "bohemian idealism." And the encouragement of individually driven, fragmentary

---

[38]Ben Malbon, *Clubbing: Dancing, Ecstasy and Vitality* (London: Routledge, 1999), 106–11, 150–5; Rietveld, *This Is Our House*, 204; Fikentscher, *You Better Work!*, 80. See also Thornton, *Club Cultures*, 99; Pini, *Club Cultures and Female Subjectivity*, 173–87.

political articulations of resistance, which, as some would argue, are not meant to actually materialize, make the clubber or raver in such accounts a realization of the archetypal neoliberal subject. The following section deals with this matter and that of other internal contradictions presented by a range of more critical dance music studies.

Critical Dance Music Studies

The literature in this section evaluates dance music neither by focusing on how a particular subgenre might be different from, and implicitly, more special than, other subgenres, nor by confirming the positive value of dance music culture overall. Instead, authors represented here take a neutral or critical tone to analyze dance floors and cultures. Sherrie Tucker's historical work about the 1940s dance club known as the Hollywood Canteen is a helpful model. It shows, firstly, that contemporary dance music and DJ culture is not the first dance culture to be romanticized as democratizing, utopian, egalitarian, or liberating. Tucker suggests that such interpretations also existed in relation to the jitterbug swing craze during the Second World War. For Tucker, "jazz and swing scholars … have often invested hopes of democracy, resistance, and freedom into jazz and swing history and practice in ways that tend to fall short of defining what we mean by democracy, resistance, and freedom." While admitting to her own interests in finding such ideas within this dance practice, Tucker argues that it is not possible to boil down the "social potential" and "political power of dancers' interactions" to anything simple. For one thing, the Hollywood Canteen took place under FBI surveillance—the kind that concerned itself with the mixing of black and white dancers. Intentional racial mixing could not be "compatible with American democracy" as it was understood by agents, and thus, must have been Communist infiltration.[39] While this may be viewed as specific and anomalous to other kinds of dance floors—such as the majority of them that, it might be hoped, are not being surveilled by the FBI or their equivalents internationally—there is a broader

---

[39]Tucker, *Dance Floor Democracy*, 6–8, 16, 279; 243–280.

sense in which Tucker's ambivalence, her radical doubt, helps her to add a scholarly contribution beyond that of what her participants give her in accounts. Tucker's evaluation of the Hollywood Canteen, the particular site and historical moment that she researched, shows several perspectives and experiences of the dance culture, and is cautiously hopeful, without being uncritically utopian:

> I approach the Hollywood Canteen with an ear for difference, negotiation, and "moments of resistance" and do not presume that these will match or add up to a "one-interpretation-fits-all" conclusion. […] If one can think of the democratic dance floor of the nation as a site of constraints and possibility, rather than a magical past where "big shots are friendly to little shots," one might even discover useful inclusive democratic dance floor strategies for the present ...[40]

In Tucker's case, the "wildly different directions" of participant narratives, an unsurprising result of her meticulously detailed archival work, constitute the generous but critical analysis of a "ready-made story about a 'democratic night club.'"[41]

The most direct and earliest disruption of the advocacy approach to dance music studies is Sarah Thornton's *Club Cultures*—where she argues that "club cultures are taste cultures," and are "riddled with cultural hierarchies." Her book constitutes an early, critical analysis of a culture that she remains on the outside of, even as she willingly goes along for the ride as a participant observer. Thornton's research is London-based, providing a snapshot of a dance music community in the well-known clubbing capital. She demystifies what it takes to be "in" or "out" in the club cultures she researches. Using a sociological analysis of taste cultures informed by Bourdieu's cultural capital, Thornton creates a parallel concept that continues to be relevant in contemporary scholarship of popular music communities: subcultural capital. This is where high culture is supplanted by cool, and low culture is supplanted by uncool. The concept of subcultural capital, among other things, includes an analysis of the figures

---

[40]Tucker, *Dance Floor Democracy*, 16–17.
[41]Tucker, *Dance Floor Democracy*, 4–5.

of Sharon and Tracy "dancing around their handbags," who are symbols of (implied, working class) women with no subcultural capital. Sharon and Tracy show up merely to dance without any particular concern for, or perhaps awareness of, what it takes to be a *real* clubber, a concept that is defined by participants who have know-how and can perform it effectively. Such women are, presumably, the equivalents of the "hairdresser types" referred to by some of my male interviewees in Edinburgh's club cultures. In addition, Thornton addresses the influence of both "mainstream" and "underground" media in dance music, through the reception of media as texts, discourse, and meaning. There is a problem with the trope that tabloid print media, or mass media in general, with conservative agendas, are the adversary in the relationship between underground club cultures and media. Instead, she argues, it is the subcultural media that help to construct the underground subculture itself, as well as to maintain this distinction between the under-threat subculture and the dominant culture that maligns it. Academic work on moral panics and the reactionary nature of mass media, according to Thornton, does not consider the ways that the subcultural construction is supported and reinforced by the conflicts, where they do exist. Mass media, that is, provide the enemy against which the subculture needs to be opposed.[42]

While Thornton's critique is not exclusively about gender, many of effects of the social dynamics she describes tend to fall disproportionately on women. This is also reflected in the way that gender issues are overrepresented in critical scholarship on dance music. Rebekah Farrugia's book-length study of gender and DJ culture, specifically about women who DJ in the Bay Area in California, is an important work that pioneers such perspectives. The location has a significant historical position in dance music culture as its countercultural legacy also made it a hub for early rave cultures in the US-American context.[43] Farrugia shows how many dance music cultures in the United States have ignored women who DJ and have limited what gender

---

[42]Sarah Thornton, *Club Cultures: Music, Media and Subcultural Capital* (Cambridge: Polity Press, 1995), 3–4, 87–162.

[43]Luther Elliott, "Goa Is a State of Mind: On the Ephemerality of Psychedelic Social Emplacements," in *The Local Scenes and Global Cultures of Psytrance*, ed. Graham St. John (New York: Routledge, 2010), 21–39.

expression for women is supposed to be. She addresses the gendered nature of DJing and production technology in dance music culture, and the ways that such media have historically been assigned gender-related symbolism and usage. The associations between electronic music technologies and masculinity are partly to blame, in this account, along with ideas of femininity normalized by celebrity and consumer culture. Farrugia analyzes discourses in fan media as one means to understanding gender dynamics in DJ culture, situating the discrimination and prejudice against women who DJ in a wider world of gender issues.[44]

Farrugia's research is corroborated in several other gender-related studies, including in Anna Gavanas and Rosa Reitsamer's study on European DJs. In their work, Gavanas and Reitsamer address both the historical baggage of gender and music technology and the exploitation by commerce of specific definitions of femininity.[45] Critical studies of dance music that deal with gender also address participation through dancing, incorporating concepts such as the material, sonic, and spatial dynamics of gender. Christabel Stirling examines such ideas in her study of grime, dub, dubstep, grime, and bass music cultures in the UK, critiquing the naturalization of such genres with certain kinds of masculinity. Specifically, Stirling argues, embodiments of masculinity in bass music are socialized over time through, for example, the cultures of roots reggae, which in turn formed in response to institutionalized aggression against 1970s London West Indian communities.[46] Other examples include McRobbie, who has reflected on and revised her earlier theorizations of feminist resistance on dance floors. In her newer work, she discusses the myriad problems with contemporary, consumer-oriented and class-hostile framings of women's empowerment. She also argues that club cultures have not only been models for, but have themselves pioneered, the entrepreneurial

---

[44]Rebekah Farrugia, *Beyond the Dance Floor: Female DJs, Technology and Electronic Dance Music Culture* (Bristol: Intellect, 2012), 11, 19–23, 43–50.

[45]Anna Gavanas and Rosa Reitsamer, "DJ Technologies, Social Networks and Gendered Trajectories in European DJ Cultures," in *DJ Culture in the Mix: Power, Technology, and Social Change in Electronic Dance Music*, ed. Bernardo Alexander Attias, Anna Gavanas, and Hillegonda C. Rietveld (New York: Bloomsbury, 2013), 51–77.

[46]Christabel Stirling, "Gendered Publics and Creative Practices in Electronic Dance Music," *Contemporary Music Review* 35, no. 1 (July 2016): 130–49.

spirit taken up as a role model for neoliberal subjectivity and attitudes to creative labor.[47]

Other critical evaluations of dance music come through examinations of race. In one such work, Saldanha addresses the tangible oppression of locals in the post-hippy psytrance scenes of Anjuna, Goa. His is an ethnographic, geographical project of colossal depth, length, breadth, and conceptual intricacy. He becomes familiar with the scene and its participants but does not adopt the perspectives of those he researches. On the contrary, he remains on the outside. He frames this as unavoidably a part of the subject position he occupies, as a "half-Indian, half-Belgian, definitely not white." This matters, firstly, because of how his ambiguous western-and-brown status places him within the complex subgroups of travelers in Anjuna. It matters, secondly, to how he is placed even as a researcher doing field work. Because of its intellectual history, "ethnography can … be seen to belong to white modernity." This long-term immersion also does not lead to any kind of watering down or meekness in his critiques of the cultures he is observing. Among the issues he examines are the ways that western party travelers' demands lead to local corruption and other problems, while also complaining about the antagonisms fostered between themselves and local authorities (including drug arrests) in relation to such problems. He notes the proximity of extraordinarily loud, all-night psytrance parties to the homes of local villagers, the years-long interconnectedness of the psytrance travelers with the local economy, and the growing hostilities of the government and locals to some of the effects of this particular kind of tourism.

In the big picture, Saldanha uses some of the philosophies of Deleuze and Guattari, among others, to theorize how a white subculture, entirely structured around the performance of "an escape from [its own] whiteness," is racist, in attitude and practice. One manifestation of this is that locals in Anjuna serve the party tourists from the West, and even wealthier Indian tourists from cities and outside Anjuna are not sufficiently schooled in psytrance subcultural capital to be allowed in as part of the hippy clique. All such dynamics, together

---

[47]Angela McRobbie, *The Aftermath of Feminism: Gender, Culture and Social Change* (London: Sage, 2009), 128–34; McRobbie, "Clubs to Companies," 519–21.

with the complicated relationships between the subgroups of tourists from the West, constitute "geographies of inequality."[48] The association of Europe with subcultural capital is also reflected in the attitudes of DJs on the Asian continent that I interviewed, many of whom believe that you have only truly made it when you have played on the European continent. Mayleen, a DJ from Taiwan, has been immersed in psytrance music and culture since 1997, and learned to DJ in 2000. Since then, she has played at parties in India, Nepal, Thailand, Japan, Malaysia, and Singapore. Despite the geographical proximity of her touring locations to the "home" of psytrance, Mayleen qualifies her list to me with, "still never in Europe," which she says it would be her "dream" to perform in (she mentions Amsterdam, in particular). Europe and the English-speaking West appear to still be the standard that many DJs aspire to, perceived as the cultural center of global dance music.

Intersectional approaches to critical research, reflecting scholarly shifts taking place more broadly, deal with various axes of identity-based oppression. Luis Manuel Garcia-Mispireta uses such an approach across his studies of dance music, which results in an ambivalence toward dance music utopianism (though there is an implicit insistence on striving toward utopias in practice).[49] Garcia-Mispireta addresses a wide spectrum of experience located in dance music: from the most beautiful, through musical affect and alternative intimacies, to the most troubling, in the erasure of people of color and queer communities from the dance music cultural canon, to the everyday, in the absorption of dance music into the cultural life and fabric of cities through tourism.[50] His ethnographies and critical historiographies of dance music

---

[48]Saldanha, *Psychedelic White*, 10, 45–46, 133, 144–65.

[49]The dance music collective that Garcia-Mispireta is part of has an overt politics of connectedness and exploration of "the political dimensions of the dance floor." See Room 4 Resistance, https://room4resistance.net/.

[50]Luis Manuel Garcia-Mispireta, *Together, Somehow: Music, Affect, and Intimacy on the Dancefloor.* (Durham, NC: Duke University Press, 2023). Luis-Manuel Garcia, "Beats, Flesh, and Grain: Sonic Tactility and Affect in Electronic Dance Music," *Sound Studies* 1, no. 1 (2015): 59–76; Luis-Manuel Garcia, "Can You Feel It, Too?: Intimacy and Affect at Electronic Dance Music Events in Paris, Chicago, and Berlin" (PhD diss., University of Chicago, 2011); Garcia, "An Alternate History of Sexuality in Club Culture"; Garcia, "Whose Refuge, This House?"; Luis-Manuel Garcia, "At Home, I'm a Tourist: Musical Migration and Affective Citizenship in Berlin," *Journal of Urban Cultural Studies* 2, no. 1–2 (June 2015): 121–34.

account for the earliest involvement of diverse queer and of color communities, not only gay cis men who are canonized in cultural histories.[51] He highlights the connection, for example, between the "stylized bodily movement" of drag and adjacent cultures from queer communities of color as early as the 1930s, and later, of disco. In service of the argument that there was not a cut and dry disappearance of queer scenes after disco, which other accounts may lead people to believe, Garcia-Mispireta discusses the 1990s deep house scene in mid-town Manhattan, which existed in a state of resistance to, while also being continuously affected and compromised by, "Mayor Rudolph Giuliani's increasingly oppressive 'cabaret laws.'"[52] Such work adds depth and breadth to existing histories of dance music.

Critiques of capitalism can also be found within critical studies of dance music. For example, Fabian Holt interrogates the cynical corporatism of an international, mostly Anglo-American and European EDM festival circuit. Market logics lead event conglomerates to commoditize and mediatize everything—including participatory social experiences associated with early dance music party cultures such as UK rave. Among other things, Holt exposes the ends to which corporations that organize dance music festivals— the same events designed to give people uplifting, euphoric experiences akin to hippy-inspired raves—are willing to go in order to safeguard their "brands," which include threats, smears, and other techniques to foreclose any kind of questioning or critique of their operations.[53] In addition, Holt's earlier study of the Red Bull Music Academy, an energy drink-sponsored program, shows the extent to which corporations set taste agendas, and in so doing, subsume culture, and even cultural capital. The corporation, in Holt's study, does not act as a mere sponsor. It employs experts and big-name DJs and producers with credibility in the niche genre worlds of dance music. This ensures that the brand name itself starts to have cultural capital, a credible art world status of its own. As Holt notes, by circulating cultural-historical material

---

[51]See also Micah E. Salkind, *Do You Remember House?: Chicago's Queer of Color Undergrounds* (Oxford: Oxford University Press, 2019).

[52]Garcia-Mispireta, "Whose Refuge, This House?," 44.

[53]Holt, *Everyone Loves Live Music*, 220–26.

such as archival information on the DJ, Frankie Knuckles, Red Bull "gains ownership of the culture" and "shapes how history is told and remembered." For Holt, such relationships ought to be questioned, even if they provide opportunities of a variety of forms where the state and other funding fail to provide them. This perspective is rooted in an understanding of models of funding specific to West- and North-European capitalist economies tempered by social democratic policies, where the arts are financed in larger programs of government-endorsed culture. The separation between "the cultural sphere" and "the corporate sphere" is particular to such settings. Holt's materialist critique of culture as a "marketing unit" does not support a Germanic nineteenth-century idea of artistic autonomy, where a notion of a "pure" *Kultur* could be free from corporatism (though those influenced by Adorno may interpret it this way).[54] Rather, it shows the effects of corporate intervention, influence, and increasingly, out-and-out taste-making agendas. The Red Bull Music Academy, as a project of the past, today calls itself a "global music institution" on its website. It has an archive of "lectures" and a list of "alumni."[55] The company's sponsorship for "underground" dance music has been part-owned by a billionaire whose inspiration for Red Bull came from the "functional drinks of the Far East."[56] Red Bull holds events in Berlin, "with help from production designer and mid-century design specialist Stephan Schilgen, with bespoke furniture created by the Bauhaus-influenced collective NEW TENDENCY and an exhibition of Berlin artists curated by one of Germany's foremost gallerists, Johann König."[57] On the other hand the fans of the Red

---

[54]Fabian Holt, "The Evolution of Sponsorship in Sensitive Cultural Spheres in the Early 21st Century: Lessons from a Culture-Producing Marketing Unit," In *Prekäre Genres: Zur Ästhetik peripherer, apokrypher und liminaler Gattungen*, ed. Hanno Berger, Frédéric Döhl, and Thomas Morsch (Bielefeld: Transcript Verlag, 2015), 102–9, 125–7; Celia Applegate, "How German Is It? Nationalism and the Idea of Serious Music in the Early Nineteenth Century," *19th-Century Music* 21, no. 3 (Spring 1998): 274–96; Weber, "Mass Culture and the Reshaping of European Musical Taste, 1770–1870," 5–22.

[55]"Red Bull Music Academy Lectures," *Red Bull Music Academy*, 2019, https://www.redbullmusicacade my.com.

[56]"Company: Giving Wings to People and Ideas," *Red Bull*, 2022, https://www.redbull.com/au-en/ energydrink/company-profile.

[57]"Berlin 2018," *Red Bull Music Academy*, 2019, https://www.redbullmusicacademy.com/about/ projects/berlin-2018.

Bull event would not likely be found at a Smirnoff vodka mixer-sponsored commercial dance music festival with celebrities and laser shows. Thus, the only thing distinguishing corporate tasteful culture from corporate tasteless culture, here, is aesthetics.

Within all the above accounts of dance music, including even the most critical among them, it is possible to see an underlying faith that there is, or at least could be, something of value to be found in dance music. If dance floors offered no potential to be inspiring, hopeful, or positive, then there would be no reason to bother critiquing them at all. This faith is clear in the works that are primarily celebratory but do not shy away from critiques. For instance, Lawrence names the brutal challenges of New York dance music cultures in the early 1980s: certain dance floors were exclusive and had a tendency to cater to cliques; the AIDS crisis impacted many participants in queer dance music scenes; criminal crack cocaine provoked extreme and draconian responses from city authorities; and groups that had previously come together on dance floors were segregating as scenes fragmented.[58] Where the coming together of celebration and critique manifests as more of an internal conflict is in works where the opposing positions are inseparable. One study where this takes place is Richard Dyer's 1979 essay in the journal *Gay Left*, "In Defence of Disco," which can be referred to as a simultaneously wholehearted and critical celebration of disco. It is an important historical document, published at a moment when disco participation was perceived as anathema to the rock and folk scenes associated with 1960s and 1970s countercultures. Dyer complicates the "eroticism, romanticism, and materialism" of disco musical aesthetics, affects, and politics" and poses a challenge to the trope that rock and folk are musics of the people, that rock and folk are uniquely accessible, and that they are, in their essence, the sole musical bearers of working-class politics. At the same time, his article was a critical response to the takeover of disco by media, marketing, and Hollywood, and to the misrepresentation and overriding of its queer, black, and minority roots.

The type of musical participation with which disco continues to be associated is different from rock in some ways, but much the same in others.

---

[58]Lawrence, *Life and Death on the New York Dance Floor,* 466.

Its differences might well, as Dyer argues, stem from the affordances of its sonic qualities combined with the conditions under which it developed. There is a link, for Dyer, between the sensory experiences brought forth by disco's aesthetics and a utopian politics. There is also a legacy of Dyer's reading of disco music's features in other authors' work, such as his notion that "open-ended succession of repetition" facilitates an eroticism different from rock's "phallic eroticism,"[59] or that house possesses a "funk impulse that frames an open sonic canvas of various cultural influences in a potentially inclusive, democratising manner," while its "amplified bass-heavy beat unites dancers under one groove."[60] In another, the political meaning of techno, within its internal musical form, is that it can "[warn] of our technological future … while advocating a DIY techno spirit in confrontation with this future."[61] Similar arguments are also made about psytrance, which is said to help participants to "enter an initiation without telos, an experience of being-in-transit … [and] a process of re-identification" while being "immersed in a social universe that is liminalized, in which spontaneity and indeterminacy are pursued and reanimated in consequential lifestyle and consumer practices."[62] No such accounts take up Dyer's ultimate ambivalence that disco and capitalism are inextricable, and not more or less than rock or any other music. Dyer's readings of the particular musical qualities of disco are coupled with a qualification (or perhaps even a capitalist realist argument) that disco is "a celebration of the world we are necessarily and already immersed in;—and disco's materiality, in technological modernity, is resolutely historical and cultural—it can never be, as most art claims for itself, an 'emanation' outside of history and of human production." As such, Dyer describes disco's material conditions as much as he does its musical and bodily *sensibility*. His discussion of the ways that disco embodies the contradictions of capitalism—its simultaneous status as a commodity and a space for opposition—is a complication of the relationship of capitalism to dance music.

---

[59]Richard Dyer, "In Defence of Disco," *Gay Left* iss. 8 (Summer, 1979): 20–23; Luis-Manuel Garcia, "Richard Dyer, 'In Defence of Disco,'" in *History of Emotions—Insights into Research*, November 2014.
[60]Rietveld, "Disco's Revenge," 8.
[61]Pope, "Hooked on Affect," 38.
[62]St. John, "Liminal Being," 253.

If this sounds over the top, let one thing be clear—disco can't change the world, make the revolution. No art can do that, and it is pointless expecting it to. But partly by opening up experience, partly by changing definitions, art, disco, can be used. To which one might risk adding the refrain—If it feels good, *use* it.[63]

The critiques included in the above overview of dance music studies are not evidence of how a pure or original culture, in its ideal form, becomes corrupted or tainted. Rather, they show that all such problems are always already present. Although dance music scholars differentiate themselves from each other, and although the differentiations often start with a distancing from the early subcultural theory of the Birmingham School, many are used, in one way or another, to serve the consensus paradigm of dance music studies, which is to bolster positive evaluations of dance music culture, politics, and aesthetics.

As all of the histories and studies of dance music have shown, regardless of how celebratory or critical they are, most dance music genres, scenes, and communities are framed by their relationships to particular locations. As the next chapter will show, none of these local manifestations is self-contained. They interact with each other through their shared mythologies, embeddedness in physical and cultural geographies, regulatory systems, and nocturnal dangers.

---

[63]Dyer, "In Defence of Disco," 23.

3

Location, Regulation, and Nighttime Danger

*This chapter contains especially candid accounts of,
or references to, violence and harm.*

Location is central to the mythos of dance music culture. Dance music genres and communities are attached to the countries, states, territories, provinces, regions, cities, neighborhoods, and venues they began in. Sometimes genres even retain the names of the locations that they are purported to have started in or where they have become well-known. As already shown, Chicago house, Berlin techno, Goa trance, and others are among the genres that this applies to. The location-based origin mythology holds that geographies, histories, politics, and demographics of given locations together create conditions that lead one or another genre of dance music to emerge, thrive, and be immediately vulnerable to either co-optation or termination. Holt refers to this idea as the "genre city," noting that it is folded into the image of the corporate, contemporary city through "tourism, heritage, and city marketing narratives." This also, it is worth noting, extends beyond music, arts, and culture, to the general belief that people hold about the same cities as emancipated or progressive places. For instance, when presenting locals with the immediate aftermath of a violent assault in Berlin, I was met with stares of disbelief, followed by head shakes and statements such as "but this never happens in Berlin" and "but Berlin is such a safe city."

Part of the drive to root dance music cultures in places is practical, based on the limits of access and resources. Put simply, it is not possible for a single researcher to get to clubs and parties everywhere in the world. It is easier to get inside of a community when focusing on one that can be accessed consistently, for a prolonged period. In addition, though, there is an underlying contention that there is no global dance music culture, only millions of distinct, local dance music cultures. Such a perspective normally means that claims about a larger scale, based on a limited research scope, are viewed as scholastically unsound and perhaps even ethically suspect. Yet it is possible to view each local dance music culture as itself already global. As the histories and dance music studies in Chapters One and Two have shown, dance music's influences span the world, from Jamaica to the United Kingdom, from the United States to Germany, from India to the Netherlands. Even people in dance music's "original" locations admit to being influenced by others. Music in a connected world is formed of an amalgam of other music, which constantly reforms itself in response to the music it comes into contact with. London's dance music culture is a hybrid of West Indian and African diasporas (or "internationalist black culture") from the mid-late twentieth century and white British cultures. Chicago house was influenced by funk New York "postdisco" dance music styles. Detroit techno was influenced by funk but also by Kraftwerk, who, in turn, had been influenced by soul, funk, and Motown.[1]

Nevertheless, there is a powerful allure to the origin story, and it remains at the center of how dance music stories are told. It is therefore the point of departure for this chapter.

Origin Stories

Origin stories wrap the tangled web of interactions, events, people, and objects, into tangible whereabouts and sequences of happenings. In other words, they help to make elusive concepts such as "music" and "culture" more comprehensible. At the same time, as Saldanha argues, "the marketing and

---

[1]For example, Sicko, *Techno Rebels*, 25–7; Melville, *It's a London Thing*, 15–17; Garcia-Mispireta, "Whose Refuge, This House?" 40; Salkind, *Do You Remember House*, 62–4.

folkloristic forces that attempt to *place* a genre or musical phenomenon ... have a conservative impulse, trying to fix what is intrinsically nebulous."[2] The conservatism is also in the desire to document, formalize, institutionalize, and preserve. The institutionalization can take many forms. One example is a German court decision to officially validate dance music venues and attribute cultural significance to clubs, which I address later. Other examples include Four Tet performing at the Sydney Opera House, Kraftwerk at the Oslo Opera and Ballet, a silent disco as part of an exhibition at a London festival curated by Yoko Ono, and a performance at the Guggenheim Museum by veteran techno DJ Richie Hawtin.[3] Beyond this, dance music studies attributes not only musical, but regional identities to house, techno, jungle, and psytrance. For instance, Lawrence shows the ways that New York's 1970s and 1980s dance cultures were the sum of many chaotic parts. In the early 1980s, he argues, New York had a thriving anti-conservative, alternative, and diverse art scene, which embraced a "less utopian" version of the 1960s counterculture. By 1983, New York City was buckling under the damage of a neoliberal capitalist regime. In practical, local terms, this meant more gentrification, more class segregation, local governments prioritizing the interests of corporations rather than people, heavy-handed mayoral governance, policing the poor, and by extension, a degradation of the kinds of dance music cultures that had been part of the fabric of the city.[4]

The cultural melting pot that Lawrence describes as pre-existing this downward slide is also found, with its own character, in the hippy-like art scenes of post-Cold War Berlin, the city that is now widely hailed as the techno capital of Europe. The events that made Berlin techno communities possible in the 1990s included the fall of the Berlin Wall and unification of East and

---

[2]Saldanha, "The Ghost of Goa Trance," 55.

[3]BFH v. Senate, "Reduced Tax Rate for the Organization of Techno and House Concerts"; NPR, "Watch Four-Tet's Sumptuous Live Performance in Sydney," August 18, 2016, https://www.npr.org/sections/allsongs/2016/08/18/490487910/watch-four-tets-sumptuous-live-performance-in-sydney; Resident Advisor, "Kraftwerk Bring 3D Concerts to Oslo," October 20, 2015, https://ra.co/news/31863; *The Guardian*, "Yoko Ono's Meltdown: Patti Smith, Boy George and Siouxsie Sioux Sign Up," April 4, 2013, https://www.theguardian.com/music/2013/apr/04/yoko-one-meltdown-patti-smith-siouxsie-sioux; Guggenheim, "Richie Hawtin aka Plastikman to Perform at the Guggenheim on November 6," September 17, 2013, https://www.guggenheim.org/press-release/gig-2013.

[4]Lawrence, *Life and Death on the New York Dance Floor*, 457, 466, 476–9.

West Germany, the abundance of leftover postindustrial spaces, unusually affordable housing and costs of living for an unusually long time compared with neighboring cities, and relatively permissive local governments at the time. The effect of the strong nightlife that resulted from such conditions included that the city attracted, and continues to attract, dance music pilgrims in the form of fans, DJs, and producers (among other kinds of artists), some of whom settle there on semipermanent or permanent basis to pursue their calling.[5] Some similar features can also be found, albeit in a more dystopian version, within former Motown and motor city Detroit. While in a state of postindustrial deterioration, a group of people started to produce and put on parties with electronic music that would later be called techno.[6]

It is possible to see more parallels. The noticeable class divide in Detroit in the 1980s also applies to London, though the class divide's geographical character differs. The "migration and settlement patterns of imperial and post-imperial subjects" from the late 1940s to the late 1960s joined the "hodgepodge of medieval streets and alleyways, suburban sprawl, property speculation and distinctly un-joined-up local-authority planning," and "the richest never live very far from the poorest."[7] Chicago, too, shares such characteristics, though again, here, the manifestation of the class divide in geography diverges: Chicago is one of the most racially and class segregated cities to the present day. Manufacturing jobs such as steel and shipbuilding declined from the 1960s, leaving people, especially young black and Latino men, unemployed, and neighborhoods in states of deterioration.[8] It is helpful to look at the processes that led to this and how academics and governments they worked for perceived such processes and their early effects. For Robert Park of the Chicago School, the consequences of continuous growth on a city spoke to problems that today's largest cosmopolitan cities encounter:

---

[5]Garcia, "Agnostic Festivities," 472; Luis-Manuel Garcia, "Techno-Tourism and Post-Industrial Neo-Romanticism in Berlin's Electronic Music Scenes," *Tourist Studies* 16, no. 3 (September 2016): 276–95; Rapp, *Lost and Sound*, 80–95.

[6]Sicko, *Techno Rebels*, 59–66.

[7]Melville, *It's a London Thing*, 15–16.

[8]Rod Sellers, "Chicago's Southeast Side Industrial History," Southeast Historical Society, March 2006; Great Cities Institute, "Abandoned in their Neighborhoods: Youth Joblessness Amidst the Flight of Industry and Opportunity," Great Cities Institute, University of Illinois at Chicago, January 2017.

As the city increases in population, the subtler influences of sympathy, rivalry, and economic necessity tend to control the distribution of the population. Business and manufacturing seek advantageous locations and draw around them a certain portion of the population. There spring up fashionable residence quarters from which the poorer classes are excluded... unable to defend themselves from association with the derelict and vicious.[9]

Of the above dance music cities, Chicago and Berlin were of particular interest to early sociology scholars. A relationship between the two manifested not only in their comparable circumstances and the way that industrialization and deindustrialization amplified the treatment of the working-class populations as temporary, even disposable, but also in their intellectual relationship. A study of *Tanzlokale in Berlin* ("Berlin Dance Halls") in the *Großstadt-Dokumente* in 1904–08 by Hans Ostwald was an influence on the Chicago School of Sociology. Ostwald both celebrated and critiqued the mass culture that resulted from urbanization in an "Americanized" Berlin—not Berlin "as the political capital, as the Prussian military city or as a seat of the emperor but as an arena of technical and cultural change."[10] This has an interesting resonance in light of the concerns of dance music studies, pointing to some of the features that eventually turn a city into a dance music city.

As the comparison between all of the aforementioned cities shows, the thriving material conditions that make a good dance music city are always temporary. At one point, all of the above cities experienced the short-term benefits of rapid industrialization and urbanization. Through population growth and an abundance of employment, they became host to vibrant urban cultures. However, when all of them later suffered from the aftereffects of either industry collapses, political upheaval, or, in the case of cities such as Glasgow, urban redesigns that firmed or worsened class divisions, those at the bottom suffered poverty, unemployment, crime, and alienation.[11] Some

---

[9]Robert E. Park, "The City: Suggestions for the Investigation of Human Behavior in the City Environment," *The American Journal of Sociology* 20, no. 2 (March 1915): 579.

[10]Dietmar Jazbinsek, Bernward Joerges, and Ralf Thies, *The Berlin "Großstadt-Dokumente": A Forgotten Precursor of the Chicago School of Sociology* (2001), 3.

[11]The Glasgow Indicators Project: Understanding Glasgow, "Post-War Housing Changes," *The Glasgow Centre for Population Health*, https://www.understandingglasgow.com/indicators/environment/housing/post_war_housing.

of these effects were deliberately enacted through neglect, punishment, geographical intervention, or a combination of all three. Significantly for dance music culture, the growth and subsequent collapse of industries also led to an emptying of large numbers of expansive industrial spaces—factories, workshops, warehouses, and so on. They took some time to become marked for demolishment or redevelopment, and until then, people would use them for parties.

Not all cities, even those that have been broadly characterized by growth, and eventually gentrification, have had large vacant spaces to throw unmonitored parties in. There are some places where this is only possible at the peripheries, or in the countryside, and even in such places it is high-risk and often suppressed. Such cities have enthusiastic, skilled DJs and producers, and many fans, but they are in a state of perpetual push and pull with authorities, local governments, and residents. The following section provides a case study of one such city, which has not had the cultural, geographic, or political conditions to ultimately achieve the status of Berlin or Chicago, but whose fans have nevertheless found ways to keep events going in the cracks.

Edinburgh: Club Culture in Struggle

Edinburgh is not counted among the key places from which dance music culture emerged. It is also a small capital city, which means it is possible to get to know more people, events, and venues within its dance music community more quickly than would be possible in huge cities with multiple neighborhoods and scattered geographical hubs. It shares qualities with other British clubbing cities. However, every city's dance music culture has its particularities, and I attempt to account for some of these here. Edinburgh's nightlife is informed both by the high concentration of students living and studying in the center of the city and visitors to the city's historical attractions. It has a high density of nightlife venues from pubs to clubs. Drinking culture is at the center of most of them. Some venues offer live music, a proportion of which is Scottish folk music. Such venues serve a mix of a local population and visitors staying in the Old Town, seeking "authentic Scottish" entertainment. The Literary Pub

Tour is one such activity, aimed at both visitors and the student population, illustrated through its official support by the Scottish Literary Tour Trust and promotion by the University of Edinburgh's student union and halls of residence. It is a tour of old pubs that are linked in fact and fiction to the literary history of Edinburgh, where "drinking is not required (although it is recommended!)."[12]

This form of institutionalized, prepackaged nightlife for the benefit of tourism and in support of the city's drinking culture differs from the club cultures in the city. From the perspectives of the dance music fans I interviewed, there are two types of clubs in Edinburgh: commercial clubs and underground clubs. Commercial clubs, or bars with dance floors belong to networks of Scotland-wide "hospitality" venues such as cinemas, hotels, bars, and restaurants. They are owned by large conglomerates (such as the Scotsman Group, formerly the G1 Group) that launch new companies (such as EH1), which use the creation of new companies to acquire other companies (such as the Festival Group), all managed by the financial services global giant KPMG.[13] Such venues appeal to people on the basis of drinks prices, reliability as spaces of social gathering, and their placement in prominent, well-trodden tourist areas. There are also clubs (and bars with dance floors) down the hill from the Old Town, in the New Town. The New Town is popular for its neoclassical and Georgian architecture and landscaping, gardens, shopping, restaurants, and cafes. The New Town is also a popular area for nighttime entertainment, but has little cultural capital among the genre-focused dance music fans and tends to be mocked as an area for people with money, but without taste.

The second, substantially smaller club community is based, for the most part, in the Old Town, geographically blended with the student and tourist venues. It is comparable, culturally, to the Newcastle clubbing communities

---

[12]The Edinburgh Literary Pub Tour, "What You Need to Know," 2019, http://www.edinburghliterarypubtour. co.uk/the-tour/what-you-need-know.
[13]G1 Group, 2020, https://www.holyroodpr.co.uk/client-hub/g1-group/; Business Sale Report, "G1 Group Acquires Several Edinburgh Pubs," July 27, 2011, https://www.business-sale.com/news/business-sale/g1-group-acquires-several-edinburgh-pubs-176681; Emma Eversham, "G1 Group Launches New Company to Increase Edinburgh Presence," Big Hospitality, July 25, 2011, https://www.bighospitality. co.uk/Article/2011/07/26/G1-Group-launches-new-company-to-increase-Edinburgh-presence.

described in Andy Bennett's research, including that its members identify with a perpetual state of struggle and vulnerability to closure.[14] The music around which such clubs orbit is dance music specific to clubbing, usually genres that neither get boosted for widespread viewing online, nor are played on commercial radio stations. While the clubs in this category operate legally, those who work and go clubbing in them view themselves as marginal. They hold club nights for a variety of music, even genres that are relatively unpopular, as a matter of principle. A semi-regular breakcore event at one club in Edinburgh, for example, brings in people who do not attend other club nights, including older clubbers with cowboy hats and boots, long hair, visible tattoos, and chaotic dancing styles to match the music. The dance floor remains relatively sparse on such nights and few people, if any, would make money from the event. But by continuing a relationship with the promoter of the breakcore night, the venue shows its loyalty to the fringe tastes of communities that are never invited to run events at the corporate nightclubs.

Some of the followers of music-focused clubs see themselves as engaged in a struggle against the culture of drinking that entertainment in general is centered on, represented by the clubs whose profit motives override any concern with music. The resistance against this phenomenon is partly enacted through attending events at music-centered venues that do not promote cheap drinks or encourage heavy drinking. While such venues promote themselves on the basis that they are different from the corporate nightclub circuit, alcohol is still the main means through which they can financially survive. Moreover, there is often a close-knit community that surrounds such venues and the promoters that have residencies with them. The communities are based in part on shared musical tastes, and in part on the oppositional imperative created by the encroachment of corporate interests on one side and the repressive policies of local government on the other. Such policies themselves serve the conservative motivations of the property owner class rather than the communities that form a city's nightlife. Those with the most anxieties about the possible loss of venues and club nights are event organizers, DJs, and

---

[14]Andy Bennett, *Popular Music and Youth Culture: Music, Identity and Place* (London: Macmillan, 2000), 73–102.

regular clubbers, the most regular of whom are friends, partners, and family members of event organizers and DJs.

The extent to which such concerns inform a music community varies. Most participants in both techno and drum 'n' bass events in Edinburgh are broadly aware that most others do not share their musical tastes. This does not necessarily translate to the oppositional sensibilities of some of their peers, nor an awareness that profit-driven venues could be a material threat to their favorite clubs. There are fans who are hardly loyal to one or another genre, venue, or community at all. Many clubbers will go wherever their friends go and dance. For some interviewees, particularly young women, this includes a disclosure of their love of "mainstream" music and venues. Qualifications of this kind happen in cases where the interviewees in question have close relationships with people who are devoted to a genre-focused scene as fans and do not like "mainstream" music. Gabi is one such person, who, at the time of the interview, lives in a share-house with a techno and psytrance dance music fan, Victor (also an interviewee), who hosts parties in his basement. Her venues of choice are not governed by what is cool according to her house mate, but what she likes to go to with her friends and where she can enjoy songs that she recognizes: "I normally go to things like [venue] and stuff, so it's all kind of mainstream music ... if my friends are with me, and it's [a] song that like, I share with my friends, it's one of those things that you want to dance with them too." Fran, a partner of a DJ, producer, and club night promoter at the time of the interview, addresses this more explicitly, by saying, "I've always liked mainstream music. I know that ... Sam and Isaac are anti-chart-toppers and stuff. But I actually like places like [venue]. They basically play chart-topping music."

Edinburgh's Old Town, where most of the clubs that my interviewees attend are located, is characterized by its centuries-old heritage architecture, with spaces occupied, burned down, abandoned, rebuilt, reoccupied, and later gentrified and reoccupied again. Strict local government laws govern legal nightlife in Edinburgh. The city has a 3:00 a.m. curfew for licensed nightclubs. There are limited times of the year during which hours are extended to 5:00 a.m. twice annually during the peak tourist seasons—the New Year (known in Scotland as Hogmanay) and the Edinburgh Fringe Festival in August. The usual 3:00 a.m.

curfews correspond with late night food venues' closing times and a lull in public transport options. Contrary to the desired effect of people going straight home, this leads to a mass exodus of (mostly intoxicated) people from venues onto the streets without alternatives. People who wish to continue their nights out without having anywhere legal to do so, go to loud afterparties hosted by friends, at cramped residential apartments in old buildings, with poor acoustic isolation.

Dance music participants view the City of Edinburgh Council as overly restrictive and conservative. If an individual makes a noise complaint, the noise exceeds the "permitted level," and is not turned down within ten minutes of a warning notice issued, the Antisocial Behaviour etc. (Scotland) Act 2004 allows that "an officer of the local authority or a person authorised by the authority for the purpose, may seize and remove any equipment which appears—(a) to be being; or (b) to have been, used in the emission of noise."[15] I have been the target of such a seizure at one of the private house parties hosted by Gabi and Victor in their basement. The party, as one of an informal series of parties, did not respect the 3:00 a.m. curfew, given that it was not a licensed venue. However, it was in a residential zone, and a single individual resident made a noise complaint. Police and City of Edinburgh Council officers entered the house, issued a warning, and shortly thereafter gave orders for us to disperse. Police instructed me to turn off the music immediately, to which I responded by asking whether I could turn the music down gradually.[16] Police ignored the request and repeated the instruction. Assuming they would not understand or respect the reason for not abruptly stopping the music, I started to gradually turn the music down. Police interpreted this as antagonistic and threatened

---

[15]P. Kerr, personal communication with author, November 14, 2012; Antisocial Behaviour etc. (Scotland) Act 2004, "Part 5: Noise Nuisance: Summary Procedure for Dealing with Noise from Certain Places," https://www.legislation.gov.uk/asp/2004/8/part/5.

[16]I saw it as a responsibility to respect people's reasons for being there, in Garcia-Mispireta's words, "to have fun, dance, enjoy music, drink, get high, get off, feel good." I was cognizant of the philosophy that Garcia-Mispireta has called, "don't mess with the vibe," which guides him in his role as an ethnographic researcher in dance music spaces, and which I also believed to be part of my role as a DJ and participant. Luis-Manuel Garcia, "Doing Nightlife and EDMC Fieldwork," *Dancecult* 5, no. 1 (May 2013): 6–7, 9. It is also important to be gentle with people who are having drug experiences associated with music, as it can be unpleasant or disturbing, even triggering negative "trips" for a sudden change in stimulus to be imposed without warning.

to confiscate my DJ equipment. A second police officer repeatedly instructed people to leave the house immediately. They appeared to be unwilling to depart until they saw the majority of people leave. The confrontation was dispiriting for all who attended. However, the main consequences were for Victor and Gabi, the residents of the house. The penalty threatened to them was an up-front £100 fine. The fear and agitation caused by the confrontation led them to wait three-and-a-half months before holding their next party.

Club nights in Edinburgh tend to be held mostly in licensed spaces. This is counterweighed by the fact that some licensed venues make themselves sufficiently affordable for promoters of genre-focused events, to the point that they often cannot cover their own margins with the income they make, due to relatively high rental costs. The likelihood of clashes with authorities is a disincentive to attempt to circumvent the law, as are permissive entry policies on club doors for both live music and DJ club nights. The cultures of security at the doors of clubs in Edinburgh are different from those at clubs of many other cities, in that they are relatively relaxed and tend to let most people in. While at genre-focused events the club promoters or those working the door for them may turn people away based on their perceived "fit," with the subtext that they appear too working class, the only people who are normally turned away by hired venue security staff are those who appear to be seeking violent confrontations, normally on stimulant drugs. Sometimes there is confusion between the two, which leads to security or promoters refusing entry to people who simply present "classed" appearances in fashion, demeanor, and accent.

The dance music and live music communities in Edinburgh underwent a period of upheaval during my primary period of research there. Clubs closed, were acquired by conglomerates, moved, changed management, reopened, renamed, audited for long term debts, and so on. Local media noticed and reported on the trends. Some of it was blamed on gentrification, some on a lack of support from the local government, some on the city's transient population, and some on material and cultural effects of the concentrated wealth derived from visitors during the August Festival season in particular. The discouragement that many fans felt at this time was compounded by the already existing perception that Edinburgh was inferior to the city of Glasgow, its larger counterpart. In the techno community, for example, Glasgow hosted

venues, events, record labels, and DJ-producers who have international reputations and careers that span decades. Edinburgh techno fans articulated the belief that Glasgow simply had a more vibrant and committed scene. Glasgow's proximity played a role in the concern that many fans had for this. While they believed many of the same qualities to be true for London and Berlin, such cities were considered in a different league because of their size, distance, and histories. The belief about being overshadowed led to what could have been humility but instead descended into self-criticism and self-depreciation on the part of Edinburgh fans. At the same time, the long-time fans, such as DJs who had been playing for decades and event organizers who had cultural capital by association (for example, an interviewee who went to the same club as the infamous *Trainspotting* author Irvine Welsh), were protective of it, or at least of the version of it that they most closely associated with their earliest experiences in the community.

In sum, the attempts of fans to protect, defend, or preserve a local dance music community will have variable effects, depending on the extent to which local authorities are convinced of the value or status of such a scene, economically or culturally. Since Edinburgh is identified with, and economically sustains itself through, its historic tourist attractions, its festivals, and its transient student population, genre-focused dance music venues and events are not a priority for those in charge. Advocates for dance music will readily be ignored for as long as there is no recognition of its value to the city. The next section deals with examples where such value *is* recognized, though not without persistence and pressure, and only by being absorbed into a tiered cultural economy.

Berlin and Oslo: Club Culture as High Culture

"It's official," said the *Guardian* article headline in November 2020: "techno is music." The German Supreme Court of the Federation for Taxes and Customs published a press release, declaring that by law, DJ nights at the nightclub Berghain, in Berlin, have a sufficiently "concert character" to be subject to a lower tax rate than venues for events that are not "concert-like." This decision

had followed a back-and-forth between the club and the court against an earlier determination that:

> DJs' musical performances were not the actual purpose of the events, it was rather about celebrating, dancing, entertaining and enjoying oneself in any way with musically like-minded people. The engagement of well-known DJs merely served as an incentive to visit the club.

The various reasons for denying the equivalency of DJ performances to other types of musical performance had been a combination of pedantry and the arbitrary, for example, that "it was completely untypical for concerts to begin with the music before all guests were present at the venue," that "the low admission price for club nights was disproportionate to the high, sometimes four-digit fees of the DJs," that "the 'interaction between DJ and audience' was also not a feature typical of a concert, but a feature that characterized party and dance events in particular;" and a concern about the focus on alcohol consumption, for which a previous court case was cited.[17]

Nevertheless, with assistance such as a written report by journalist Tobias Rapp, the judgments were overturned, and techno lovers in and outside of Germany celebrated. Social media reactions from the DJ networks ranged from subdued approval to jubilation. There was more money to put on events and less tax to pay for them. Along with the financial victory, people celebrated the prestige of having their courts affirm their cultural contributions to Germany. As Garcia-Mispireta notes, the German word for "high culture" was avoided in the ruling itself, though it was used by media liberally. In a couple of exceptions, a *Resident Advisor* article questioned when other clubs might acquire the same status and an article from the *Guardian* suggested that "the ruling was not a

---

[17]BFH v. Senate, *Judgment of the 23rd of July, 2020* V R 17/17, "Reduced Tax Rate for the Organization of Techno and House Concerts," https://www.bundesfinanzhof.de/en/entscheidungen/entscheidungen-online/decision-detail/STRE202010223; Press Services of the Federal Fiscal Court, "Reduced VAT Rate for Techno and House Concerts: Judgment of 10 June 2020V R 16/17," press release, no. 049/20, October 29, 2020, https://www.bundesfinanzhof.de/en/press/press-releases/detail/ermaessigter-umsatzsteuersatz-fuer-techno-und-house-konzerte; Luis-Manuel Garcia, "Agnostic Festivities: Urban Nightlife Scenes and the Sociability of Anti-Social Fun," *Annals of Leisure Research* 21, no. 4 (2018): 471–3.

decision of basic principle but specific to Berghain," corroborated by the fact that another Berlin club, which later closed, had had its appeal rejected.[18] It would have been interesting to learn on what basis different clubs might have been determined *not* to be a cultural contribution to the life of the city.[19]

A similar story comes from the city of Oslo. A club manager, booker, and promoter of an Oslo venue, Sylvi, also a record label owner and DJ herself, sent me a request for a voluntary expert defense of her venue, which was being threatened by a higher tax bracket. If the full tax rate were to apply, the venue would not be financially viable and would need to close. The act of contacting me was part of a formal appeal by the venue of this earlier determination. The tax office argued that the club had a higher proportion of hours per week with DJs than with live bands or instrumental music and that DJing was not equivalent to the skill required to play an instrument or sing. As such, they could not grant the venue the same reduced tax rate that was granted to venues focused on live (instrumental) music. It was my job to assess their judgement and convince them that DJing was, in fact, a musical skill. The fact that Sylvi had access to an "expert" made a difference: the case turned out to be sufficiently strong, the club maintained its reduced tax rate, and business was able to continue as usual. Since the venue is a social and cultural hub with a significant role in the city's small but vibrant nightlife, this was a positive outcome.

Both cases show the degree to which workers are willing to fight to survive systems that are, by default, hostile to dance music culture. It also shows the power of bureaucrats, faced with budgets and decisions about where public money must go, to determine where legitimate art or cultural contributions

---

[18]Garcia, "Agnostic Festivities," 471–4; Philip Oltermann, "High Culture Club: Berghain Secures Same Tax Status as Berlin Concert Venues," *The Guardian*, September 12, 2016, https://www.theguardian.com/music/2016/sep/12/berlins-berghain-nightclub-classed-as-culturally-significant-venue; Matt Unicomb, "German Court Deems Berghain 'Cultural' Space Along with Theatres and Museums," *Resident Advisor*, September 13, 2016, https://ra.co/news/36363.

[19]Matthew Strauss, "Berlin Declared High Culture Venue by Berlin Court," *Pitchfork*, September 12, 2016, https://pitchfork.com/news/68211-berghain-declared-high-culture-venue-by-berlin-court/; Alexander Iadarola, "Berghain Officially Given High Culture Status and Lower Tax Rate," Vice, September 13, 2016, https://www.vice.com/en/article/8q7vd3/berghain-high-culture-german-court; Oltermann, "High Culture Club."

end, and "mere" entertainment begins. Where government employees and lawyers decide on the relative worth of cultural activities and institutions, centuries-old hierarchies are reaffirmed rather than challenged. The imperative for venues to compete both in the marketplace and for the support of government for high cultural status, where the punishment for not succeeding is manifestly material, only makes the escape from such hierarchies seem even more unlikely. Representatives of cultural institutions have no choice but to actively lobby, in one or another way, for their status to be raised. And where a venue or type of culture has already received legitimation, it would have to vie for its status to be maintained each time an audit takes place.

Dividing culture along status lines by punishing the have-nots materially is not in line with the purported emancipatory values of dance music. The same system is the source of, and continues to fortify, the larger divisions of high and low culture. The embrace of being "let in" to the category of valued culture is an affirmation of class and class-related social divisions. The acceptance of dance music venues into the high culture social club, endorsed by government, joining with the contributions of the western art canon—the opera, the ballet, the symphony, the fine art exhibition, the history museum, or officially endorsed popular music activity, is the acceptance of the high culture social club. It is to be absorbed into, and become a beneficiary of, old-world cultural hierarchies. Rather than stopping at the point of their initiation into the top tier, a greater challenge to those representing dance music would be to direct their attentions to opposing, or at least questioning, such a system at its core.

Nightlife, Regulation, and Danger

"The night" as a temporal and institutional construct is simultaneously central to the life of a city while also being subject to ongoing contestation and tension. Night studies continues the tradition of the early sociologies of popular dance and music discussed earlier, as well as the studies of "deviant" activities that were of concern to social policy makers. It has also expanded to include matters of cultural and economic revitalization and includes constructions of interdisciplinary theories of the night. For example, Will Straw addresses the

way that the 24-hour temporality of contemporary life has been absorbed and reconstituted by media, while Robert Shaw sees the night as an assemblage that ties together the social and natural, "a collection of precarious relations."[20] The particularities of the night have been a common point of departure for various themes in dance music research, including: dance music and the night as synonymous signifiers of amoral and illicit activity; the reversal of wake/ sleep patterns as a subversion of mainstream temporalities; the possibility of community participation for people who are excluded from such participation in the light of day; and the incongruity of a sustainable daytime life with nighttime partying, to name just a few. *Dancecult* has published a special issue to address some of the above issues, positing that nightlife field work is a methodological challenge for dance music researchers. A few key methods emerge, such as respect, trustworthiness, and appropriate boundaries for privacy on the part of participants, and health and financial burdens on the part of researchers.[21]

Surge in research into night life—not only academic—is at times reactive, spurred on by local issues such as new curfews, street violence, drug-related fatalities, and residential property development that shift demographics and lead to clashes between residents, venues, and nightlife participants. In other cases, it is proactive, addressing how a city and its stakeholders can capitalize on its existing successes for the purposes of increased tourism, economic investment, or global cultural credibility. Where existing local governance, urban planning, and social policy are seen to be effective, the concern is to plan for their long-term sustenance. Where such systems are determined as negatively impacting on nightlife, research includes strategies for change, whether economic, material, cultural, or social. As Garcia-Mispireta notes, such fields as tourism studies can uncritically take on "managerial discourse

---

[20]Howard S. Becker, "Becoming a Marijuana User," *The American Journal of Sociology* 59, no. 3 (November 1953): 235–42. See also Robert Shaw, *The Nocturnal City* (London: Routledge, 2018), 2–3; Will Straw and Collaborators, *The Urban Night: An Interdisciplinary Research Project on Cities and the Night*, last updated May 13, 2022, https://theurbannight.com/night-studies-publications-by-will-straw/; Global Cities After Dark, 2022, https://www.globalcitiesafterdark.com/; Will Straw, "Media and the Urban Night," *Articulo: Journal of Urban Research* 11 (2015), https://journals.openedition.org/articulo/3098.
[21]Garcia, "Doing Nightlife and EDMC Fieldwork," 3–17.

of the 'night-time economy' as their sole frame of analysis." For example, there is an assumed notion that tourism has a "trickle-down" positive effect on permanent residents of cities that have a vibrant nightlife. While positive effects may occur in some ways, for example, through new ways for residents to make money, growth in tourism often also breeds resentments due to the priorities of tourism overtaking the needs of residents. The most challenging effects are the rising costs of living, generally, and housing, specifically.[22] At the same time, if the priority is a thriving musical nightlife, some basic conditions need to be in place. Sufficient material infrastructures, population densities, economic might (not channeled toward the rich), diverse demographics, and political will, are among the elements required to sustain activity between dusk and dawn.

Entertainment, including music, is associated with night because in the modern city, day-bound "business hours" apply to the bulk of a population's work and family lives. The thrill of the night comes in part from an almost exclusive bracketing of certain types of adult fun. To what extent nighttime cultures are ageist, or whether they are conducive to participation by adults in their older years, is another issue of growing interest. On the one hand, youth cultures associated with nightlife have had their relationship with particular popular music scenes severed by a mismatch between the demands of nighttime participation and their post-youth social lives and physical states. On the other hand, the extent to which different musical communities welcome participation regardless of age varies substantially from place to place. During my Edinburgh-based research, genre-specific club nights included a small but regular cohort of participants over 50. In Oslo, on the other hand, the mean age at club nights was noticeably younger, except for the DJs, promoters, and their friends.

Overall, the allure of nightlife comes through some research in the form of advocacy and recommendations for how to best support it—defined in various ways, both qualitatively and quantitatively. On the one hand, the night

---

[22]Garcia, "Agnostic Festivities," 466–7. For examples of political will being exerted, see Garcia-Mispireta's description of the installation of the "night czar" in London to bring night culture back to life, and the lobby groups against the Berlin municipal government's move toward private property development.

as a cultural, social, and political realm requires defending and advocating because not everyone in a modern city participates in it by choice. Groups that do participate and value it are therefore charged with proving how the consequences of its suppression are demonstrable, if not measurable, and proving that a thriving nightlife provides quantifiable benefits. In organizations devoted to music nightlife such as Sound Diplomacy, a "global research and strategy consultancy," success stories are cited from Asunción to Amsterdam, and Berlin to Bogota. The argument is made that a vibrant and active nightlife is necessary for the wellbeing of a modern city, even reducing crime, and where such activities are repressed and forced out, a city suffers culturally and economically.[23]

Attitudes to nightlife, and the policies that stem from such attitudes, tend to fluctuate, swing, or cycle. A particularly stark example comes from New South Wales (NSW) in Australia. The NSW state government enacted strict "lockout laws" in 2014 in a particular precinct of Sydney known for its nightlife, including a red light district, Kings Cross. The lockouts were ostensibly reactions to two separate deaths from "one punch" alcohol-driven attacks in a short space of time, and fifteen such attacks in six years.[24] According to Shane Homan, the laws were put into place due to pressure from various interest groups, including the families of the victims and the newspapers *The Daily Telegraph* and *The Sydney Morning Herald*. Homan analyzes such campaigns and the lockout laws themselves with reference to the moral panic model as it has been applied to alcohol.[25] However, an interdisciplinary economics and drug and alcohol research study suggests that the policy may not have reduced the number of assaults overall, because while they fell in the specific area that the lockout

---

[23]Sound Diplomacy, "About Us," 2022, https://www.sounddiplomacy.com/about; Sound Diplomacy and Andreina Seijas, "A Guide to Managing Your Night Time Economy" (London: Sound Diplomacy, 2017).

[24]Alexandra Smith, "Sydney's Final Lockout Laws Axed to Revive CBD," *Sydney Morning Herald*, February 9, 2021, https://www.smh.com.au/politics/nsw/sydney-s-final-lockout-laws-axed-to-revive-cbd-20210208-p570nf.html; Caitlin Fitzsimmons, "Violence Spread Across City by Lockout Laws Could Hurt Sydney's Nightlife Revival," *Sydney Morning Herald*, January 23, 2022, https://www.smh.com.au/national/nsw/violence-spread-across-city-by-lockout-laws-could-hurt-sydney-s-nightlife-revival-20220111-p59nfv.html.

[25]Shane Homan, "'Lockout' Laws or 'Rock Out' Laws?: Governing Sydney's Night-Time Economy and Implications for the 'Music City'," *International Journal of Cultural Policy* 25, no. 4 (2019): 500–14.

laws applied to, they increased in the adjacent neighborhoods.[26] Moreover, from the perspective of those who participated in the nightlife, including entrepreneurs whose interests were economic as much as cultural, such incidents were excuses to adopt policies that were aligned with conservative religious agendas.[27] Importantly, they provided an opportunity for the State to enact what the agents of gentrification, property developers, and wealthy residents had already supported: a prohibitive new set of curfews, which ultimately led to a mass-scale closure of venues in an area that had previously been known for its nightlife. The state granted exemptions to the Star Casino and a new development of the billionaire James Packer. The queer nightlife, which was known globally, was especially affected. In 2009, it was still possible for clubbers to party all night on Sydney's infamous Oxford Street and emerge in broad daylight, while daytime shoppers and workers were already several hours into their days. It did not take long after the lockout laws came into place for those parts of Oxford Street to be almost as quiet as residential streets after nightly restaurants and sit-down bars had closed.

In February of 2021, the lockout laws were lifted by the NSW government, stating that "this move will help stimulate the local economy and boost jobs, while maintaining a focus on community safety." Like London's relatively new night czar, the government employed a "24-Hour Economy Commissioner" to assist with implementation.[28] Yet counterintuitively, the government's approach to the policy reversal is aligned, not in conflict with, the gentrification process. According to the State Premier Gladys Berejiklian at the time of the policy change, "Kings Cross has transformed considerably since these laws were introduced over six years ago … the precinct is now well positioned to continue to evolve into a vibrant lifestyle and cultural destination with a diverse mix of small bars, live music venues and restaurants." There is no

---

[26]George Athanasopoulos, Vasilis Sarafidis, Don Weatherburn, and Rohan Miller, "Longer-Term Impacts of Trading Restrictions on Alcohol-Related Violence: Insights from New South Wales, Australia," *Addiction* 117, no. 5 (May 2022): 1304–11.

[27]Kishor Napier-Raman, "Sydney Finally Scraps Lockout Laws—Was It Worth It?" *Crikey*, February 11, 2021, https://www.crikey.com.au/2021/02/11/sydney-lockout-laws/; Matt Barrie, "Would the Last Person in Sydney Please Turn the Lights Out?" LinkedIn, February 3, 2016, https://www.linkedin.com/pulse/would-last-person-sydney-please-turn-lights-out-matt-barrie/.

[28]Fitzsimmons, "Violence Spread Across Sydney by Lockout Laws Could Hurt Sydney's Nightlife Revival."

mention of nightclubs or sex work. Instead, the "mix" of venues in question fit within ideas of gentrified acceptability. Moreover, the only way that the city can revitalize and be "a vibrant, diverse, inclusive and safe precinct," according to State government definitions, is by means of surveillance, through the use of identification scanners.[29] As such, while such initiatives may be beneficial to those who are interested in the benefits of a nightlife to a city, state, or country's economy, it remains in question whether such benefits do, in fact, "trickle down." What is more, the latter responses to tend to make things less safe. People feel monitored and intimidated by the institutionalized hostility of street police and additional security staff at venues. When queer-friendly or queer-focused venues that would take people in danger of being victimized off the streets, people will need to seek such spaces elsewhere, including in places that are not legal, and that are potentially high-risk in other ways, which will be discussed at length in the latter part of this chapter.

What emerges from the above discussion is the night's relationship with danger. Geopolitical circumstances such as licensing laws, local government policies, cultures and practices of policing and security, drug laws and attitudes toward drugs are among the elements that affect interviewees' safety-danger nexus.[30] But the tools of surveillance and policing described above also take "softer" forms. For example, a program in Oslo, "SALUTT" (*sammen lager vi utelivet tryggere*—together we make nightlife safer), is a course and certification run by the City of Oslo.[31] It involves police and the municipal government in the training and then monitoring of responsible service of alcohol, under the proviso that it is excessive drinking that leads to increases in violence. While the police force states the program's success, with a noticeable decline in violence, a study of the program funded by the Research Council of Norway

---

[29]NSW Government, "Lockout Laws Lifted for Kings Cross," February 9, 2021, https://www.nsw.gov.au/media-releases/lockout-laws-lifted-for-kings-cross.

[30]On the relationship between drugs, danger, and gender, see also Fiona Hutton, *Risky Pleasures? Club Cultures and Feminine Identities* (Aldershot: Ashgate, 2006), 49–90.

[31]City of Oslo, "Salutt Course," last accessed May 18, 2022, https://www.oslo.kommune.no/english/licence-to-serve-food-and-alcohol/salutt-course/#gref.

challenges this.[32] Like the conflicting evidence about whether or not violence was reduced by lockdowns within NSW, this shows how difficult it can be to parse whether such programs work when the official data are presented by those with a clear vested interest in portraying their success.

Other solutions proposed by governments and the organizations that collaborate with them take more creative forms. Incidents of street violence have prompted some organizations to research the nature of people's experiences qualitatively, rather than merely counting the number of such incidents and adding them to statistics. This leads, in turn, to yet more interventions, like those based on the phenomenology of street safety, which can involve surveys, focus groups, or the use of apps. One such project, now complete, is *Free To Be*, an initiative of the Australian branch of humanitarian organization *Plan International*, which worked with Monash University and a Melbourne online mapping software, *Crowdspot*. The project publicly documented the relative safety or lack of safety that women and girls feel in urban and suburban areas of Melbourne. They asked people to map their "sad spots" and "happy spots" on specific streets, represented in red and green respectively. They had the option of adding comments to describe why a spot was happy or sad. The replies to their comments were sometimes abusive "trolling." For example, in response to a woman who said a park she had to use as a thoroughfare is poorly lit and isolated, one person responded, "It's ok Leena you are safe. You're simply paranoid because you've been brainwashed by man-hating feminist propaganda." In response to a person who reported two men throwing several glass bottles in her direction while she walked past them, one respondent said, "What should they do? Go kill them for throwing a bottle near you as a joke, which they would've done whether you were there or not." The reporting is also complicated by the fact that some people report a "sad spot" when they simply *see* homeless or drug-addicted people.[33] It would be hard to argue that

[32]Willy Pedersen, Torbjørn Skardhamar, and Silje Bringsrud Fekjær, "Utelivsvolden og overskjenkingen i Oslo bare fortsetter," *Aftenposten*, March 9, 2017, https://www.aftenposten.no/meninger/debatt/i/4aRkG/utelivsvolden-og-overskjenkingen-i-oslo-bare-fortsetter-willy-pedersen-torbjoern-skardhamar-og-silje-bringsrud-fekjaer; Olav Eggesvik and Erlend Tro Klette, "Forskere: Har ikke lykkes med å redusere utelivsvold i Oslo sentrum," *Aftenposten*, March 9, 2017, https://www.aftenposten.no/oslo/i/epkdR/forskere-har-ikke-lykkes-med-aa-redusere-utelivsvold-i-oslo-sentrum.
[33]*Free To Be*, "Free To Be Archive Map," *Plan International*, https://bit.ly/3UpBHv5.

such encounters belong to the same category as being verbally or physically attacked, even if seeing a homeless person leads one to feel fear. To this end, the comments, as the primary qualitative data, help to mitigate the potential conflation of attacks or aggression with fears alone. In other examples, *Plan International* released a global report on urban street safety in five cities (Sydney, Delhi, Lima, Madrid, and Kampala) titled "Unsafe in the City."[34] In addition, there is a volunteer-led organization in Oslo called *Natteravene*, or the Night Ravens. It is made up of small groups of people who walk around the streets of Oslo and other municipalities, who wear yellow vests with reflectors and blue logos with black ravens on them. The goal of the groups is to help to keep streets safe from violence and make themselves available for assistance to people when needed. *Natteravene* has been in operation since 1990. According to their website, Night Ravens volunteers must "hold a positive view of humanity." The ethos of the role is further described as follows:

You don't need to know karate to be a Night Raven. You don't have to be able to bench press 10 kg in one go. We use words instead. The Night Ravens never intervene in violent situations but observe and call the police if needed. You won't be paid a penny, but you will learn a lot about the town and your local environment, get plenty of fresh air and make new acquaintances—and it does wonders for the conscience![35]

All these examples provide alternatives to the more punitive approaches of restrictive alcohol licensing and explicit policies of aggressive policing and security, though none of them can cover all areas of safety.

Evidently, negative incidents that take place at night can be used to fuel fears of the night and the mistaken belief that the only way to prevent such incidents is to make nighttime spaces illegal. More broadly, however, the question of how to foster an open and free nightlife that is also safe is always in tension. The dangers

---

[34]*Plan International*, "Unsafe in the City: The Everyday Experiences of Girls and Young Women," *The State of the World's Girls Report*, July 8, 2018 (Monash University), https://www.plan.org.au/publications/unsafe-in-the-city-the-everyday-experiences-of-girls-and-young-women/; Nicole Kalms, Gill Matthewson, and Pamela Salen, "Safe in the City? Girls Tell It Like Is," *The Conversation*, March 27, 2017, https://theconversation.com/safe-in-the-city-girls-tell-it-like-it-is-72975.

[35]Natteravene, "Hi, Join the Night Ravens! Helping to Keep the Streets Safe Since 1990," 2018–21, http://www.natteravnene.no/resources/infobrosjyrer/Natteravn-brosjyre_Engelsk.pdf.

that come from the social environments around dance music are not coincidental, nor have they historically existed "just for fun." They were born from necessity. For example, precariousness and danger inflicted upon queer lives and the lives of people of color in the light of day has made the night a safer alternative for many. This has been the case for a long time, and for many groups that have needed to hide. Furthermore, the very institution of the nightclub is associated with subversion and gritty underworlds in the western imagination because of its histories. Prohibition in the United States contributed to such ideas, as did the after-hours nighttime entertainment in Britain during the First World War and the 1920s. Licensed venues were obliged by law to close by half past ten, but illegal after-hours clubs nevertheless flourished and were associated with drug use (alcohol, cocaine, and opium), dancing, stripping, and prostitution. Such venues were viewed as dangerous and corrupting to society. By some accounts, the notion that youth was a distinct group with cultures and behaviors that differed from the respectable adult world also surfaced during this period—tantamount to the enjoyment and appropriation by white people of the vernacular music and dance styles of the Black Atlantic.[36] These are among the histories that show that when certain types of activity do not gain legal or social approval, they do not stop happening altogether, but are driven underground. Of course, the associations endure even in the dance music cultures that are fully absorbed into commercial entertainment industries. But the subversion of temporal norms is not, by itself, a subversion of other societal norms. It is the social purpose such a subversion serves that matters, like whether it meets the needs of people in struggle.

Where things get more complicated is that the same characteristics that make the night ideal for hiding from surveillance and authority—its slipperiness and conduciveness to invisibility and stealth—can also make it unsafe in a number of ways. For example, according to data collected from the Lincolnshire Police in the UK, the majority of sexual violence occurs at night, offenders are usually intoxicated, and people are less likely to report harassment due to the fact that such behavior is expected.[37] DJs who have to

---

[36]Marek Kohn, "Cocaine Girls," in *The Clubcultures Reader: Readings in Popular Cultural Studies*, ed. Steve Redhead (Oxford: Blackwell, 1997), 120–6.

[37]Hayley Child, "Collectively Tackling Sexual Violence After Dark," *Global Cities After Dark Outcomes Paper*, November 2018, 12.

travel alone late, after most clubbers have already left, are therefore more likely to be exposed to harm. When people are less visible due to a lack of light, when there is a relative lack of visibility, and when intoxication is common, people who wish to commit acts of harm and violence are freer to do so with less fear of consequence. Such incidents vary in form and degree.[38] One example comes from a DJ, Gabriela, in Buenos Aires.[39] Gabriela stated that she has not felt as though she was "treated differently" in her DJing work due to her gender. However, she does not feel the same safety travelling home late from gigs. The specific reason for this is what she referred to as a "growing paranoia around rape and murders—*femicidios, Ni Una Menos*." *Ni Una Menos* refers to "Not One (Woman) Less," the feminist activist movement in Argentina that has been protesting femicides and the attitudes that normalize them since 2015.[40]

Another example comes from Veena from New Delhi. Veena has been a target of both gender and homophobic violence, the latter which, at the time of the interview, was still legitimated by Indian law, though this has changed since 2018.[41] Veena refers specifically to two semirural/rural areas outside New Delhi, Uttar Pradesh and Haryana, from which many men at her gigs would come. Veena associates specific parts of these regions with prevalent gender-based violence and honor killings, for example, New Delhi's satellite cities of Noida, in Uttar Pradesh, and Gurugram (Gurgaon) in Haryana, both of which Veena explained had recently been subsumed into New Delhi's expanding geopolitical boundaries. Media reporting and research highlights the scale of such incidents.[42] As a result, when she has played at larger events that she

---

[38]Of course, problems with street safety are common at all hours and in all spaces. If anything, both the *Me Too* and *Black Lives Matter* campaigns have shown the extent to which people enact violence and harm in plain sight—and get away with it. However, it is these environments and circumstances, within which dance music primarily operates, that can foster and amplify such problems.

[39]We communicated using email instead of video or audio on her request, to allow her to feel more comfortable to form her responses more fully in English.

[40]María Luengo, "Gender Violence: The Media, Civil Society, and the Struggle for Human Rights in Argentina," *Media, Culture and Society* 40, no. 3 (2018): 397–414.

[41]Newly Paul, "When Love Wins, Framing Analysis of the Indian Media's Coverage of Section 377, Decriminalization of Same Sex Relationships," *Newspaper Research Journal* 43, no. 1 (March 2022): 7–28.

[42]M. E. Jaleel Ahmad Arupendra Mozumdar Khan, and Deepthi S. Varna, "Gender-Based Violence in Rural Uttar Pradesh, India: Prevalence and Association with Reproductive Health Behaviors," *Journal of Interpersonal Violence* 31, no. 19 (2015): 3111–28; *Times of India*, "Honour Killings: More than 300 Cases in Last Three Years," September 22, 2018, https://timesofindia.indiatimes.com/india/honour-killings-more-than-300-cases-in-last-three-years/articleshow/65908947.cms.

has anticipated will attract men from greater-Delhi, the ends Veena goes to in order to ensure her safety are more extreme than those of the other DJs I have interviewed.

> V: For most parties I used to have a gunman ... a bouncer.
>
> TG: Do you know whether other women DJs in India do the same thing?
>
> V: They try. But ... I mean, these security guards aren't cheap. But because one of my friends ... ran an agency back in the day. He'd be like, "dude, just have this guy for the night, it's fine. I'll take care of it. And just pay whatever ever you want to whoever you can," sort of thing. And I made friends with one particular person, so that particular person would keep coming. Again and again. You know. And ... it's not as if the gun is loaded or anything. But still carrying around a gun on his shoulder would just keep the people at bay. I don't think we ever had the gun loaded. Never. Because I'm not fond of guns. The gun was never really loaded, but it was just hanging on his shoulder, yeah? Makes people think twice about messing.
>
> TG: And would you take this bouncer with you to every city?
>
> V: Oh, just in Delhi. Just in Delhi. Never needed a ... bouncer outside Delhi.

Veena also recounts how safety is not only a concern due to the homophobia and gender-related prejudices of clubbers, but also in relation to managers and bookers, who exploit their power to harmful ends:

> For me it was hard because ... men did not like the fact that I am a lesbian. They did not do well with that at all. They were not very happy. And the number of times you would get "oh, you just haven't met the right man yet." And ... men expect a lot of favors in return for helping you out. Like ... so ... I mean, being made uncomfortable with awkward sexual advances. And ... guys being like, okay, I can get you to play in this club but what do I get in return. I'm like, oh ... you can have some cash or you can take a card or whatever. You're getting that anyways, it's not like you're giving me everything you're getting, so what the fuck are you guys on about?" But there is always that. I mean that is really annoying ... I mean ... god. I was sexually abused, I mean, sexually molested once or twice ... by a

few men … This manager put his hand in my thigh and squeezed it really hard and said, "you know what I want." Then another one grabbed a boob. There was a festival which I wouldn't want to name but the organizers at that festival, wanted to … well … sort of left me in a very, very, very tragic position.[43]

There are also stories DJs have accounted of danger inside venues. Some do not feel safe in the hands of nightclub or festival security staff, often because security staff are either unresponsive or combative. Sydney-based DJ Patricia describes an encounter in a DJ residency she held in Dubai:

> P: The security didn't believe me that I was there to DJ. They didn't believe that that's what I was there for. I was just like "I've just been flown over, I'm resident here." I was literally booked to play there. And it wasn't until I actually got to know the security each time that they were okay with it. They just wouldn't even let me in the DJ booth!
>
> TG: How did you … get around it in the end?
>
> P: I actually had to go, okay, just think about where you are, actually had to go and find an Australian male who worked there who (I knew there was one) to vouch for me. [*Laughter.*] Which was quite unbelievable. And even, like … heaps of ex-pats that are over there, they just turn into pigs … one English guy came up and put his hand on my leg and called me a whore. And I'm just like, what the fuck, like, this is hectic. Security's just like "tell me he bashed you and then we can fuck him up and put him in jail." And I'm like, "I'm not saying that!" Like, it's just [*laughter*] nuts. It's absolutely nuts … I haven't been back for awhile, mind you.

In other situations, security staff treat the DJs themselves as the threat, adding an additional layer of disempowerment. This is an issue particularly for transgender, nonbinary, or gender nonconforming people. Some interviewees have recounted provocations, taunting, verbal harassment, and physical

---

[43]Another interviewee from India who identifies as a lesbian, Falak, said that she does not experience the kinds of gender issues that women who present heteronormatively do, on the other hand, because people think she is a cis man.

violence as commonplace experiences. Christine from Melbourne describes examples of her experiences at length in the below excerpt.

> C: I had my CD launch at [venue] about two months ago, and I went for a cigarette out on the street, and a guy who was drinking in the front bar was also out on the street having a cigarette, and he started … well he just started having a go at me for what I was wearing. And started calling me a poofter and everything. And I kind of walked up to him and said, "no, I'm actually a trans woman." I said "I'm a woman." He said, "no, not to me you're not." And I said, "no, I am." And he said, "don't get fuckin' smart with me or I'll punch your fuckin' head in." And the bouncer did absolutely nothing. I said to the bouncer, "what are you going to do about it?" And the bouncer just pressed his lips together and did nothing, just shrugged his shoulders. And then I ran inside to get some help and the dude at the front bar came out to kind of sort it out. And then the guy who wanted to punch my head in started punching the window with his fist repeatedly and smashed the window. And then the bouncer walked up to me and said, "if you don't get out of the front bar, I'm going to put you out on the street." And I had to play a show, half an hour later. And I was like, "you've got to be kidding me." I had to be calmed down. It was really scary. And this was probably two months after the bashing of [name] in New South Wales. Violence for us is a very serious thing. It's something that we have to navigate in and out of …
>
> I had to go to [venue] the next day. And … they fired their bouncer. They explained all this stuff, "oh, it was an ice addict, it could have happened to anybody." I said, "no, it couldn't have happened to anybody. Trans folk violence doesn't happen to anybody. Just because it's an ice-head doesn't mean that ice is making this person …" I was like, "don't blame it on drugs and don't say it can happen to anybody. It's different and you've got a responsibility in the end. And, like, you don't just solve the problem by putting it out on the street. If the bouncer needs to protect the person that's vulnerable, putting me out on the street, I'm going to get killed. I want to do more shows at [venue]. What

are you guys going to do about saving your reputation as a place that's going to protect trans women?" And there's been incidents since. ... I got in a fight. I got in another fight with somebody about three weeks ago, four weeks ago. So, you know.

TG: A physical fight?

C: Yeah. They came up to me and started hassling me and I pushed them into the speaker. Such is, I guess, the fear that I have about being attacked, that if anyone comes near me, I just ... get on the front foot and put them down.

Christine also recounts how security staff, even when briefed, either show poor training, or willfully misinterpret instructions designed to ensure trans and queer people are safe at venues:

I organized the [name] party at a club. And, I put in my contract with the venue that security and bar staff needed to provide a safe space. It was a queer and it was a trans party and I didn't want anyone to be hassled. I also didn't want dickheads to be let in who might hassle. So [security staff's] attitude in doing that was to basically tell everyone who walked up […] to say, "oh it's a queer party and it's a trans party tonight, you probably won't like it." So we ended up not getting enough people on the door, they shut us down early, we lost our deposit. And then I'm trying to pack up the party on my own and then the security guard comes up to me and starts verbally intimidating me to get out of the venue. And I'm packing up lasers and ripping up tape and taking down décor and packing up instruments all on my own. I'm like, "can you give me 20 minutes to pack down?" And he was pretty upset, because I was stopping him from having an early night. So there are some places that we just won't go back to ... so then we don't have venues, so then we've got to do things in warehouses, or we've got to do things at house parties, or we've got to sort of take it into our own hands. You know, do things in squats. You know, and meanwhile, there are touring queer DJs who play at places like [venue], or places like ... wherever. But they don't book any local queer DJs. We're too scared to go to those venues. Some women are too scared to go to those venues. Because the men there

are just going to be really problematic. We just don't want to deal with that. There are just places that are just notorious for being (*sic*) sexually assaulted. You know, grabbed on the arse, groped, having drinks spiked, all that kind of stuff. You know, there's just … you've got to be really careful. It completely affects DJ culture, it affects dance culture.

Another problem is the physical character of venues themselves. The use of warehouses and abandoned industrial spaces for unregulated parties has been understood as fulfilling a need for people marginalized across various axes to be free and socially and physically safe to party and express themselves where they would otherwise not be able to (actual clubs, bars, or legal festivals). Unregulated, abandoned, old buildings can often be structurally unsound, or, where they are rebuilt or refurbished, such work is often undertaken in an ad hoc, patchwork manner with no oversight or regulation applied. One community still suffering as a consequence of this kind of situation is the residents and artists of the Ghost Ship in Oakland, and their families and friends. The Ghost Ship was a warehouse that functioned both as a living space and a working space for artists, some of whom continue to struggle to afford housing.[44] In December 2016, not long after my interviews with DJs who had friends in this community, the Ghost Ship caught fire during a party, probably due to poor electric wiring and other structural issues. The fire killed thirty-six people, including one of the residents, together with DJs, producers, and other dance music fans. Many victims belonged to, or were involved with collectives of, queer and other marginalized groups.[45] A long-term, multiple-stage lawsuit against the master tenant and rent collector followed, which finished in a restitution order and a plea deal in July 2021. The families of victims argue that this is inadequate as a consequence for the criminal negligence (as the prosecution called it) of

---

[44]Erin Baldassari, "Former Ghost Ship Residents Struggle with Trauma, Finding Permanent Housing," *East Bay Times*, April 30, 2017, https://www.eastbaytimes.com/2017/04/30/former-ghost-ship-residents-still-struggling-with-trauma-finding-permanent-housing/.

[45]Julia Prodis Sulek, "Oakland Fire: The Last Hours of the Ghost Ship Warehouse," *East Bay Times*, December 11, 2016, https://www.eastbaytimes.com/2016/12/11/oakland-fire-ghost-ship-last-hours/; "Oakland Fire Victims Remembered," *BBC*, January 4, 2017, https://www.bbc.com/news/world-us-canada-38218022.

the tenant.[46] One letter to the editor from a local resident argued that it was the responsibility of the warehouse's landlord and the City of Oakland as much as the tenants.[47] The City spent tens of millions on the legal defense and the settlement overall, in contrast to what victims' families received: USD 5800 each to "cover funeral costs and the cost of victims' lost property."[48]

Such a tragedy epitomizes the darkest sides of gentrification pushing people to the fringes and of also denying people the formal approval of their activity or community. Where society and law does not support the rights of people to be free to participate in a social and cultural life of their choosing, there is a justification for the fight for acceptance by institutions. Being "above board" is one way to avoid life-endangering risk, for example, in the right to use buildings that are structurally sound and fire safe. The fights may result in success for specific venues based on changes to local laws. But they then need to either be government or privately owned. The former requires a trust that government does not abuse its ownership via attempts to control or micromanage the way that a venue is used or the purpose for which it is used based on its ideological or economic interests. The latter, on the other hand, requires money, which, in turn, must either come from formal institutions such as governmental or nongovernmental organizations, or more realistically from the people who wish to hold events at the venue, who then also need to pass on costs to those who attend such events. While the broader political fight is to make all unused spaces legal to use, it is not clear how it would be possible to do so democratically and without the intervention of interests informed by capital or by the dubious interests of states, in a system where property and space are treated as commodities rather than basic rights. In sum, the drive into the underground, while glamorized or celebrated as edgy by people who can opt in or out as they wish, can be dangerous for those who are forced into it.

---

[46]Nate Gartrell, "Ghost Ship Criminal Case Ends with Restitution Order: Victims' Families Ordered to Receive $5,800 each, but are doubtful they'll ever see the money," *East Bay Times*, July 23, 2021, https://www.eastbaytimes.com/2021/07/23/ghost-ship-criminal-case-ends-with-restitution-order-victims-families-ordered-to-receive-5800-each-but-are-doubtful-theyll-ever-see-the-money/.

[47]Sean Williams, "Letter: Owner, City also at Fault in Ghost Ship Tragedy," *East Bay Times*, December 13, 2017, https://www.eastbaytimes.com/2017/12/13/letter-owner-city-also-at-fault-in-ghost-ship-tragedy/.

[48]Gartrell, "Ghost Ship Criminal Case Ends with Restitution Order."

The last form of intervention worth addressing, which contrasts with some of the top-down approaches imposed by governments and collaborating organizations discussed in this chapter, is the grassroots kind, whose scale is too large to do justice to here. One open and simple act that ballooned during my research on gender was to incorporate deliberate policies of inclusion within booking contracts. At times, the instigators of such policies would publicize them, while at others, they would be private transactions with venue managers, promoters, and festival organizers. During the same period of research, another method of direct action became an increasingly commonplace move for bookers, venue managers, club promoters, or festival organizers: the cancelation of bookings of DJs who acquired reputations for misogynistic, racist, or homophobic acts, who support political ideas that are seen as oppressive, or who had been accused of assault.[49] Cancelling performers is, in some senses, a comparable move to the older idea of the boycott, a technique often applied to nation states and corporations as a form of withholding support for regimes, policies, or acts. Any behaviors or ideas that a vocal enough group in the general public (including but not only fans) considers to be a problem are subject to the same method of withholding or withdrawal. It is an imperfect method of response, since, in cases where an accusation is untrue, there is no recourse for those who are "cancelled."[50] Yet due to its starkness, and due to the impossibility of ignoring it in the public sphere (fans are affected whether they agree or not), it is possible to view cancellation as an example of the most effective and public call to attention for such issues to date.

In conclusion, location is a key means through which to understand dance music, both from the perspective of its origin stories, the formation of a

---

[49]For example, Katie Bain, "Datsik Breaks His Silence in Lengthy Video Statement After Sexual Assault Allegations," *Billboard*, May 5, 2019, https://www.billboard.com/music/music-news/datsik-video-statement-sexual-assault-allegations-8542801/.

[50]For example, see Janice Du Mont, Karen-Lee Miller, and Terri L. Myhr, "The Role of 'Real Rape' and 'Real Victim' Stereotypes in the Police Reporting Practices of Sexually Assaulted Women," *Violence Against Women* 9, no. 4 (April 2003): 466–86; and more recently, Shyamala Y. M. Gomez, "A Measure of Justice: Alternatives to Pursuing Criminal Accountability in Conflict-Related Sexual Violence in Sri Lanka," *Violence Against Women* 28, no. 8 (June 2022): 1824–41; Dean Peacock, "Moving Beyond a Reliance on Criminal Legal Strategies to Address the Root Causes of Domestic and Sexual Violence," *Violence Against Women* 28, no. 8 (June 2022): 1890–907.

narrative of key (extraordinary) dance music cities, and what even ordinary dance music cities' specific features can have on their dance music cultures and nightlife. Constructing and framing a social nightlife is a way to make sense of one of the greatest determining factors on dance music: the regulatory framework of a location through licensing, the law, and policing. Within this, the conceptions and realities of danger, as well as responses to them by the law, work together or against each other in complex ways to affect the actual safety of dance music participants around the world. The chorus of voices that identify the dangers that have existed for a long time is becoming louder, which, in turn, impacts both regulatory responses and broader cultural shifts about how society can better treat people who wish to enjoy dance music at night. Whether the changes are sufficient to curtail actual violence and harm, as opposed to only identifying and punishing individuals who inflict harm, is yet to be seen.

What is extraordinary is that regardless of the challenges to dance music spaces in ordinary locations with regulations and nighttime dangers, people nevertheless continue to seek out any such spaces—in the hope of a time and place where some of those ordinary experiences just might be transcended.

4

Transcendence

On an empty dance floor at the beginning of one club night in Edinburgh, a couple of hours before I am due to DJ, I dance with my friend Holly. Her eyes are closed, and she appears to be oblivious to (or at least unconcerned about) who can see her or what is happening around her. Her dancing is not dictated by "moves" or by interacting with other people, but by allowing herself to be carried by sound, darkness, and space. She remains fixed to one spot in the middle of the otherwise empty dance floor. I dance some distance away, to honor whatever it is that she has carved for herself.

Within half an hour, people begin arriving. At this time, the DJ starts to build up the volume of the music, and any conversation increasingly must be shouted rather than spoken. The dance floor is still largely empty, with most people at the bar buying their first drinks or sitting on stools behind the dance floor to greet or wait for friends. But one man—a stranger—comes to the dance floor and begins dancing some distance behind Holly. He appears to be seeking a clear view of the DJ, but as he continues to shuffle toward her, it becomes clear that the DJ is not his focus. After several minutes, and despite an otherwise empty dance floor, the stranger has moved so close to her that he is all but making bodily contact with her from behind. Remarkably, despite how close he is, he manages to stay almost in perfect sync with her movements without any touch or contact for several minutes. Given that her eyes are still closed, Holly is not aware of him. I recognize the futility of saying anything, as I would need to shout directly into his ear to make myself heard. Holly's dancing becomes more dynamic and expansive. She eventually collides with him. Having been jerked out of her state of flow, she opens her eyes and turns to look at him. I anticipate a confrontation, but it does

not come. Instead, she turns to her original position, takes a few steps forward,
closes her eyes, and continues to dance. She seems unfazed. As the dance floor
fills, I give the stranger a glare and a dismissive wave. He sidles away.

Anyone with exposure to the cultures and claims of western art music would be
broadly familiar with the assertion that higher experiential states can be achieved
with the right kind of listening, in the right kind of listening environment. Such
states come from an intuitive, embodied knowledge of the material affects/
effects of sound, music, dance, and togetherness. They also, though, come from
a learned standpoint, influenced by certain kinds of Romantic idealism, that the
symbiosis of music, dance, and in the case of dance music, usually drugs, help
partygoers to *transcend* something. In the case of dance music, it is their egos,
their identities, worldly problems, the drudgery of everyday life, the constraining
temporalities of labor and leisure in an industrialized, bureaucratized society,
and political disaffectedness. What occurs at the other side of transcendence
ranges from Being with Nature (for example, at forest raves), coming to an
understanding of the essence of human experience (for example, through drug-
and-music-induced euphoria), and connecting meaningfully with others (for
example, through dancing and tripping together). There does not need to be a
pot of gold at the end of that rainbow; the rainbow is the means *and* the end.

At the same time, several versions of the above story about Holly and
the stranger, which came from participant observation on a dance floor,
occur everywhere—regardless of genre, regardless of how "commercial" or
"alternative" music is, and even regardless of the absence or presence of any
music. Electronic dance music contains a confluence of sounds, cultures, and
circumstances that together work to make the above incident commonplace:
openness to nonnormative and "eccentric" behavior; darkness and loudness;
a focus on sensual (and in some contexts, sexual) bodily pleasure, to name
just a few. Yet it is hardly remarkable or unfamiliar that Holly's agency is
undermined, her personal space intruded on, and her activities disrupted by a
man who she does not know. In Holly's case, the disruption is a mere hitch in
her ability to "get into it."[1] But in many other scenarios, for many other people,

[1]See Mihalyi Csikszentmihalyi, *Beyond Boredom and Anxiety* (San Francisco: Jossey-Bass, 1985), 104–5, 109.

getting back into it is not possible at all. For others, finding "it" was impossible in the first place.

It is possible to jump to a couple of conclusions. One is that Holly has figured out how to do it right, either through denial, determination, or by accepting that some people will not respect her boundaries and deciding to have a good time despite this. The implication here is that women who would allow such a man to disrupt their connectedness to music and space are getting it wrong by allowing others to get in their way. Positive psychologist Mihalyi Csikszentmihalyi would say that Holly has found a way to put her "'inner' skills and 'outer' challenges ... in balance [so that] the flow state can be experienced."[2] Another conclusion is that the specific conditions of *this* dance floor are not right, that it is failing at what it is supposed to socially provide. Since these rely on either the triumph of an individual will or a nostalgia for a mythologized dance floor golden age, neither of these conclusions is satisfactory. Rather, the dance floor is part of a world that makes such incidents, the stranger's behavior, and the behaviors of countless others like him, entirely the norm.

Based on the celebrations of dance music culture outlined earlier, it is not surprising that stories of the ruptures to the transcendent experience get buried.[3] It is hard to stay on message about the power and potential of a musical culture while also pointing out that whatever the music, wherever the party, people will be people, which sometimes means they will do bad things to others. At the same time, many dance floors provide profound and transformative experiences to a great many people, even helping some of them to transcend something—whatever that may be. The first part of this chapter describes what different kinds of transcendence are and what techniques and technologies (such as sounds and drugs) people use to make them happen. As the descriptions of sonic experience will show, the techniques to reach states

---

[2]Csikszentmihalyi, *Beyond Boredom and Anxiety*, 191.
[3]The notable exceptions are typically from feminist critiques of dance music cultures. See, for example, Farrugia, *Beyond the Dance Floor*; Gavanas and Reitsamer, "DJ Technologies, Social Networks and Gendered Trajectories in European DJ Cultures," 51–77; Thornton, *Club Cultures*. For a more nuanced argument, see Malbon, *Clubbing*, 42–5. However, other feminist analyses argue that so-called subcultural or underground dance music cultures can be liberating for gender and sexuality compared with more "mainstream" spaces. See, for example, Hutton, *Risky Pleasures?*, 103–4; McRobbie, *Postmodernism and Popular Culture*; Pini, *Club Cultures and Female Subjectivity*.

of transcendence are held in a delicate equilibrium with the ordinary, material reality within which they take place, and, more than this, are a part of that reality. It is this delicate balance, together with the tensions that belie it, that the final part of this chapter directs its attention to.

What is a transcendent experience or encounter at a dance music event? What leads someone to have one, and what characterizes it? To say that a person can "have" such an experience may not even be the most helpful articulation, since the phenomenon emerges from an infusion of affect, sensation, nostalgia and memory, connection, intensity, and various kinds of stimulus. While many of the accounts summarized earlier note that other aspects of dance music matter, in the end, they point to the core significance of dance music as a place where something ordinary can (and even ought to) be transcended. To begin with, expectations of transcendence can be self-fulfilling, in that the intention to experience the transcendent will often lead to behavior that helps to facilitate it.[4] This is as true for producers and DJs as it is for dancers. Producers knowingly make their music, and DJs knowingly plan their sets, not only to bring people to, and keep people on, dance floors, but to take dancers on a journey to transcend their usual senses of their bodies, time, and sound while they are there. At some electronic dance music events, tactile encounters between moving bodies, sound, light, and space—or what Maria Pini calls the "mind/body/technology assemblage"—are the means through which some dancers can enter into states that they experience as beyond the ordinary.[5] Such states are transcendent in the broadest sense possible (not to be confused with the specific nineteenth-century American Transcendentalist literary movement and philosophy). For many people, this higher state is simply the contrast to what happens every other day, beginning with the rituals of getting ready to go out on a Friday or Saturday night.[6] For others,

---

[4]Several authors discuss the confluence of such elements to create a kind of alchemy or magic in similar ways: Ben Malbon describes an oceanic experience (Malbon, *Clubbing*, 105–10); Graham St. John refers to liminal-being (St. John, 2015, "Liminal Being," 254); and Kai Fikentscher and others write about the vibe (Fikentscher, *You Better Work!*, 80–2). See also Becker, "Becoming a Marijuana User," 235–42.

[5]Maria Pini, "Cyborgs, Nomads, and the Raving Feminine," in *Dance in the City*, ed. Helen Thomas (London: Palgrave Macmillan, 1997), 124.

[6]For a humorous and realistic depiction of such rituals, see *Human Traffic*, directed by Justin Kerrigan (Cardiff: Irish Screen & Fruit Salad Films, 1999; In2Film & Metrodome Distribution, 2007), DVD.

experiences are attached to specific dance floors or certain nights out. For a third, perhaps rarer group, dancing at certain places, with certain people, to certain music, can lead to transcendent experiences that outlast their nights out and percolate their everyday lives on a long-term or permanent basis.[7] Put another way, the transcendent experience ranges from the most mundane to the most profound. At the mundane end, there is still a humble power in the demarcation of a time and space exclusively for pleasure, away from the toil, routine, or boredom of daily life. At the most extreme end, people might be able to enter what is sometimes described as a trance state. Judith Becker describes being in trance as "a state of mind characterized by intense focus, the loss of the strong sense of self and access to types of knowledge and experience that are inaccessible in non-trance states."[8]

Another form of transcendence that is often talked about in conjunction with trance is ecstasy. Trance and ecstasy both connote an intensity that makes them of particular interest to anthropologists of ritual. Gilbert Rouget, for example, posits a dualism of trance and ecstasy, where ecstasy is a clearly recalled experience and trance involves dissociation and "amnesia." Ecstasy includes visual and auditory hallucinations, trance does not. Ecstasy brings forth "sensory deprivation," while trance elicits "sensory overstimulation." Rouget takes this binary classification to its outer limits with many more characteristics: ecstasy equals immobility, trance equals movement; ecstasy equals silence, trance equals noise.[9] Yet while going to great pains to distinguish between them, he also argues that the words are used in a variety of ways (and far less schematically) in early Greek, Christian, and Muslim texts. As descriptive terms for what happens on DJ-driven dance floors in the twentieth and twenty-first centuries, they also tend to be fluid and interchangeable in their use. In addition to trance and ecstasy, flow describes a state sometimes elicited by dancing or listening to dance music.[10] Several other adjectives could

---

[7]See Malbon, *Clubbing*, 173–9.

[8]Judith Becker, "Music and Trance," *Leonardo Music Journal* 4 (1994): 41.

[9]Gilbert Rouget, *Music and Trance: A Theory of the Relations Between Music and Possession*, trans. Brunhilde Biebuyck and Gilbert Rouget (Chicago: University of Chicago Press, 1985), 9–11.

[10]See Alice O'Grady, "Interrupting Flow: Researching Play, Performance and Immersion in Festival Scenes," *Dancecult* 5, no. 1 (May 2013): 18–38; Csikszentmihalyi, *Beyond Boredom and Anxiety*.

stand in for "transcendent," such as "mystical" or "spiritual." However, for the purposes of this discussion, the "transcendent" is sufficient to summarize any of the above elements, without necessarily referring to one more than another.

There are several more specific aspects of dance music environments that can contribute to, or together constitute, transcendence: music's extreme loudness and sub-bass frequencies; the various "tactile" qualities of the electronic sounds; and the music's repetitious, looping, and unfolding form.[11] Sonic affect in transcendent dance floor experience is not just about what sound is doing to the body, but what the body is doing in response. Dance and rhythmic movements activate the sonic impacts of music, also adding to the overall sensation of bodily pleasure through physical exertion and serotonin release. Other common methods for seeking transcendence include the use of alcohol, ecstasy, LSD, or other drugs.[12] Particular locations can add depth to transcendent experiences. Goa, for instance, is a symbolically and mythologically significant place, known by psytrance (psychedelic trance) fans as the geographical starting point for the parties and culture that they participate in. Recounting her pilgrimage with other psytrance partygoers, Mayleen, the DJ from Taiwan introduced earlier, describes Goa as "a very magic place" with "a very pure energy." There are many other elements designed to facilitate transcendent dance floor experiences, more than can be addressed in any meaningful way here.

Sound

Sound, in general, and its relationship to bodily sensation, in particular, is at the center of transcendent dance floor experiences. When successful, sounds deliver the fine balance of immersion, tension, and release that help partygoers

---

[11]For an exploration of tactility and the senses in the sounds of electronic dance music, see Garcia-Mispireta, "Beats, Flesh, and Grain," 60.

[12]There are several scientific studies of the capacity of music to induce "chills," a common term used in music psychology and neuroscience experiments to describe physiological arousal of various kinds. See for example, Oliver Grewe, Reinhard Kopiez, and Eckart Altenmüller, "The Chill Parameter: Goosebumps and Shivers as Promising Measures in Emotion Research," *Music Perception* 27, no. 1 (September 2009): 61–74; Valorie N. Salimpoor, Mitchel Benovoy, Kevin Larcher, Alain Dagher, and Robert J. Zatorre, "Anatomically Distinct Dopamine Release During Anticipation and Experience of Peak Emotion to Music," *Nature Neuroscience* 14, no. 2 (February 2011): 257–62.

to dance and to ultimately enter into a state that might be called transcendent.[13] Bass is one of the first and most conspicuous encounters with sound that people are met with on arrival to a dance music space, augmented significantly by overwhelming loudness.[14] Such "extra-cochlear," low-frequency sounds and loudness lead to "whole-body vibrations" and sensations of "auditory abundance" where "bodies are placed inside sound."[15] This constitutes a kind of propulsion and drive to dance that goes beyond a mere desire or wish to do so. The sensation or affect of such extreme loudness and low frequencies is described by Julian Henriques as a "sonic invasion," a violent invocation of what is only possible through technologies such as electronic sound production/reproduction and loudspeakers.[16] The potency of such encounters with bass lies partly in the unknowability of how they work. While people recognize them and can say that they are significant, they may have a hard time explaining how or why.[17]

The theoretical and material interest in bass by scholars is affirmed by several fans and clubbers, revealed when asked what makes them dance. A clubber in Sydney, Kylie, says: "The bass. God … and you see I don't know the technicalities behind the music so I can't sort of go … 'it's *this* thing.'" Without access to the "expert" know-how of DJing and producing, Kylie is lost for words when asked to reduce her corporeal experience to a verbal summary, especially in a setting (a Skype interview) detached from the source of the encounters she

---

[13]For experimental scientific studies on this, some of which also overlap with phenomenology, see, for example, Maria A. G. Witek, "Filling In: Syncopation, Pleasure and Distributed Embodiment in Groove," *Music Analysis* 36, no. 1 (March 2017): 138–60; Maria A. G. Witek, "Feeling at One: Socio-Affective Distribution, Vibe, and Dance-Music Consciousness," in *Music and Consciousness 2: Worlds, Practices, Modalities*, eds. Ruth Herbert, David Clarke, and Eric Clarke (Oxford: Oxford University Press, 2019), 93–112; Ragnhild Torvanger Solberg and Nicola Dibben, "Peak Experiences with Electronic Dance Music: Subjective Experiences, Physiological Responses, and Musical Characteristics of the Break Routine," *Music Perception* 36, no. 4 (April 2019): 371–89.

[14]A famous exception to extreme loudness as a standard is the Loft in New York and later London. A focus on sound quality over loudness reflected David Mancuso's sound system philosophies and practices. See Lawrence, *Love Saves the Day*, 6–13.

[15]Julian Henriques, *Sonic Bodies: Reggae Sound Systems, Performance Techniques, and Ways of Knowing* (New York: Continuum, 2011), xvi.

[16]Henriques, *Sonic Bodies*, xvi.

[17]Paul Jasen, *Low End Theory: Bass, Bodies and the Materiality of Sonic Experience* (New York: Bloomsbury, 2016), 35. See also Steve Goodman, *Sonic Warfare: Sound, Affect, and the Ecology of Fear* (Cambridge, MA: The MIT Press, 2010); Henriques, *Sonic Bodies*.

is trying to recall (warehouse parties or nightclubs). Although Kylie finds it difficult to explain the effects of bass because of what she perceives to be a lack of technical knowledge, other clubbers describe in simple terms what it does to their body. Another Sydney clubber, Rachel, when asked to expand on what bass does to her, says, "two words: booty shake." A clubber in Edinburgh, Fleur, says, "the louder it gets, the harder the bass, the more you jump." Rick, a DJ originally from Sydney, says that the kick drum and bass "anchor your knees and your gut." Edinburgh DJ, Dom, makes an effort to provide substantive detail about how he experiences sound in his body. He refers to the bass line as "*hitting* you … especially when there's a good sound system … It's harder to stand still than to dance … it's like human activation." Visual metaphors and real-world analogies will stand in for the lack of specialized language for "aqueous" sensations of sound and "being roughed up" by bass.[18] Edinburgh DJ, Cam, and Scottish Borders radio DJ and clubber, Rob, both describe bass as "growly." For an Edinburgh-based psytrance partygoer from France called Sarah, bass can "make you feel like you're in a cloud." Sarah's analogy for her affective state under the influence of bass (and LSD) departs from the evocations of ferocity of violence that others make.[19]

Bass is not alone in its impact on the body and its capacity to move people. Some electronically produced music includes "risers" for the serotonin rushes and "sensations of upness."[20] They also contain extended reverb effects or long decays, and "granular" and "textured" sounds that evoke kinesthetic memory of friction or grating of rough objects against one another.[21] The "riser" is the engine-like *swoosh* sound effect, usually without definite pitches. It does what its name suggests: it crescendos during build-ups and induces intense adrenaline rushes. Other sound effects such as those resembling sirens can elicit feelings of danger, but in a leisure setting where there is no actual emergency—such a feeling manifests as thrill. Various synthesizers that

---

[18]Jasen, *Low End Theory*, 2.

[19]Sarah addresses LSD experiences in relation to psytrance at length. For the material, historical, and symbolic connections between bass and violence, see Goodman, *Sonic Warfare*; see also Rodgers, *Pink Noises*, 6–16.

[20]Malbon, *Clubbing*, 107.

[21]Garcia-Mispireta, "Beats, Flesh, and Grain," 64–9.

provide riffs or melodic material can lead to "shivers in your spine moments," as Dom puts it. Dom goes on to describe what he calls "synth stabs" as sounds that function in a similar way to risers in terms of their effects on the body. They gradually ascend in pitch, which is a form of tension building that causes people to want to "dance their bones out of their skin" before a plunge into the groove of staccato basslines:

> Your arms almost lift with the music. I think that's one of the most powerful effects you can use as a DJ is that sort of sireny, lifting sound, that elevation of music, the ascendance. You sort of feel it inside yourself as well, it lifts you. It's all about this tension, this pushing of tension. I think, when people … when they're listening to huge sounds like that, it's almost like they're trying to dance their bones out of their skin, you know, it's just kind of *pushed*. Something's pushing, whether it's in your body or in your head, you know.

Dom goes on to discuss breakdowns as an additional example of tension-building:

> The breakdown is just like this noise going [*makes growling sound*] and then [*makes growling sound*] and just lifting, lifting, and again it's that lifting, lifting, lifting, lifting. And it just goes on for so long and then the white noise starts coming in and by the end, you're actually sort of like [*enacts trembling arms*] like "please!" But it's not that you're not enjoying the breakdown, the breakdown is about to put *you* into a dance frenzy. It's like if you get an elastic band and you pull it to very … it's completely taut and then you release like that [*mimes an elastic band releasing*], that's what I find breakdowns do to me.[22]

Even apparently subtler sounds have profound affective capacity in dance floor contexts. A sound that is significant both for people's desire to move and for how producers make electronic music, but one without the high profile of bass lines or the sonic prominence of risers, is the hi-hat. It constitutes

---

[22]See also Ragnhild Torvanger Solberg, "Waiting for the Bass to Drop: Correlations Between Intense Emotional Experiences and Production Techniques in Build-Up and Drop Sections of Electronic Dance Music," *Dancecult* 6, no. 1 (June 2016): 61–82.

an illustrative case study for the variety of ways that sounds are used in electronic dance music. The hi-hat in dance music can be a sampled sound of an actual physical hi-hat (closed cymbal) from a real-life drum kit, it can be any synthesized percussive sound that plays the same rhythmic and metric function, whether it resembles it precisely or loosely, or it can be a sample from acoustic sound (whether a hi-hat from a drumkit or an entirely different source). Producers and DJs sometimes identify some hi-hat sounds with specific analog drum machine models such as the Roland TR-909 and 707, or as is more likely now, digital sound replicas of them. Depending on the genre or producer's predilections, samples are often manipulated digitally to the point that it is no longer possible to recognize their acoustic origins. Therefore, while the hi-hat is sometimes identifiable through its recognizable sonic character, it is more consistently identified through its relationship to other sounds: in terms of time (between kick drum downbeats), its place on the frequency spectrum (normally higher), and its loudness (less than other parts of the digital percussion ensemble). As such, the act of calling an electronic sound a hi-hat, even when it sounds nothing like the hi-hat on a drum kit, is to demonstrate a cultural familiarity with drum kit sounds from jazz and popular music *and* with their approximations in electronically produced sound. Some hi-hats have a longer decay than others, providing a closer association to the acoustic reality of two cymbals striking each other in a physical space.

Whether the sound is a close digital replica of an acoustic hi-hat, a sample of a physical one, or identifiably similar, is generally of no concern to dancers. What matters is its effect/affect. As producers, DJs, and fans note, its capacity to set people into motion is just as potent as bass lines, risers, and other, louder sounds. When a hi-hat is introduced into the mix, a robotic four-to-the-floor kick drum and bass line march can become buoyant and allow a dancer to find a groove to move to. Sometimes producers accentuate the syncopation by skewing the hi-hat slightly away from the precise meter so that a more "natural" or "swing" feel is achieved. Such an effect is not particular to electronic dance music but is more noticeable when there is less sonic activity surrounding it.[23]

---

[23]This technique is not new in popular music. Richard Middleton shows how this takes place in Elvis Presley's "Heartbreak Hotel." The off beats are the focus, "jerking the body into activity." See Richard Middleton, *Studying Popular Music* (Milton Keynes: Open University Press, 1990), 18–19.

As Dan, a DJ and producer from Edinburgh, explains, the hi-hat "gives you something to dance *off*." Dom, again, expands on this idea by examining the importance of contrast:

There's things that producers use. Like for example, I always talk about a hi-hat. And how a hi-hat can completely freshen a passage of music. If you're just listening to *hvoomda ... hvoomda ... hvoomda ...* and then suddenly a *ts, ts, ts*, you automatically do that [gestures] it freshens, it's like someone's just opened the window on your techno you're blasting and cool air's come through it. And they know what they're going to do next, they're going to add a snare drum and that's when you see people jacking because it completes the pattern, you know what I mean, it's almost like putting pegs in the right-sized ... in the right-shaped holes. So these techniques are used and producers know exactly what they're doing when they're using it, you know, it's not fluke (*sic*), that they'll leave the hi-hat out of it for awhile, so when they do chuck in the hi-hat, it does feel like a ... When you see a track building up, going through its motions, as it were, you see that reflecting on the way people dance. As soon as that hi-hat comes in people start moving a bit harder, and then when you add that snare, that's when people start really going pretty nuts. Like I said, the pattern is complete, if you like. And people are ... it's ... (*sighs*) it's hard to explain! It is a hard thing to explain, but (*laughs*) ... but yeah, as I say, these things all affect people differently, but they all affect them the same ...

After circling around the same ideas, Dom continues:

I think people like the offbeat to dance from. I think because it gives you the ... when you're dancing, you generally dance down and up hitting the off beat on either the down or the up. And when you've just got the one, the one steady, the main beat, [claps] *deh DO deh DO deh DO deh*, that can ... but when the hi-hat comes in, it just ... the thing I always say is that I'd be freshening the music and I think that reflects in the way people dance as well. And they go [inhales sharply] and you can see them maybe move an arm up and then you put in the snare drum and that's when people really groove. Because it *is* that ... groove. It's ... that pattern is complete.

In other words, hi-hats provide a sensory relief from the heaviness of the kick and the bass.

Based on observation during fieldwork, the hi-hat visibly and immediately alters how people move their bodies. Dancing is pulled toward a downbeat when bass, kick, and snare parts are not complemented by hi-hats, though may syncopate movements based on snare patterns, if present. However, when a hi-hat enters the mix, people have more options for interpreting rhythm. While some people maintain a kick drum, downbeat emphasis, others dance *to* the hi-hat. Dancing uniformity, which can be a way that dancers connect with each other socially, dissipates as the number of sounds increase in general, heads begin to move in different directions, and clubbers achieve more freedom of movement.

The dancing body's encounter with sound involves the sense of touch—both with sound itself and with other people.[24] The tactile aspects of sound are amplified (literally) by the sounds' loudness, and, as the next section shows, can be brought into focus with the use of sense-altering drugs. The effects of drugs also include altered senses of time and if the circumstances are right, a type of transcendence known as a flow experience.

Drugs and Flow

Another technique that people use in dance music to seek experiences of transcendence is drugs. For most participants that were part of the research for this book, the primary drug of choice was MDMA.[25] People have taken intoxicating substances to facilitate transcendence for millennia, and this continues to be a component of many human cultures. MDMA can also help people to forget their troubles for a few hours, and to enjoy losing their minds and feeling "wasted." It can allow them to become absorbed in both the bodily

---

[24]Garcia, "Beats, Flesh, and Grain," 71–3.

[25]Ecstasy and MDMA are not the same thing, even though MDMA is often referred to by the street name ecstasy. Ecstasy pills are often deliberately mixed with other substances such as amphetamines or hallucinogens to produce slightly different effects to MDMA. They are often also diluted with "filler" substances or chemicals so that production can be cheaper and profit margins higher.

experience of sound and the social bonding with people on dance floors. 1960s experiments using MDMA for psychotherapy showed that the drug facilitated a greater willingness to feel empathy and express feelings candidly.[26] Such effects can help to facilitate more enduring and profound transcendent states that for some, lead to shifts in perspective, attitude, or even disposition.[27] MDMA's effects are visible to anyone paying attention, dramatically altering the mood, pace, and range of movement amid groups of people who have "dropped" at the same time. It is common to see people waiting until they feel the effects before they venture onto the dance floor. Many people even appear bored, indifferent, or anxious until they "come up" (feel the full effects of the drug), at which point they may have a sudden burst of energy and excitement, and only then, begin dancing. For such people, dancing to electronic music and taking drugs are activities that always happen together.

MDMA acts on sensory perception in a way that augments the intensity of affect brought on by such sounds such as the "low pass filter sweep."[28] It increases focus on, and immersion in, not only the sensual encounter with sound, but also with light and dark (since color, shape, and movement look different), with surfaces such as the floor, and with the company of other people. For this reason, some scientists and social scientists call it an entactogen, which means "to touch inside," though, unofficially, the drug has come to be known as an "empathogen." Along similar lines, the etymology of the drug's street name ecstasy is *exstasis*—to be within *and* outside oneself.[29] One of my interviewees recounts that during her first experience of taking ecstasy, she

---

[26]See Ram Dass and Ralph Metzner, *Birth of a Psychedelic Culture: Conversations about Leary, the Harvard Experiments, Millbrook and the Sixties* (Santa Fe, NM: Synergetic Press, 2010), 22, 95, 191, 219.

[27]Along such lines, there are popular and journalistic accounts of rival English football teams letting go of their hostilities while on ecstasy. Of course, football tribalism did not disappear in any enduring sense, but the image of macho football "lads" hugging it out at raves is too good a story not to tell. See Brewster and Broughton, *Last Night a DJ Saved My Life*, 428–43; Push and Silcott, *The Book of E*, 62–71; Reynolds, *Energy Flash*, 44–60.

[28]Reynolds, *Energy Flash*, xxx, 491–2.

[29]Alana R. Pentney, "Exploration of the History and Controversies Surrounding MDMA and MDA," *Journal of Psychoactive Drugs* 33, no. 3 (2001): 216; Push and Mirelle Silcott, *The Book of E: All about Ecstasy* (London: Omnibus Press, 2000), 8; Jerome Beck and Marsha Rosenbaum, *Pursuit of Ecstasy: The MDMA Experience* (Albany: State University of New York Press, 1994), 79; Pentney, "Exploration of the History and Controversies Surrounding MDMA and MDA," 216; Malbon, *Clubbing*, 49.

became fascinated by the sensation and the appearance of her arms in motion while dancing and focused on them for an extended period.[30] Another says that the greatest pleasure of MDMA is the touch of other people in the form of hugging, stroking, and massage. A third says that one of the effects of the drug is that loudness becomes more pleasurable.[31] There are whole genres of dance music produced specifically to act on some of the common sensory effects produced by drugs. Journalist and music critic Simon Reynolds has a particular flair for describing this effect:

> Today's house track is a forever-fluctuating fractal mosaic of glow-pulses and flicker-riffs, a teasing tapestry whose different strands take turns to move in and out of the sonic spotlight. Experienced under the influence of MDMA, the effect is synaesthetic—like tremulous fingertips tantalizing the back of your neck, or like the aural/tactile equivalent of a shimmer. In a sense, Ecstasy turns the entire body-surface into an ear a [sic] ultra-sensitized membrane that responds to certain frequencies.[32]

Affect is the primary focus of such descriptions. Yet not only did psychedelic experiments in the 1960s show what neurological and physiological effects drugs could have on people, but today researchers know that spatial and social settings can completely alter people's trips.[33] The social rituals that people perform when seeking transcendent experiences through drug use in dance music communities matter as much as, if not more than, how "well-matched" particular sounds might be to the effects of drugs. Dance music fans who use MDMA take for granted the association of the drug with times and spaces of leisure, fun, and in some cases, transcendent experiences.[34] At the same time,

---

[30]Accounts of drugs by interviewees are integrated rather than directly included, even though the vast majority of interviewees in this book have opted for pseudonyms. Such details are intimate and delicate as they involve admissions of illegal activity. Paraphrasing, rather than quoting, ensures that there is no risk of identifying responses by individual speech idiosyncrasies that come from other parts of this book.

[31]See also Reynolds, *Energy Flash*, xxxi.

[32]Reynolds, *Energy Flash*, xxxii.

[33]For example, Dass and Metzner, *Birth of a Psychedelic Culture*; Ido Hartogsohn, *American Trip: Set, Setting, and the Psychedelic Experience in the Twentieth Century* (Cambridge, MA: The MIT Press, 2020); Karen McElrath and Kieran McEvoy, "Negative Experiences on Ecstasy: The Role of Drug, Set, and Setting," *Journal of Psychoactive Drugs* 34, no. 2 (April–June 2002): 199–208.

[34]McElrath and McEvoy, "Negative Experiences on Ecstasy," 206.

it is the social associations that allow the drug to be an actor in facilitating those experiences. People are "taught" the rituals and techniques of use that correspond with a particular community of users, if not explicitly, then by mimicking others.[35] For MDMA, such rituals and techniques are geared toward helping people dance for longer, reach heightened states of pleasure while dancing, and bonding with others. Such effects are not always the "natural" or first responses to the sensations that people feel when they take the drug. People learn them from others—either by observing them, by being explicitly taught, or most often a combination—and become practiced at them. At some point, they feel natural—such effects are just what happens.

One of the relationships between MDMA and the transcendent dance floor experience is the way that it can alter people's perception of time. A night out can be over very quickly, or a minute can feel like an hour. In addition, the tactility and intensity of drug effects facilitate being more present, or "in the moment." Given that being less concerned with the past or the future can be one aspect of transcendent experiences, this allows people to take pleasure in the feeling of time passing more quickly or slowly than they are accustomed to when sober. Along with the stimulant effects of the drug, such shifts in how people feel about time passing also allow people to dance for much longer than they would while sober, when it is more likely that they would get caught up in questions of how they will get home or what they are doing tomorrow. What is more, given that music mediates experiences of time, and electronic dance music is defined partly by a relatively unchanging speed of repetitive beats, the combined effects may add considerably to the experience of a time warp.[36] This may include smaller timescales such as the ways that people perceive the speed

[35]Becker, "Becoming a Marijuana User," 237; Beck and Rosenbaum *Pursuit of Ecstasy*, 62–3; Brian C. Kelly, "Mediating MDMA-Related Harm: Preloading and Post-loading Among Ecstasy-Using Youth," *Journal of Psychoactive Drugs* 41-1 (March 2009): 24.

[36]Jörg Fachner, "Drugs, Altered States, and Musical Consciousness: Reframing Time and Space," in *Music and Consciousness*, eds. Eric Clarke and David Clarke (Oxford: Oxford University Press, 2011), 266, 269–71; Reynolds, *Energy Flash*, xxxii; Harry Shapiro, *Waiting for the Man: The Story of Drugs and Popular Music* (London: Helter Skelter Publishing, 2006), 253; see also Maria A. G. Witek, Tudor Popescu, Eric F. Clarke, Mads Hansen, Ivana Konvalinka, Morten L. Kringelbach, and Peter Vuust, "Syncopation Affects Free Body-Movement in Groove," *Experimental Brain Research* 235 (April 2017): 995–1005.

of music they are dancing to or how they experience their own bodily rhythms as they synchronize with rhythms in the music.[37]

To summarize some of the aspects of transcendent experience addressed above, then, people encounter the sonic onslaught of repetitive electronic sound, which can elicit feelings not only of being affected by the material impacts of sound, but of being affected by the co-presence of other people who are present for a similar experience. Therefore, while the transcendent experience may lead to out-of-body sensations and experiences, it is rooted firmly *in* the body.[38]

Another conceptual apparatus through which it is possible to understand the transcendent experience on dance floors, whether on or off drugs, is one known as flow, sometimes expressed as the flow experience or flow state. For writers who want to capture the affective qualities of dancing to electronic music, flow is both a description of a bodily, material phenomenon and a potent metaphor.[39] It is also familiar across other fields, most famously through the theories of flow attributed to Csikszentmihalyi, whose work spans several decades and has been adapted to contemporary management theory. Csikszentmihalyi defines it as the "the holistic sensation that people feel when they act with total involvement."[40] One way to enter into a state of flow while dancing to electronic music is to find a rhythmic synchronicity with the music. As noted by Danielle, a clubber from outside Edinburgh, dance music is repetitive and contains looping musical fragments and a larger-scale looping form. Such a repetitious, looping form allows a dancer to latch onto aspects of the rhythm and remain there for long periods of time.[41] It also has

---

[37]Sean Leneghan, "The Varieties of Ecstasy Experience: An Exploration of Body, Mind and Person in Sydney's Club Culture" (PhD diss., University of Sydney, 2010), 53–4.

[38]See Garcia (2015) for a fleshing out of this body-music-affect interaction in his article "Beats, Flesh, and Grain."

[39]For example, Malbon, *Clubbing*, 138–44; O'Grady, "Interrupting Flow," 18–38.

[40]Csikszentmihalyi, *Beyond Boredom and Anxiety*, 36.

[41]Eugene Montague, "Moving to Music: A Theory of Sound and Physical Action" (PhD diss., University of Pennsylvania, 2001); Luis-Manuel Garcia, "On and on: Repetition as Process and Pleasure in Electronic Dance Music," *Music Theory Online* 11, no. 4 (October 2005), https://www.mtosmt.org/issues/mto.05.11.4/mto.05.11.4.garcia.html. For different language and a different disciplinary description of a similar phenomenon, see Eugene Montague, "Entrainment and Embodiment in Musical Performance," in *The Oxford Handbook of Music and the Body*, eds. Youn Kim and Sander L. Gilman (Oxford: Oxford University Press, 2019), 177–92. From the sciences, see Tomas E. Matthews, Maria A. G. Witek, Torben Lund, Peter Vuust, and Virginia B. Penhume, "The Sensation of Groove Engages Motor and Reward Networks," *NeuroImage* 214 (July 2020). See also Butler, *Unlocking the Groove*, 5–6, 90–1.

an open-ended sense of time for those committed to staying on dance floors and experiencing the full shape of a DJ set or multiple DJ sets.[42]

It is easier for a person to enter into a state of flow on a dance floor if they are able to set aside concerns about how they appear to others, what other people are doing, the passage of time, and thoughts or anxieties about the past or the future. In relation to this, and in a discussion of the challenges of doing research on dance floors, Alice O'Grady's description of the flow experience is applicable to clubbing more broadly:

> True understanding of flow comes from direct experience of it. Being fully immersed, losing our sense of self, either through harmonious concentration or through relinquishing control, provides a route through which flow might be achieved.[43]

O'Grady notes the kinds of internal monologues that people engage in as they move into and out of states of flow. This means that *not* to do them requires a deliberate set of special actions.

By playing continuous music with a relatively consistent meter and tempo for hours, DJ work provides a good start at helping to facilitate flow states. But more than this is often needed. Gordon, Danielle's partner, refers to the time they spent in India in the 1970s and says that the ebb and flow of release and focus helps him to reject "the chattering monkeys" in his mind:

> I don't know if Danielle said as well, we sometimes go and see a Shaman called Emaho and he does a thing called the fire dance … And the fire dance goes on for sometimes … he's got a very interesting website. And we've gone to see him for a long time. We haven't been recently, but as part of his ritual, and his ritual was kind of created to an extent … in Scotland (so he tours the world), but it kind of came out … I think it was in Glasgow that it was born. It's a similar thing. You know, you dance, you get into that headspace by dancing for a very long time. And the fire dance goes on for hours and hours and hours. And it's a total work out, it's a meditation, it's a dynamic meditation. And I mean, similarly, I went to India in 1976

---

[42]On how DJs musically sculpt their sets, see Butler, *Unlocking the Groove,* 240–54.
[43]O'Grady, "Interrupting Flow," 31.

and I went to see Rajneesh. And, you know, there were a lot of dynamic meditations, and it kind of tunes into that headspace as well. So yeah, I've always regarded it as that kind of … it's a great focusing device. And you know, all your problems, you know, the day by day stuff, just … it gets set on one side. And it's a bit like any meditation where you can get rid of the chattering monkeys in your head, all the problems that you've got, and you just focus on that one thing and the shared experience as well. I mean you can do it on your own, we dance on our own here, I dance on my own sometimes, but it's much more fun with others.[44]

The flow experience, in Gordon's account, is the sharing of what he calls the "mass experience," on drugs, with others that makes it fun, though, and not simply a therapeutic technique. Danielle can get into a flow using the sensory aspects of dance music, particularly how she feels in her body, and her relationship with the space. She says that "the atmosphere, the feeling in the room, and the music" are important features for her. There are several components that constitute each of those three features:

There's something that's very primal, which is about the heartbeat isn't it? In a particular beat you can sense that your body's responding innately to it, which does feel tribal. Obviously, there can be a sense of … if you *know* the music and you love it and you hear it … it's the volume also really, other people's responses to it as well as your own. Or else, if you don't know the music but it just feels right. There's something about the atmosphere, really. And the space, of course. You've got to feel safe. Because you can feel vulnerable dancing, so you have to feel secure. And safe.

Danielle suggests that when she can set aside a consciousness about how she dances once she feels safe, her flow experience includes setting aside her self-consciousness:

---

[44]The explicit link that Gordon makes between the flow state of the contemporary electronic dance music space and the shamanic, dynamic meditation sessions in India also underscores the relationship between post-disco dance music and some of the hippy countercultures of the 1960s and 1970s. This is relevant later in the analysis.

It's not ego led, eventually. The mind is put aside and your sense of being self-conscious is erased to the point whereby you can allow your body i.e., the physicality and your mind … not quite meditation, but your mind is not standing in your way.

Other than the mind not standing in the way, a feature common to both Gordon and Danielle's accounts is the sense of connectedness with other clubbers. The experience of dancing may be different for each body on the dance floor, but it is heightened by the collective nature of the dance floor and its surroundings. This may be thousands of people at outdoor dance music festivals, intimate clubs, or warehouse parties. But in such accounts, a singular figure—a DJ—is trusted to bind the group's flow states together through music.[45] In turn, drugs facilitate "sensations of extreme flow," as Malbon refers to them, helping people to forget time and lose themselves in feelings of pleasure and connectedness with music and dance and with other people.[46] For Malbon, "the relationships between self and those that constitute the surrounding dancing crowd are, at the least, unsettled and in certain cases temporarily re-cast completely."[47]

Transcendence: Not for All

In the opening vignette of this chapter, Holly dances with her eyes closed, and in doing so, creates an imaginary private haven. The closed state of her eyes is the social boundary she creates for her absorption into the music and dance. This imagined boundary meets its social limits when it is breeched by someone who does not observe it. We come, therefore, to the first point of discord: that not everyone who seeks a transcendent experience has one, or, in this case, not everyone undergoing such an experience can remain in it. Participant observation and interviews show that on many dance floors,

---

[45]Sometimes DJs play in pairs or groups, but in such cases, which are the minority, the effect is much the same.
[46]Malbon, *Clubbing*: 139–40.
[47]Malbon, *Clubbing*: 142.

men prevent or disrupt the transcendent experiences of women by directly interfering with their capacity to reach transcendent states. This can start at the door of a venue. For some groups, security and door staff at venues use ethnic, classist, ageist, and ableist standards to determine that some people are not suitable for a dance music venue or event.[48] There are clubs that are difficult to get into because the goal is to prioritize people that are sidelined elsewhere, but these are not the norm. In my first experiences clubbing in Sydney, racial and class profiling took place at the doors of certain nightclubs under the cover of a concern for dress codes. Clothes such as tracksuits or sports shoes, which were also associated with specific ethnic communities and/or working-class communities, were an easy tool to exclude people with, under the pretext of dress codes articulated by venues. To say that the policies were applied inconsistently would be putting it generously.

Ageism was also prevalent at these venues. When the security staff on the door of a nightclub asked a couple, perhaps in their 50s or 60s, why they wanted to be there, the couple told them that they wanted to have a dance on their anniversary night. They were turned away because the door staff determined that they would not "fit in" and that it was not their "scene." As addressed in the previous chapter, while such screening was less common in Edinburgh, visible markers of lower classes were used to reject potential clubbers. Normally, when such people got beyond security, the rejections were framed with reference to cultural capital, and therefore extended to gender as well as class. Women in a group, out for a bachelorette party, for example, were assumed not to "understand" the purpose of a club night, and thereby would not contribute to the "right vibe." Questions used by promoters or their door staff would often begin with "what are you here for?" or "who is playing tonight?" The scrutiny of door staff can set the tone for an event, even for those who are bearing witness to another person's interrogation. Such interactions can disrupt or entirely prevent the transcendent experience.

Transcendence can even be prevented by the anticipation, fear, or reliving of experience where safety is not felt by someone as a certainty. This speaks to what Danielle states (above) about feeling safe as a necessary condition

---

[48]See Knudsen, "Vakten dro meg ut av utestedet og la meg på hodet ned i trappa," 38.

to trust that she can relax and enjoy the social space of the dance floor. It is worth pausing here to mention that Danielle and Gordon, who are the mother and father of two other interviewees, tend to go out together on the same nights. Yet the safety and comfort that Danielle says she requires to be able to enter a state of flow does not feature in Gordon's accounts. Interspersed with her description of the things that *do* facilitate her state of flow and sense of connectedness with others on the dance floor, Danielle raises the matter of safety again (unprompted) in a later part of our interview:

> D: I think you have to feel, as I said, secure. The space needs to feel okay. The people within that space, i.e., are there too many people? Depends if you're in a mosh pit or not, that's not something I'm particularly comfortable with. Although it's a sort of … the word I'm looking for is … collective. It's almost like a consciousness, a collective … whereby you sometimes feel that, especially with dance music or techno, that you're moving as one. You know, you're experiencing this journey together. The room doesn't matter so much as the quality of the music you're listening to. It would be very different if you were outside around a fire, of course. I think … I can't stress too much, it's not so much the place, it's feeling *in* the place. However, I would be aware of fire exits, for example. If there were hundreds of us packed in somewhere, I need to feel … I need to check it out, before I'll let go.
>
> TG: And do you think, did you do that, did you know where the fire exits were at [venue]?
>
> D: No [*laughs*] I didn't actually. I just knew the space, and I knew it from theater. And I knew that it was an ancient space, and I assumed that it would be the case. But having said that, no I didn't particularly check it out, it just felt okay, to be honest … it's site specific. [Venue] is established, there's a trust already there.

The specific reference to fire exits is notable. There are clearly a range of things that could prevent Danielle from entering a state of flow.

Malbon, for whom oceanic and "extreme flow" experiences are a central tenet, also argues that "experiencing of flow through play is by no means automatic, and clubbing can also be an experience laden with anxiety." Not

unlike the argument here, he identifies a key point of anxiety or rupture to flow as taking place when a person's ability to fit in is compromised. The focus is on the inability to meet the expectations of subcultural capital (to import Thornton's term), for example, through self-presentation, including dancing style or "body techniques" more broadly, attitude, and fashion. Another point of disruption to flow that Malbon identifies is the interrupting of dancing that calls to mind the story of Holly at the beginning of this chapter. For Malbon, "a dancer may be interrupted in their dancing practices, they may experience a 'break in the flow' and become self-conscious. A dancer may even get ambiguous or unpleasant feedback from those within the crowd."[49]

There is no mention by Malbon of sexual harassment, an especially common form of unpleasant dance floor experience. His focus, instead, is the notion that attempts to "belong" or "be cool" are unsuccessful or that others on the dance floor are not receptive to it. Such anxieties exist for clubbers, for various reasons. Danielle, for example, feels social anxiety at events with one or both of her adult children:

> D: … I'm old. And I don't want to feel inappropriate. To begin with, that's my mind. And I was a little bit anxious about going with Dana and her friends, and young friends. I know I've known some of them for many years, and I still didn't want to feel inappropriate. So yes, I was very self-conscious at first, and then I thought …
>
> TG: Is this generally the case these days overall? Or just on that night?
>
> D: No, I don't go clubbing. I mean it's the first time really in a big scene … in a big club that I've done … I mean in here [the house] we've had you know, nights, and decks, and you know … parties. So I've been in that experience, certainly, quite a few times, but not in a club. So it was … I was a little anxious. Will I feel that I belong, or will I feel that I shouldn't be here? But I felt *incredibly* welcomed. And I felt … many people communicated with me … Yes, it was a lovely sense of … not belonging, it sounds too … but you know, just really loving it. And

---

[49]Malbon, *Clubbing*, 142–3.

not … it was just something about … I think it's just like a collective, really. I don't mean a collective consciousness, but something about, we're … you know, you're not quite nine million sparrows swarming, but you're part of a something, you're in it.

In the end, Danielle's anxieties at this event were quelled by what she saw as a welcoming space. The sense of being part of a "collective" supersedes her focus on how she appears to others.

Other interviewees also relate the importance of who they are with as the most significant factor for them in whether or not they feel anxious. This is an issue for Ron, a clubber interviewed in Edinburgh. Ron, who considers himself both self-conscious and sensitive, states that the group of people he is with, including a "nice mix" in gender balance, are elements that allow him to "enjoy dancing or take it for its own worth instead of as a means to something else." For Fleur, also a clubber in Edinburgh, the moods of those around her directly impact her. Her receptiveness to people's moods extends beyond the other clubbers, reinforcing the earlier point that a fulfilling dance floor experience can be established before even setting foot into a venue:

I get a buzz off other people … So if I see other people having a good time, then it makes me have a good time. The bar staff as well … It's kind of important for me. If I see that they're a bit snappy or whatever, it's going to put me in a bad mood. And bouncers as well. They're the first person you see before you go in a club. And if they're bitchy about things, you're not going to want to go in.

At the same time as transcendence is not possible for everyone in dance music to achieve, it is also not something that everyone seeks. Participant observation and interviews reveal that what people seek on dance floors is, unsurprisingly, heterogeneous. There are people who talk about the first time they took ecstasy or LSD on a dance floor as life changing, and those who consequently incorporate such experiences into a life philosophy. But in most cases, no matter how much a line of interview questioning aims to uncover the spiritual significance of dance music, it is clear that for many people, the

point of dance music is to dance.[50] People drink, talk (or rather, shout) with friends, look at others, and pay attention to things taking place on and around the dance floor. People go to dance music events to hear a DJ they like, to take drugs that make them feel good, and to punctuate their week with something that brings them pleasure. They may enter a state of flow when they dance and feel "at one" with the crowd of people who share their taste in music, as well as appreciating the shared bodily vocabulary of dancing to it. But most people rarely express such experiences as transcendent or anything similar—it is simply a fun night out.

Countercultures, Nature, and Alternative Spiritualities

This chapter has taken as its starting point the question of some of the forms that the transcendent experience takes in dance music, how it looks, and how it feels. From there, a pastiche of practices—seemingly disparate, but linked by symbols, histories, philosophies, and intellectual schools of thought—emerges to illustrate where such ideas come from beyond the level of individual phenomenology or physiological drive. The transcendent experience is channeled through the 1960s counterculture, nineteenth-century interpretations of paganism and medievalism, and appropriations of indigenous objects and rituals by white hippy ravers in colonized settings. All of this is not in addition to, but indistinguishably enmeshed within, the technocapitalism of the present, bolstered by neoliberal practices and beliefs.

The means by which people seek transcendent experience on dance floors is often through invocations of the past, whether knowingly or through participation in derivative forms of ritual or use of symbolic cultural objects.

---

[50]The assumption underpinning this is that the wisdom is latent and interviewees simply do not know how to articulate it properly. This is a confession. In my first research project, I doggedly pursued a line of questioning that was about reinforcing my belief that sound was the primary trigger for dancing. I withdrew from this agenda and was humbled by interviewees such as Fran, who told me that while she likes some of the electro that her boyfriend produces, and *will* dance to it, what really makes her dance is when she recognizes a tune, when her friends are dancing to it, and when she is sufficiently drunk to do so.

Psytrance DJ Mayleen enacts this quite literally: she owns and runs a shop that sells psychedelic paraphernalia in the outskirts of Taipei. Such a venture was designed to financially counterweigh her years of living a transitory life, from the island of Ko Phangan in Thailand to Nepal and India, especially Goa, where her goal was to "learn about the hippy spirit and the hippy life." Mayleen is the primary carer of her young son and manages the shop on her own, while her husband, a promoter, runs large outdoor parties in Kop Phangan during the months-long "high" season each year. She emphasizes, "I only play outdoors," as this aligns with the psytrance philosophy and lifestyle. Not only does she embrace such a lifestyle fully herself, but she also believes it is her role to "push" the lifestyle in Taiwan. This was also a motivation for opening a psychedelic-themed shop rather than simply taking a waged job:

> I want to push psychedelic trance music in Taiwan. Because in Taiwan, the people, now, they don't understand much. In Taiwan, our psychedelic trance age is [from a] long time ago, twenty years old. But [since then], they have [had] many kinds of music, like house, techno; many [kinds of] music [have] come in. And then the new people, the new generation, they don't understand, so they're [a] little bit confused. And I want to push my music, our style [of] music … can teach more young people, [the] new generation to understand our music. So I hope that my shop [is] not only for sales, [it is] for sharing the decorations, art, and also the psychedelic dance music *spirit*.

Such visual signifiers of the "hippy spirit and the hippy life" are not only continued on the fringes within psychedelic trance music communities but have more recently been reconstituted in the mass-scale commercial form of the EDM festival, in the 2010s.[51]

As the usual account of the extraordinary case of dance music will claim, the attraction of dance music to ancient (or ancient-*inspired*) ritual and symbolism lies partly in the embrace of the bodily experience and encounter, which is rejected by centuries of logocentrism of western culture, the Cartesian

---

[51]Holt, *Everyone Loves Live Music*, 220–38; Michelangelo Matos, *The Underground Is Massive: How Electronic Music Conquered America* (New York: Dey St., 2015), 321–36, 339–64.

separation of mind and body, and the elevation of cerebral endeavor over and above mere flesh. The fact that a genre called Intelligent Dance Music (IDM) emerged in the 1990s, in contrast to dance music that a group of fans determined to be unintelligent, at least by implication, reinforces just how pervasive such thinking is.[52] Rupert Till notes the ways that Christian morality, and by extension, European cultural norms, conflict with the overt corporeality both of popular music and dance, and Paganism.[53] Paganism is among the traditions that inform ritual practice in dance music cultures, particularly outdoor or "nature"-based events. Its wide repertoire of symbolism has informed practices spanning Romantic art worlds in the nineteenth century, to the extensive symbiology of the counterculture of the 1960s.

It is the most recent of these that electronic dance music events—especially the outdoor kind—most visibly and most obviously replicate today.[54] Certain countercultural music scenes in the 1960s and early 1970s adopted such Pagan symbols in the service of "challenging the dominant technocratic discourse at the time" through premodern back-to-nature (or, "back-to-the-land") ideals and spirituality in opposition to rationalism and modernity.[55] For Bennett, Pagan ideas and symbols can be found in musical aesthetics (harmony, timbre through production techniques), lyrics, and media from bands such as Led Zeppelin, Black Sabbath, and Jethro Tull. Beyond the aesthetic invocations of Paganism, however, it is not clear what the challenge to the technocratic discourse is. One answer may lie in Till's suggestion that contemporary uses of Pagan rites provide an alternative to the oppressive aspects of Christianity. In this argument, Paganism in its modern forms attracts participation in its facilitation of "new forms of religious expression that are free from cultural ossification and the weight of hundreds of years of religious law and dogma."

Further, the uptake of Paganism and other ancient ritual practice is not merely about opposition to Christianity but an overall move away from

---

[52]See Reynolds, *Energy Flash*, 526.

[53]Rupert Till, "Paganism, Popular Music and Stonehenge," in *Pop Pagans: Paganism and Popular Music*, ed. Donna Weston and Andy Bennett (London and New York: Routledge, 2013), 26–8, 40.

[54]Donna Weston and Andy Bennett, "Towards a Definition of Pagan Music," in *Pop Pagans: Paganism and Popular Music*, ed. Donna Weston and Andy Bennett (London and New York: Routledge, 2013), 3.

[55]Andy Bennett, "Paganism and the Counterculture," in *Pop Pagans: Paganism and Popular Music*, ed. Donna Weston and Andy Bennett (London and New York: Routledge, 2013), 14–16.

prescriptive, organized religious practice and toward its individualization—and in the case of popular music, the individual's experience of group ritual.[56] This is not to detract from the incorporation of ancient rituals, beliefs, and symbols as potential sources of collective experience in electronic dance music culture and other popular music settings.[57] At the same time, the personalization, and indeed, individualization of religious experience in the western context— including when it takes the form of profound, transcendent dance music experience—forms in close relationship with Protestant types of morality that Paganism ostensibly opposes.[58] It is possible, on the one hand, to perceive an appeal to alternative spirituality as an indirect, or even direct, challenge to the foundations that technocratic discourse is built on. But such appeals appear to stop at the cultural, self-contained utopia, at the transformation of the inner spirit, and the rebellion of the Temporary Autonomous Zone, or TAZ. When opting to remain at the level of culture rather than to intervene directly in exterior politics, it is also possible to see such appeals, at best, as pleasant, temporary interventions, and at worst, as fundamental to the maintenance of the technocratic discourse—and the stability of the capitalist system of which such discourse is a part.[59]

The relationship of alternative spiritualities and the transcendent dance floor encounter to technocapitalism itself is not arbitrary or coincidental. The practices and philosophies within the 1960s alternative cultures and their beneficiaries in dance music have a close relationship with Silicon Valley. As the work of Fred Turner shows, such ideas and aesthetics are derived quite directly from, and not at all opposed to, the technocratic, ideological machinery of the American empire in the 1960s and earlier. According to Turner, a particular branch of the countercultural communities of the 1960s, which he refers to as the New Communalists, decided that organized political action and struggle against injustice in institutions and systems of power were

---

[56]Till, "Paganism, Popular Music and Stonehenge," 39–41.
[57]For example, Douglas Ezzy, "Dancing Paganism: Music, Dance and Pagan Identity," in *Pop Pagans: Paganism and Popular Music*, ed. Donna Weston and Andy Bennett (London and New York: Routledge, 2013), 118.
[58]Max Weber, *The Protestant Ethic and the Spirit of Capitalism* (New York: Charles Scribner's Sons), 85.
[59]Luis Suarez-Villa, *Technocapitalism: A Critical Perspective on Technological Innovation and Corporatism* (Philadelphia: Temple University Press, 2009).

not the main object of their interest. Instead, the New Communalists focused on the idea that music, arts, and the right sort of literature, brought together by consciousness-expanding drugs, futuristic architecture, and machine technologies could facilitate transcendence, self-realization, and communal belonging. Furthermore, within such communal belonging, the "liberation of the individual"—the ideal at the center of the United State's Cold War policies, involvement with foreign wars and imperial expansion that is still ever-present at the time this book is in press—was the ultimate goal. Moreover, such liberation, which involved a breaking down of existing hierarchical structures and bureaucracies, could only be realized, for the people at its fore, through information technologies, and technological innovation in general. As Turner notes, "if the self was the ultimate driver of social change, and if class was no more, then individual lifestyle choices became political acts, and both consumption and lifestyle technologies—including information technologies—would have to take on a newly political valence." Importantly, the 1960s countercultural utopian ideal also constituted a denunciation of "traditional forms of governance" and an embrace of entrepreneurialism. By the time the New Communalist section of the counterculture had matured to middle age in the 1990s, they had amalgamated their beliefs in the capacity of technology (and specifically digital technologies and the Internet) to free society from Big Government and Big Corp, their utopian ideas of consciousness, and their belief that individual actualization is more desirable and important than organized political action. All of this coalesced with capital and they became the owners of Silicon Valley's startups.[60]

In addition to the military-industrial geneses of the counterculture's preoccupation with technological innovation, which manifests centrally in dance music culture through the valorization of the DJ, their *gear*, loudspeakers, lights, and drugs, there is a persistent presence of the Romantic. Far from an incidental link between the counterculture and the adoption and adaptation of Paganism, Romanticism is one of the core genealogies that inform the practices and self-perceptions of participants and how music, musical events,

---

[60]Fred Turner, *From Counterculture to Cyberculture: Stewart Brand, The Whole Earth Network, and the Rise of Digital Utopianism* (Chicago: The University of Chicago Press, 2006), 3–14, 31–8, 45.

artists, record labels, technology brands, and experiences are marketed. Strangely enough, one of the standout features is the Romantic interest in Medievalism, which is exactly as it sounds: a set of ideologies and symbols that refer to, and were adopted in the aftermath of, the Middle Ages. While Medievalism includes nonreligious themes, there are overlapping aesthetics with Paganism and the mysticism drawn on in some electronic dance music cultures. Medievalism appears in early and later Romantic art worlds—for example, in Liszt's compositions and Wagner's operas—and concerns itself with fantasies and idealizations of the past, including with ritual.[61] References to medieval spirituality or religion in some of Wagner's operas are, as Barbara Eichner argues, loose interpretations of medieval ideas—akin to the retelling of folklore undertaken by the Brothers Grimm. Themes of magic, miracles, and mysticism as they manifest in Wagner's operas portray an all-encompassing form of transcendence that contrasts with the monotheistic Christianity that dominated during the periods to which Wagner's operas refer.[62] It did not stop at the turn of the twentieth century. In the 1940s, Allan Ginsberg responded to the brutality and inhumanity of rationalism, modernism, and mechanization by drawing on the writings of American Romantic poets such as Walt Whitman, to address the full depth of personal experience and mysticism. Such poetry and other similarly inspired literature made a significant philosophical and cultural influence on the 1960s counterculture.[63] It is such fairy-tale adaptations of medieval philosophy and symbiology—via Romanticism and later, via the 1960s counterculture—that show up through the exaltation of nature and the "ancient" in the dance music cultures centered around psychedelic drugs and outdoor dancing.

Connectedness to nature, magic, and miracles, the core components of Medievalism and Paganism that Romantics embraced and blended, are at the core of how twenty-first-century dance music cultures, especially psychedelic trance and other "free party" cultures, relate to the idea of the transcendent

[61]Kristin Yri and Stephen C. Meyer, "Introduction," in *The Oxford Handbook of Music and Medievalism*, ed. Kirsten Yri and Stephen C. Meyer (New York: Oxford University Press, 2020), 1–9.
[62]Barbara Eichner, "Richard Wagner's Medieval Visions," in *The Oxford Handbook of Music and Medievalism*, ed. Kirsten Yri and Stephen C. Meyer (New York: Oxford University Press, 2020), 182–3.
[63]Turner, *From Counterculture to Cyberculture*, 62.

experience. Michel Maffesoli is popular in dance music studies, a fitting tool for analysis if the goal is to foreground the transcendent experience and related aspects of dance music. For Maffesoli, the late twentieth century is an age of "disindividuation," and "return to a vitalism." Vitalism, as he uses it, has a theological and mystical basis, with the help of Gershom Scholem, a founder of the scholarly study of Kabballah (Jewish mysticism): "these powers are the primordial elements 'upon which all reality is founded'; thus 'life flows externally and vitalizes creation while remaining at the same time deeply internal, and the secret rhythm of its movement, of its pulse, is the law of the dynamics of nature.'"[64]

Maffesoli is expressly anti-instrumentalist, and his notion of the social divine is born from the contemporary, postmodern world:

> There are times when the social "divine" is embodied in a collective emotion that recognizes itself in one or another typification [...] [The mythical type's] sole purpose is to express, for a precise moment in time, the collective spirit. This is the main distinction to be drawn between abstract, rational periods and "empathetic" periods of history. The rational era is built on the principle of individuation and of separation, whereas the empathetic period is marked by the lack of differentiation, the "loss" in a collective subject: in other words, what I shall call neo-tribalism.[65]

Ancestry is another significant artefact from Romantic preoccupations with nostalgia and idealized versions of "the ancient" that continue to be central to outdoor-oriented dance music. Ancestry can mean a range of relations, whether to land, animals, past humans, or deities. This idea has been realized through enacting Paganist rites in popular music contexts since the 1960s, at events such as the Stonehenge Free Festival and later, eclipse psytrance festivals.[66] According to Graham St. John, in the latter, where participants are "in search of transpersonal, transnational and transformative knowledge, the sociocosmic event potentiates the simultaneous loss of ego and the gaining

---

[64]Scholem in Michel Maffesoli, *The Time of the Tribes: The Decline of Individualism in Mass Society*, trans. Rob Shields (London: Save, 1996), 4.
[65]Maffesoli, *The Time of the Tribes*, 10–11.
[66]Till, "Paganism, Popular Music and Stonehenge," 39.

of the world."[67] Ideas such as spiritual connectedness to ancestors are at times lifted from western characterizations of eastern philosophies, Indigenous cultures, and Kabbalah (Jewish mysticism)—often all blended together in a druggy mishmash of ecological "techno-mysticism."[68] In both the writing and practice of dance music cultures, the DJ is frequently compared with, described as, or treated like, a shaman.[69]

Again, the 1960s comparison is helpful. The countercultural uses of psychedelic drugs such as LSD and music to achieve states of transcendence and higher consciousness were as much about primitivism—paradoxical as this might seem—as much as they were about what new technologies could facilitate. As Turner notes, the interactions between the New Communalist groups getting together for psychedelic gatherings and Native Americans involved, at least to begin with, a perception of First Nations peoples as possessing an intrinsic earthiness—as "custodians of the American landscape and, as such, guides to the preservation of the American wilderness." Later, such perceptions broadened to "symbolic figures of authenticity and alternative community"—inviting the white Hippy man to *himself* become an embodied participant in the idealized tribal community, accessing the "cosmic consciousness," where "the Indians had been ... all along."[70]

In sum, the 1960s New Communalists interpreted nineteenth-century Romantic representations of Indigenous symbols, eastern philosophy, Paganism, Medievalism, and other ancient rites. Such symbolisms and rituals are still present in psytrance forest parties in the American or Australian (colonized) desert, which draws into focus the persistent white "explorer" fascinated by (and desiring to be emancipated by) the cultures of exotic Others as an escapist alternative to western modernity.[71] The politics of incorporating

---

[67]Graham St. John, "Total Solar Eclipse Festivals, Cosmic Pilgrims and Planetary Culture," in *Pop Pagans: Paganism and Popular Music*, ed. Donna Weston and Andy Bennett (London and New York: Routledge, 2013), 131.

[68]Turner, *From Counterculture to Cyberculture*, 50.

[69]See Alice Beck Kehoe, "Primal Gaia: Primitivists and Plastic Medicine Men," in *The Invented Indian: Cultural Fictions and Government Policies*, ed. James A. Clifton (New York: Routledge, 1990), 193–209. See also Graham St. John, "Civilised Tribalism: Burning Man, Event-Tribes and Maker Culture," *Cultural Sociology* 12, no. 1 (March 2018): 8.

[70]Turner, *From Counterculture to Cyberculture*, 59.

[71]Saldanha, *Psychedelic White*, 11–20.

Indigenous and tribal cultural symbolisms—whether or not they are well-intended, respectful, and even approved by local Indigenous peoples—remains in question, particularly in dominantly white-participant contexts where Indigenous people materially suffer disproportionately compared with others.

It remains in question whether the transcendent encounter with dance music is an ideal state for participants to strive for, or whether its attainment is an inherent good. A DJ in Taipei, Su, believes it to be true:

> The thing that distinguishes DJing/Electronic music scene from other performance arts is that it blurs so many boundaries and frames between realities and dreams, between people from different races and genders, between performers and audiences. And as a DJ, I'm free from being the center of the space, being watched as I used to be as a singer and guitar player. Whether with the darkness and smoke in clubs or in forests or other natural landscapes at outdoor parties, I'm just a small element of the whole scene in the whole universe. My gender and my image just doesn't matter that much anymore. What matters is how lives can vibrate, resonate and be connected in the moment, sharing the sense as a collective. And I think this kind of culture helps to change the unbalanced situation of modern society: too much individualism and too little collectivism.

For Su, this kind of experience is where the societal change can be located: in material *and* metaphorical resonances, with discarding her ego and constructed identities. This hinges on a belief that there is a politics in the very act of engaging the spiritual or mystical aspects of dance music cultures in the right places and settings.

It is also possible that the transcendent experience can produce some of the opposite effects. For example, what results from an acceptance of the delimited, temporary nature of the radical mystical or spiritual experience, is a compartmentalization of the radical way-of-being from compliant participation in rational institutions with conservative practices. This is not to argue that, where individuals are incapable of fully opting out of the system they exist in, their political acts of rebellion and opposition are of no value. To demand all or nothing of political engagement would be a cheap shot and an unproductive nihilism to which this book does not subscribe. The point

of critiquing the limitations of alternative culture is rather that the status quo remains stable and self-reinforcing if subversion is defined and understood as being self-contained, and as belonging only to some groups, and not to others. The potential for the effects of the transcendent experiences described here could be extraordinary, but they would need to be harnessed for use in a structurally transformative political philosophy and action. There are aspects of participation in some dance music cultures that are not normative, such as use of illegal spaces, dancing at "anti-social" hours, illegal drug use, and various expressions of sexuality and sexual encounter. These require an openness to behavior, aesthetics, temporalities, and identities that are unacceptable or unusual in other settings. Aspects of such openness in one context can certainly lead to political shifts in another. The broadening of modes of dress and self-presentation considered acceptable without persecution or discrimination, the licensing and policing of electronic dance music nightlife no differently from other forms of culture, and the decriminalization of drugs are just some examples. The transcendent dance floor experience may be an important turning point for an individual's decision to engage in such efforts. When this happens, the spiritual experience can take a decidedly worldly form.[72] Yet this potential is unlikely to be realized if it stops short at the edge of the dance floor, since the dance floor always reflects what is brought to it from beyond its edge.

---

[72]There are dance music communities, such as Room 4 Resistance, that have a deliberative, conscious, and active set of practices that transfigures the dance floor ethos into the wider world. These are currently the exceptions, not the rule.

5

"This One's for the Ladies":
Gender Trouble in Sound
and Dance

Over the past decade or more, public discourses about gender have not only shifted in their nature but also moved to a greater extent than ever before from the fringes to mainstream. More people than ever are talking about gender as one of the many axes of inequality in contemporary society, bolstered in no small part by the #MeToo campaigns of 2017, which were in turn taken from the work Tarana Burke had been doing with sexual assault survivors in black communities in the United States since 2005.[1] Mainstream media, who had started to publish stories of people hurting others by virtue of their gender, began to do so more regularly. The headlines normally foregrounded people across celebrity culture, politics, and other spheres of high influence. However, the social media campaign's power appeared to come from the huge numbers

This chapter includes reworked sections from "Resistance or Reiteration?: Rethinking Gender in DJ Culture," *Contemporary Music Review* 35, no. 1 (February 2016): 115–29; and from "'I Don't Play Girly House Music': Women, Sonic Stereotyping, and the Dancing DJ," in the *Routledge Research Companion to Popular Music and Gender*, ed. Stan Hawkins (London: Routledge, 2017), 196–210.
[1]Tarana Burke, *Unbound: My Story of Liberation and the Birth of the Me Too Movement* (New York: Flatiron Books, 2021), 10.

of people admitting that they, too, had been "Harvey Weinsteined." The tone of many people who had previously been either indifferent or outright hostile to feminism and other gender-related discourses began to shift. Colleagues and friends discussed the latest news on who had harassed, raped, exploited, or all three, and what to do with such information when it involved leading figures in an industry or politics. Across populations and demographics, people reconsidered gender's meanings and protested injustices—in some cases for the first time. In other cases, people across scholarly and broader spheres debated old issues and raised new ones, refuting and redefining them as a means of making sense of the reconfiguration of their understanding of gender and power. Story after story of one celebrity after the other—musical ones included—abusing people (women and girls, in particular) for years, with the excuses and facilitations of those around them.[2] Here was a collective potential of enormous scale, calling for a feminist mass movement that could be genuinely plural, transcend national boundaries, and exceed the western hemisphere. Change did feel as though it was afoot.

As the narratives in state and corporate media developed in tandem with big business, validated by academic institutions, the emphasis shifted from the large-scale, collective chorus of #MeToo to individual stories of retribution and punishment on the part of perpetrators and on healing on the part of victims. Story after story came out of individual vulnerability, adversity, and crisis, and in some of the more uplifting cases, these were followed by resilience, grit, and empowerment. Stories of struggle and change within dance music and DJ culture, which had previously, like other forms of gender discussion, been only occasional (addressed by music journalists such as Tricia Romano) entered the mainstream media discourse to a greater degree.[3] There was an increasing admission that musical practices associated with power and authority, such as conducting, producing, and in most spaces, DJing, continue

---

[2]Catherine Strong, "Towards a Feminist History of Popular Music: Re-Examining Writing on Musicians and Domestic Violence in the Wake of #MeToo," in *Remembering Popular Music's Past: Memory-Heritage-History*, ed. Lauren Istvandity, Sarah Baker, and Zelmarie Cantillon (London: Anthem Press, 2019), 217–32.

[3]Tricia Romano, "Women Edging Their Way into the DJ Booth," *New York Times*, November 1, 2013, https://www.nytimes.com/2013/11/03/arts/music/women-edging-their-way-into-the-dj-booth.html.

to be dominated by men and that clubbers are still harassed regularly, which reflected the research I had done to this point.[4] The mass media response had been preceded by a consciousness and action *within* dance music culture, to challenge intersectional discrimination.[5] One dance music community's reckoning concerned a DJ and promoter in Oslo, known as a central figure in the history of Norwegian club culture. It was a short time later that the stories of his court charges started to materialize in the Norwegian media, with analogies to Harvey Weinstein among the analyses made in them.[6] The issues were not straightforward. The DJ's defense attorney, for example, objected to the "lack of respect for the rule of law" with respect to a street protest that happened in response to the court's acquittal of eight of nine rape charges

---

[4]Marietta Nien-hwa Cheng, "Women Conductors: Has the Train Left the Station?" *Harmony: Forum of the Symphony Orchestra Institute* 6 (April 1998): 81–90; Carol E. Robertson, "Power and Gender in the Musical Experiences of Women," in *Women and Music in Cross-Cultural Perspective*, ed. Ellen Koskoff (Champaign: University of Illinois Press, 1987), 225–44; Farrugia, *Beyond the Dance Floor*; Gavanas and Reitsamer, "DJ Technologies, Social Networks and Gendered Trajectories in European DJ Cultures," 51–77.

[5]See Diana Hubbell, "Meet Nakadia, the DJ from Rural Thailand Who Is Underground Techno's Rising Star," *Vice*, February 4, 2016, https://www.vice.com/en/article/8q7xv5/nakadia-mungphanklang-interview-thailand-dj-sven-vath; Kish Lal, "Meet the DJs Challenging Melbourne's Blokey Club Scene," Inthemix, July 6, 2016, https://inthemix.junkee.com/meet-the-new-djs-challenging-melbournes-blokey-club-scene/(last accessed 2016); Carl Loben, "Who Are the Women Pioneers of Dance Music?" *Huffpost Entertainment UK*, April 28, 2016, https://www.huffingtonpost.co.uk/carl-loben/women-pioneers-of-dance-music_b_9794186.html; Michaelangelo Matos, "Nightclubbing: Your Sisters' House," *Red Bull Music Academy Daily*, February 17, 2015, http://daily.redbullmusicacademy.com/2015/02/nightclubbing-your-sisters-house Mitchell 2016; Michaelangelo Matos, "The Techno Feminists Next Door," NPR Music, November 6, 2015, https://www.npr.org/sections/therecord/2015/11/06/454946162/the-techno-feminists-next-door; Resident Advisor, "Between the Beats: The Black Madonna," August 11, 2016, https://ra.co/features/2793 2016; Sophie Weiner, "Can Teaching Young Women to DJ and Produce Solve Gender Equality in Electronic Music?" *Vice*, February 26, 2016, https://www.vice.com/en/article/bmajww/can-teaching-young-women-to-dj-and-produce-solve-gender-inequality-in-electronic-music.

[6]Morten Schwencke and Harald Stolt-Nielsen, "Derfor frikjennes Gaute Drevdal for åtte voldtekter," *Aftenposten*, January 28, 2022, https://www.aftenposten.no/norge/i/lVL6v9/derfor-frikjennes-gaute-drevdal-for-aatte-voldtekter; Ola Mjaaland, "Voldtektsdømte Gaute Drevdal med nye forsvarere og ny strategi før ankesaken," *NRK*, October 14, 2021, https://www.nrk.no/norge/voldtektsdomte-gaute-drevdal-med-nye-forsvarere-og-ny-strategi-for-ankesaken-1.15685321; Ola Mjaaland, Kirsti Haga Honningsøy, Eirin Tjoflot, and Emily Louisa Millan Eide, "Gaute Drevdal får stor reduksjon i straff—anker erstatningskrav," *NRK*, January 29, 2022, https://www.nrk.no/norge/gaute-drevdal-far-stor-reduksjon-i-straff-_-anker-erstatningskrav-1.15827803; Farid Ighoubah, "Kulturprofil Gaute Drevdal frikjent for åtte av ni voldtektsanklager," *Nettavisen*, January 29, 2022, https://www.nettavisen.no/nyheter/kulturprofil-gaute-drevdal-frikjent-for-atte-av-ni-voldtektsanklager/s/12-95-3424237555.

against the DJ.[7] In another, in 2019, a successful DJ from Glasgow publicly shared that revenge porn was used to shame her in 2013 and that police did not take her initial report seriously.[8]

This chapter takes this broader background into account when addressing a number of issues that relate to how gender issues interact with dance music culture. What they all come down to is that DJing and production are "male-coded spaces," which is to say that they exclude or discriminate against women in various ways.[9] Participants use compound terms, "girl DJs," "female DJs," or less frequently, "women DJs." Men, by contrast, are just DJs. Women are treated as though they are less competent at DJing, are excluded from the informal spaces of learning and exchange, and are often pressured into proving their worth in other ways. Corporate constructions of hypersexual femininity influence how women who DJ stylize themselves. Through fashion and other methods, they present in ways that reaffirm the Enlightenment understanding of beauty, which is that it is a feminine phenomenon and also "an inferior aesthetic category" to the masculine "sublime."[10] Some participants also experience sounds that they hear in dance music through enculturated understandings about gender. For example, participants equate "fluffy" sounds to "girly" music and believe that "femininity" is incongruous with "sophisticated" or "good" music (and that "good" music has "masculine" features). Labelling music with so-called girly appeal as low culture is a familiar concept for anyone who has encountered dismissals of music that is most popular among adolescent girls. The treatment of higher-profile women who DJ—those who achieve fame and success on an international scale—is worthy of note. The DJ Nina Kraviz is a compelling case. Her success has upset and

---

[7]Farid Ighoubah, "Forsvarer for Gaute Drevdal reagerer på demonstrasjon mot voldtektsom," *Nettavisen*, February 2, 2022, https://www.nettavisen.no/nyheter/forsvarer-for-gaute-drevdal-reagerer-pa-demonstrasjon-mot-voldtektsdom/s/12-95-3424240661.

[8]Gordon Blackstock, "Revenge Porn Victim Says Police Scotland Fobbed Off Complaint So They Could 'Solve Murders,'" *Daily Record*, May 19, 2019, https://www.dailyrecord.co.uk/news/scottish-news/revenge-porn-victim-says-police-16166386.amp?__twitter_impression=true.

[9]Gavanas and Reitsamer, "DJ Technologies, Social Networks and Gendered Trajectories in European DJ Cultures," 57.

[10]Judy Lochhead, "Theorizing Gender, Culture, and Music: The Sublime, the Ineffable, and Other Dangerous Aesthetics," *Women and Music: A Journal of Gender and Culture* 12 (2008): 64–70. See also Gadir, "'I Don't Play Girly House Music,'" 197.

discredited the binary often imposed on women who DJ. Women must either be attractive for commercial ends and possess no cultural capital or musical "underground" credibility, *or* they must be musically credible and occupy the "cool" scenes, where physical appearance may not fit modern western beauty standards. Kraviz has done both, the result of which is that she is an object of resentment for other DJs—most vociferously, though not exclusively, for high-profile men. Such resentment manifests through various media and commentary on issues ranging from whether her photo shoot in a bubble bath was acceptable in 2013 to whether she performs the "correct" (western) position on the conflict in her home country, to her social media followers in 2022.[11] Finally, different forms of media, from videos to written commentary, play a central role not only in providing a visual vehicle for her performances to be viewed beyond the club, but also in their facilitation of blaming and shaming.

Sexy and Incompetent

In typical industry practices, there is a clear strategy of segmentation of the market for DJs. Women who DJ tend to be categorically, commercially separate from men.[12] To achieve such segmentation, gender, as it is constructed by commodity culture, helps to portray the DJing jobs of women as radically distinct from those of men. Companies and networks such as femaledjagency.co.uk use web space dominated by "sexy" photographs of DJs and persisting visual symbols of femininity such as pink and purple color

---

[11]Greg Wilson, "Nina Kraviz: The Mistress of Her Own Myth," *Greg Wilson: Being a DJ* (blog), April 8, 2013, https://blog.gregwilson.co.uk/2013/04/nina-kraviz-the-mistress-of-her-own-myth/; Nina Kraviz, "Greg Wilson wrote an article about me," Facebook, April 8, 2013, https://www.facebook.com/permalink.php?story_fbid=556948164349995&id=192110944137172; *Factmag*, "Russian DJ Nina Kraviz Addresses *that* Bath Scene after Greg Wilson and Maceo Plex Have Their Say," *Fact*, April 9, 2013, https://www.factmag.com/2013/04/09/russian-dj-nina-kraviz-addresses-that-bath-scene-after-greg-wilson-and-maceo-plex-have-their-say/; Nina Kraviz (@NinaKraviz) "I'm praying for peace! #mir #мир," Twitter, February 27, 2022, 7:41 a.m., https://twitter.com/NinaKraviz/status/14976732577 71745281?s=20&t=ColMvbqEspi1o4iY_zihBw.

[12]Gavanas and Reitsamer, "DJ Technologies, Social Networks and Gendered Trajectories in European DJ Cultures," 51–77.

schemes.[13] Furthermore, "She Can DJ" is among a number of woman-specific DJ competitions that have promoted not only candidates' DJing, but also their aptitude for fashion and make-up—usually of a commoditized, hyperfeminine kind. Key sponsors of the "She Can DJ" competition have included not only EMI Music but corporations such as Rimmel cosmetics and "designer bargain" clothing chain DFO (Direct Factory Outlet). Such blatantly gendered corporate branding prevails across contemporary dance music settings. It also epitomizes the close relationships between gender stereotyping, commerce, and capitalist ideology. Finally, it is a stark example of just how far gender performance can go.[14] Many interviewees raise the theme of conscious feminine stylization. Some counter the above trends (and pressures) in their DJ work by consciously enacting antifemininity, in how they dress, in how they behave, and in what music they play. Others simply indicate a lack of interest in doing gender in any sense. Others adhere to the unwritten rules of gender market segmentation. Hannah, for instance, a commercially successful Sydney DJ, has expressed that many women DJ feel compelled to draw attention to sexualized images of their bodies.

> A lot of girl DJs are sexy, and they do put out sexy images ... Guys say that on my Instagram, I've noticed that: "You only get shows 'cause you're hot" ... We have a common understanding that it's important to look hot to work as what we do ... Like, we all understand that you have to be marketable, and people will have to want to be engaged with what you're doing ... you get that that's part of the job ... I suppose, if you've got a good-looking woman in a position of power doing something that they kind of wish that they could do .... I definitely think it's problematic, because ... for example, if I was short and really overweight, with bad acne, but I was a killer DJ, no one would come listen to me! And that sucks.

Melbourne-based DJ Christine also believes that the criteria on which many women are judged is sexual desirability:

---

[13] "We Run the World Female DJ Agency™," 2022, https://femaledjagency.co.uk/about-us/.
[14] See Judith Butler, "Performative Acts and Gender Constitution: An Essay in Phenomenology and Feminist Theory," *Theatre Journal* 40, no. 4 (December 1988): 519–22.

Being a trans woman, I've been on both sides of the nightclub. I've had the discussions, presenting as male. And I've been privy to the discussions about why someone would like a particular DJ. And they're not great, they're pretty awful discussions. They're like, "they're a babe, they're hot. Oh, and they really know about their music too." It's so misog[ynistic] …

In order to survive in the dance music milieu, then, women must continuously negotiate how to "deal with" their appearance.

The barriers that women face as DJs also take place while agents are booking them for events. Take the following example from Edda, a trance DJ in Oslo:

I remember this one [e]mail that I got from Portugal. They wanted to book me. And then they were asking, "are you a model?" And I was like, "no, why?" "No, 'cause, then you won't get the job, because you're not a model, because that's what we want." So I'm like, "okay, so what about the music quality? What about the technical quality?" And it didn't matter. So I was like, "fuck off!" I don't want this. This is not me … [Another time,] this one place I played … I went there to play, and I got so much good feedback, and I was like, okay, good, maybe I'll come back here … And then … [the booking agent] told me … "you're not worth the money … you should have been a lot more undressed for that price."

Further examples of disturbing harassment take place during DJ performances too, such as in the following account by Hannah:

I actually finished 15 minutes early, [and] walked off stage, because everyone was screaming, "tits out for the boys, tits out for the boys." Even the girls …[15] And, so … I pulled the sound down, got on the mic, and I was like: "I find it really rude that you're saying that when I'm performing for you guys. If you want to see tits, go home and ask your girlfriend to [show you] her tits." … And they kept doing it … There [were] five hundred people in the venue, and probably half of them were screaming this chant, over and over … And

---

[15]As this incident illustrates, women can be complicit in upholding the same prejudicial attitudes that lead to their own and other women's oppression.

then the third song, I mixed it in, and I was almost in tears. I was like, this is so shit. So I just said to the [next] DJ, "can you jump on? I'm leaving."

As well as walking off the job on singular occasions such as the one described by Hannah, above, DJs also reject gig offers when they experience difficulties. María, a wedding and events DJ in Reykjavík, Iceland, explains her decision to turn down Friday and Saturday night performances "because I simply cannot deal with the harassment of people not in the same state of mind as I am." It is not only that such people are intoxicated, which she explains in the interview, but that their responses are built on a widely shared assumption that women are less competent than men at DJing. As María notes, "it has to do with the fact that I'm a girl. People come to the booth, and they pretend that I don't know what I'm doing."

Relatedly, there can also be a lack of willingness of men to share their skills with women who are beginners. A New York house DJ, Jennifa Mayanja, had her initial interest in DJing met with encouragement by some of her peers, but with resistance by others:

Some friends had started to get into DJing that I knew … and they was kind of playing around, and I was like, "Oh, well, you know, I've always been into DJs and what have you … and you know, maybe you could show me," and they were like, "No. You're not going to learn because you're a girl."

This kind of resolute refusal to help is also reflected in psytrance DJ Mayleen's story. Mayleen faced resistance to her interest in learning how to DJ for the same reason. Instead, she learned by seeking a job at a nightclub and arriving to every shift early enough to practice before the club DJ would arrive.

In addition to the feedback that women receive for their supposed lack of practical and technical competence and the lack of willingness to help them improve, their musical tastes are also in doubt. Specifically, participants consider men's music, whatever its form, to be authentic. Women's music, on the other hand, is manufactured and lowly.[16] At times, this prejudice is so entrenched that when a woman performs music that a man believes is "good,"

---

[16]Simon Frith and Angela McRobbie, "Rock and Sexuality," in *On Record: Rock, Pop, and the Written Word*, ed. Simon Frith and Andrew Goodwin (New York: Pantheon Books, 1990), 371–89.

it must be due to the influence of her male mentors, not her own tastes or skills. Fenfang, a psytrance DJ from China, based in Taipei, describes a common encounter at gigs that illustrates such attitudes:

It's totally annoying that after I play, people would say: that was awesome! What's the song played around 40 min? Is that from your boyfriend? ... And no one asked him if I gave *him* music.

This attitude also manifests through the idea that particular music technologies, such as DJ hardware and software, are masculine in essence, which, in turn, means that women do not possess the capacity for audio-technical expertise.[17] Many women, nonbinary, or transgender DJs interviewed for this project describe incidents that convey this perception. In their accounts, sound engineers, promoters, booking agents, clubbers, and other DJs suggest that the competent operation of DJ hardware and software in performance is unlikely or unusual for women to be able to achieve. The attitude is so routine that some interviewees take them for granted. A DJ duo from Oslo, Lill and Sabine, insist that being women in dance music constitutes a substantial advantage rather than a problem. They express bewilderment at women DJs' complaints about being singled out as women. When asked whether their abilities to use DJ technologies have ever been called into question, however, the answer is "yes, of course." They describe one incident in which a booking agent offered to provide them with a premixed CD to "perform." Such an act implies that the DJs do not know how to mix music themselves, and since Lill and Sabine could mix their own music, they took this as an insult.

What is striking about such stories is the extent to which agency is taken away from women by men in relative positions of authority. The removal of agency is also reflected in the conviction that men who DJ know what sounds

---

[17]Gavanas and Reitsamer, "DJ Technologies, Social Networks and Gendered Trajectories in European DJ Cultures," 53–9. See also Victoria Armstrong, *Technology and the Gendering of Music Education* (Farnham: Ashgate, 2011), 29–30; Georgina Born and Kyle Devine, "Music Technology, Gender, and Class: Digitization, Educational and Social Change in Britain," *Twentieth-Century Music* 12, no. 2 (September 2015): 135–72; Veronica Doubleday, "Sounds of Power: An Overview of Musical Instruments and Gender," *Ethnomusicology Forum* 17, no. 1 (June 2008): 15–18; Susan McClary, *Feminine Endings: Music, Gender, and Sexuality* (Minneapolis: University of Minnesota Press, 1991).

women, especially women in groups, are attracted to. In doing so, men who DJ task themselves with determining what women on their dance floors will hear or dance to according to these criteria.

"This One's for the Ladies": What Women Want to Dance To

In many dance music genres—for instance drum 'n' bass, dubstep, house, techno or psytrance—where musical sound is a topic of conversation, references to the ways that sounds appeal to different genders come up.[18] The most overt manifestation of this concerns the question of which types of sounds women—usually portrayed as a homogeneous group—enjoy dancing to. In their interviews, DJs (mostly men) identify three elements that "get women to dance": prominent or catchy melodic riffs, particularly those in high registers; vocal lines, particularly those involving female voices; and soft or "fluffy" timbres. Such beliefs determine a simple formula, understood as follows: if a DJ plays dance music with any of the above features, women will dance. If women are dancing, men—whom, it is assumed, are attracted to women—will then also dance and the DJ has done their job right. One ex-psytrance DJ and producer from England, Warren, describes what he observes in the below interview excerpt:

> If you use some sort of melodic element, what we used to call fluffy—fluffy techno, or fluffy trance—then that's a way to get the girls dancing, very often, and once the girls start dancing, then everybody else starts dancing. That sounds like a cliché, but … it's just what happens every time I've seen it.

Cam, an Edinburgh-based DJ and promoter, also reflects on the techniques that he uses to attract women to dance floors:

> There's always the old tricks like playing a record that's got a cheeky vocal in it or something. Get girls dancing, generally you'll get boys dancing … that's

---

[18]For broader discussions of sound and gender, see Farrugia, *Beyond the Dance Floor*, 8–10; Stirling, "Gendered Publics and Creative Practices in Electronic Dance Music," 130–49.

a good rule to follow, and it's not something that I particularly like using, because I don't really try to categorize my records as being, you know, "oh that one's a bit more for the ladies." I don't really like records like that, I like good electronic music. But there will be records where you know this one might get a few girls up dancing, and if you can get a wee troop of girls up (five girls up there that are on their own night out), then generally they will be followed by a pack of lads. And once you're on to, like, ten or fifteen people on the dance floor, it's much easier to build a dance floor. You know, one or two people: you've got to kind of pull out the stops.

Cam and Warren's comments are among the many that emerged not only from interviews but also from a year of intensive work at a mobile events DJing business. On the one hand, their comments are based on observations, which in and of themselves do not constitute prejudices. Indeed, it is possible to take the observations that Warren and Cam make and use them to argue that women have a great deal of agency in dancing-focused spaces, in a way that is not necessarily true of pubs or of music studios. The "wee troop of girls" in Cam's account, who respond well to melodies or catchy hooks, or the girls at Warren's psytrance gigs who like "fluffy" sounds, are in one sense, uniquely empowered by their command of the entire "vibe" of the dance floor. Such a perspective reaffirms the work of Maria Pini, that includes quotations from women who feel that rave cultures allow them to "own" the space in a way they do not feel is possible elsewhere. Pini's argument is that this cannot happen in more "commercial" music settings because women are more likely to be hassled or harassed. However, it is also the case that at a Top 40 club night or at a wedding, women of all ages steer dance floors. Men from Anglo-Saxon and West-European cultures are not, in a widespread sense, socialized to dance and, on the contrary, are often socialized to believe that it is not something they should do. In contexts where dancing does take place, they can feel very challenged by, and excluded from, such social situations. But the broader point remains that DJs such as Cam associate their understandings of "good electronic music" with broader perceptions about gender and taste. In the above excerpt, Cam explicitly contrasts tracks he deems to be attractive to women with his appreciation of "good electronic music." When he says

that there is a particular type of "cheeky vocal" music that makes women (or "girls") dance, then, this is *not* good electronic music. This is a musical taste compromise that he must make, to appeal to the people on his dance floor who are most likely to dance.

The belief that women prefer to dance to vocal lines comes from the association between the voice and the feminine body in music. In popular music, the notion that women sing and men play instruments reaffirms this, as does electronically produced dance music produced by men while "featuring" women's voices—especially those of black women. In some dance music genres, the voice is at the center of an otherwise exclusively electronic soundscape. Most electronic dance music that has made it into commercial club charts has singing in it. This is unsurprising, because of the centrality of voice to popular music in general, the universality of it across cultures of human music. Even when certain kinds of technological mediations and effects detach the listener from the bodily sources of the producer, remixer, instrumental player, or singer, voices serve as reminders that such bodies are still there, somewhere. What is more, the voice expresses aspects of physical and emotional feeling, phenomena that are linked to femininity in the western Enlightenment paradigm.[19] If the voice is simultaneously charged with two traditionally feminine aesthetic qualities—the expression of emotion and an aural reminder of the body's materiality—then it is no surprise that the voice is also understood as the most feminine sound. It is not a coincidence that the DJs who distinguish themselves from commercial dance music culture express a common distaste for vocal lines. According to one interviewee, his favorite club in Frankfurt had a no vocals policy. The voice is treated differently in a lot of electronic dance music (for example, genres such as techno) from

---

[19]Frith, *Performing Rites*, 191–2; Middleton, *Studying Popular Music*, 261–4; see also Nick Prior, "Software Sequencers and Cyborg Singers: Popular Music in the Digital Hypermodern," *New Formations* 66 (March 2009): 91–4. For a different perspective on the voice-technology relationship, see Nick Prior, "On Vocal Assemblages: From Edison to Miku," *Contemporary Music Review* 37, no. 5–6 (2018): 488–506. Stan Hawkins, *The British Pop Dandy* (Farnham: Ashgate, 2009), 123–51; Colwyn Trevarthen, Jonathan Delafield-Butt, and Benjamin Schögler, "Psychobiology of Musical Gesture: Innate Rhythm, Harmony and Melody in Movements of Narration," in *Music and Gesture II*, ed. Anthony Gritten and Elaine King (Aldershot: Ashgate, 2011), 11–43; Lochhead, "Theorizing Gender, Culture, and Music," 63–124.

other popular music, in that it is either not used at all, used sparingly, or used as a part of the overall texture of a track. However, there are several genres in which it is prominent and commonplace. In the end, beliefs that women prefer vocals, initiate dancing, and that men will invariably follow are used selectively, and continue to motivate DJs to reinforce such ideas and perform with them in mind.

Attitudes to taste as they are expressed by women in groups do not relate only to specific sounds such as vocal lines but also to musical genre. Dom explains, for example, how women on hen nights (bachelorette parties) do not fit the normative, implicitly masculine, styles of dancing that are fitting for techno club nights:

> When you get an influx of girls on a hen night, they don't dance the same way … even though they're listening to the same music. So they normally would maybe not [listen] to dance music, maybe more sort of R 'n' B, or chart orientated; so you get more of the girly dancing like that. You see, girls who are in with the electronic music crew dance the same way as the guys do.

Dom implies that women who are out on a hen night either do not understand techno, or do not understand how to dance to it properly. Women on hen nights are the specific targets for Dom's criticism; men at stag nights do not receive a mention. For Dom, a division exists between the "girly" dancing style of women on hen nights, honed by listening to R 'n' B or chart pop (which must be feminine genres), on the one hand, and women "*in* with the electronic music crew," because they are techno fans who dance like male techno aficionados, on the other. The participation of women who are "in" is validated partly by their choice to adopt masculine styles of dancing. Interviews with Dom and other techno DJs reveal an attitude to contemporary R 'n' B that equates it with "low" popular music genres whose associated dancing styles in club settings are not only feminine but sexual. In sum, the music and the dancing are signifiers, for Dom, of hen nights (and thus larger groups of women), low musical taste, dancing in a "sexual" (feminine) manner, and not "fitting in."[20]

---

[20]Simon Frith and Angela McRobbie's discussion of the prejudices in the rock world directed against women with regard to their "pop" (low) musical tastes are still applicable to attitudes in a number of music scenes today. Frith and McRobbie, "Rock and Sexuality," 371–89.

Attitudes to gender via genre are prominent in many genre-focused musical communities, not only dance music, because distinctions between a specific genre or subgenre and all the others are a core point of identification and belonging for fans. In dance music, DJs are similarly concerned with how their practices and music differ from "commercial" club music and practices.[21] It is nevertheless striking that male DJs in twenty-first-century dance music communities identify a formula (or at least, a trend) for making women dance, and that this comes with a qualification that they need to lower their musical standards to achieve this.

Given that another dimension of twenty-first-century dance music experience is that it is now possible to watch club nights through high quality video media, gender prejudices are reflected, even amplified, when the DJ is turned into a spectacle for the screen. It is therefore worth examining the broader relationship between DJ culture and media to provide context for how such dynamics play out.

Media, Dance, and Gender Stereotyping

Music has been a mass televised event since the first live "talkie" television broadcast of Adèle Dixon performing "Magic Rays of Light in 1936 for the BBC.[22] Beyond sensationalist media reporting on the conflicts between ravers and the state, on the one hand, or screen documentaries celebrating rave culture as extensions of the electronic music avant-garde, on the other, there are other dance music precedents for the Boiler Room YouTube channel, which is the way that most contemporary dance music fans would view videos of club nights today.[23] For as long as there has been recognition of an audience for dance music, there has been a niche in broadcast media for DJs to play it. When it came to radio, shows such as WBLS in New York had mix-DJ shows reflecting both disco and hip-hop scenes locally and Capitol Radio in London

---

[21]See also Thornton, *Club Cultures.*

[22]David Hendy, "The Birth of TV: Opening Night: November 1936," BBC 100, last accessed May 20, 2022, https://www.bbc.com/historyofthebbc/100-voices/birth-of-tv/opening-night/.

[23]See Cultures of Resistance Films, *Modulations*, directed by Iara Lee, produced by George Gund, January 18, 2020 (original film released 2000), https://youtu.be/icpDt6aQDww.

had house and techno playing, with material from the party scenes in Ibiza. Both of these inspired the long-running BBC Radio 1 *Essential Mix* program.[24] As for television, in the late 1980s and early 1990s, Detroit had its own local program specifically for techno parties, *New Dance Show*, complete with a lively presenter.[25] The focus of the show was the dancers and their moves, not the DJ, who was generally in the background.

Since they began in 2010, *Boiler Room* events have developed their own style that began with "a webcam taped to a wall" and developed into professional-quality videos of the world's best DJs.[26] Their funding model includes commercial partnerships, including from alcohol (such as Miller Genuine Draft and Ballentine's), and music technology brands (such as Technics). They stream and record events that would rarely, if ever, appear on state or corporate media broadcasts. They include the authentic atmospheres of club nights and genuine fans enjoying their favorite dance music genres. The videos have a considered intimacy to them, as viewers can imagine that they are in the club, should they wish to. The dancing takes place with no choreographed dancing or performance. However contradictory it may seem to broadcast or stream a type of event to people sitting at home where the primary activity is dancing, the *Boiler Room* is, in fact, centered on what the screen shows to the people sitting at home. The camera and lighting make DJs' faces appear clearer than they would be for most people encountering them at a club in the flesh. In most cases, DJs face the camera, and the clubbers are behind them so that everyone faces the camera, rather than the usual setup of clubbers facing DJs, or in some cases, of DJs being in the center and clubbers dancing around them. Clubbers are aware of the cameras and know that they are part of the cast. Like in *New Dance Show*, the clubbers are part of the

---

[24]Elias Leight, "The Essential Mix at 25: Pete Tong on Creating One of Dance Music's Most Important Mix Shows," *Rolling Stone*, October 26, 2018, https://www.rollingstone.com/music/music-news/pete-tong-essential-mix-dance-music-bbc-radio1-745904/.

[25]Vivian Host, "Don't Stop Now: Revisiting the New Dance Show of Detroit," Red Bull Music Academy, May 24, 2019, https://daily.redbullmusicacademy.com/2019/05/rj-watkins-lawanda-new-dance-show. There are a few YouTube archives of the show, for example, by user Caprice87. See Caprice87, "Dance! New Dance Show 1990: Recorded in November 1990 at Key Wat TV Studios, Detroit, MI," video, https://www.youtube.com/watch?v=DVBE4mcBiSo&ab_channel=Caprice87.

[26]*Boiler Room*, 2022, www.boilerroom.tv/about.

appeal of the *Boiler Room* events, as distinct from watching DJs livestream or post videos of their mixes on their own.[27]

It is precisely such screen orientations that invite the intense scrutiny of how women who DJ appear, behave, and perform. This manifests in the early comments on Nina Kraviz's *Boiler Room* YouTube videos from 2013 and 2015, where people accuse her of deliberately playing sexually provocative dance moves as part of her DJ set. Commentary on her YouTube videos is but one small fraction of an enormous constellation of attention and smearing that has corresponded with her growth as a DJ-producer with an international profile. Criticism of her femininity, sexualization, desirability, and skill takes up the same media spaces as all forms of celebrity "controversy."[28] It has included the responses to what should have been a promotional documentary by the online dance music publication Resident Advisor, in 2013, which included an interview conducted with her in a swimsuit at the beach, and another from a bubble bath in a hotel. It is very plausible that such framings could well have been designed in part to foreground her appearance and attract attention in the age-old "sex sells" marketing approach. However, this does not justify the viciousness with which viewers and some of her peers reacted, the claims that it was in "bad taste," the notion that such a documentary showed a lack of integrity, and that she was doing an injustice to all "the ladies playing amazing music and pushing the scene forward with nothing else than sick records and

[27]For a detailed analysis of the ways that club night experiences are remediated in *Boiler Room* sets, see Guillaume Heuguet, "When Club Cultures Goes Online: The Case of Boiler Room," trans. Luis-Manuel Garcia, *Dancecult* 8, no. 1 (November, 2016): 73–87. See also Philip Auslander, *Liveness: Performance in a Mediatized Culture* (London: Routledge, 2008), 25, 69.

[28]Marcus Barnes, "Maceo Plex on Nina Kraviz, the Return of Maetrik and Juggling Fame with Family Life," The Independent, April 25, 2013, http://blogs.independent.co.uk/2013/04/18/maceo-plex-on-nina-kraviz-the-return-of-maetrik-and-juggling-fame-with-family-life/; Ilenia Cangelosi, "The DJ Sex Battle: Maceo Plex Speaks Out on Nina Kraviz' RA Video," *Less Than 3*, April 9, 2013, http://blog.lessthan3.com/2013/04/the-dj-sex-battle-maceo-plex-speaksout-on-nina-kraviz-ra-video/; *Factmag*, "Russian DJ Nina Kraviz Addresses *that* Bath Scene after Greg Wilson and Maceo Plex Have Their Say,"; Henry Johnstone, "Maceo Plex Calls Out Nina Kraviz Over 'That' RA Video," *Pulse*, April 9, 2013, http://pulseradio.net/articles/2013/04/maceo-plex-calls-out-nina-kraviz-over-that-ra-video-feature; Jacob Reamer, "Nina Kraviz Video Scandal Explained," TickPick: Where Smart Fans Buy Tickets, April 12, 2013, https://www.tickpick.com/blog/nina-kraviz-video-scandal-explained/; Greg Wilson, "Nina Kraviz, The Mistress of Her Own Myth".

studio time."[29] Similarly, the *Boiler Room* set commentaries included that her appearance has allowed her to succeed in the absence of real DJ skills, accusing her of "eye-fucking the camera" and making "self-conscious sexy dance moves," and criticizing her desire to "strike a pose and pout for the camera."[30]

All such responses reaffirm the distinctions that continue to keep women on the outside when they do not correctly participate in the rules of the (sub) cultural game. If people in a "cool" musical community claim that a woman is acting in a way that draws attention to her sexual desirability, she has no business being in that community. She is tainting the seriousness of the pursuit of music and culture with her performance of sexiness. The video of the 2015 set shows Kraviz using more of her body, across more space, to dance in a way that is not all that common to techno DJs. However, it is not that dissimilar to the fist pumping and arm flapping that many men do while they DJ, as a way to "get into" the music and contribute to the energy of their DJ sets. When clubbers see DJs enjoying themselves, it feeds into their own responses to the atmosphere. Yet stereotypes of femininity and masculinity have their own manifestations in DJ culture, where it is women who interact with crowds more directly, while men DJ with smaller body movements and introverted postures, focusing their attentions on their tools of performance (mixers, laptops, turntables, CDJs, effects units, MIDI controllers), and showing their cool by effectively ignoring the crowd and being absorbed with their toys. For her critics, Kraviz, who takes up more booth space and engages her hips to dance along with the rest of her body, must be trying to seduce her crowd through exaggerated sex appeal. Kraviz does occasionally interact with her crowds and the fans at home by smiling and blowing "air kisses" toward particular people who she appears to know personally in the two *Boiler Room* sets that are the object of this analysis. It is even possible to say that particularly in the 2013 Berlin *Boiler Room* set, her movements are as minimal as, if not more than, many of her counterparts. But the moments where she "betrays"

---

[29]Maceo Plex in Cangelosi, "The DJ Sex Battle: Maceo Plex Speaks Out on Nina Kraviz' RA Video"; Johnstone, "Maceo Plex Calls Out Nina Kraviz Over 'That' RA Video."

[30]Edward Clowes, YouTube Comment on Nina Kraviz, 2015, https://www.youtube.com/watch?v=YIcbIIHcx44&ab_channel=BoilerRoom; Fig Les, YouTube Comment on Nina Kraviz, 2015, https://www.youtube.com/watch?v=YIcbIIHcx44&ab_channel=BoilerRoom.

her femininity or sexuality are sufficient to threaten the idea that DJs must be men or masculine to be legitimate. Such moments take place fleetingly within long DJ sets, and yet receive a great deal of attention and are used to cast aspersions on her character, her intentions, and her skills—can she truly be good if she is "cute," and worse, *knows* it?[31]

Despite all of this intense, negative attention, Kraviz has a million Instagram followers and has been DJing internationally for over a decade. It is even possible to interpret the below description on her website as a conscious incorporation of negative attention she has received into a bigger marketing strategy:

> Kraviz has charisma to spare and she knows it. The way she commands the DJ booth and the camera has made her a vital force in the eradication of stone-age attitudes to female talent and sexuality, and the feeling from intimidated men that the two are somehow mutually exclusive. As long as Kraviz is here to stay, techno will continue marching forwards.[32]

Reflecting the broader changes between the period of research and the present, the positive comments on the videos of the DJ performances have noticeably outweighed the negative. This may be because attitudes have changed. It may also be a result of the cultural change propelled by #MeToo, which has included that hateful expressions against women have moved from the mainstream to the fringes of media. While this may be more agreeable as an experience for people reading YouTube comments, such a change is not a sign that bigotry and misogyny have disappeared—only that those who do it feel more justified and victimized themselves.

Just as dance music community participants have become more engaged with gender politics together with the wider public and have exercised their collective power to stop working with people who have done others harm, a growing minority of promoters, club managers, and booking agents have implemented a broader shift in booking practices. An increasing number

[31]microglitch, YouTube Comment on Nina Kraviz, 2015, https://www.youtube.com/watch?v=YIcbIIHcx44&ab_channel=BoilerRoom.

[32]Mixmag, "Nina Kraviz: Biography," accessed May 8, 2015, https://mixmag.net/artist/nina-kraviz.

of DJs, regardless of gender, have written policies into their contracts that allow them to reject event bookings that do not also include women DJs. Correspondingly, some bookers have established policies of booking women, transgender, and nonbinary DJs for every gig they organize. For some, this is not a completely new concept. Melbourne DJ and booking agent Cory said that while he has never had a formal policy, he has always invited women as a substantial proportion of his regular line-ups, if not a majority of them, as a matter of principle:

> C: [When I started playing in 2001,] ... we kind of went, okay, how do you make a night happen? And we decided we needed three or four resident DJs. And part of that conversation at the time was "we need a chick." You know, there's got to be a female presence here. Because the techno bro thing, that's always been there. But it was pretty clear to us that we couldn't continue the lineage that way and that we needed to acknowledge that there were good female DJs out there. There was no talk at all at that time anything beyond "he" and "she." That was definitely not part of the conversation. But we weren't ever going to proceed without a resident female DJ in our crew of what ended up being four DJs.

Beyond more equitable booking practices, which will be at the center of the case study in the next chapter, some club nights incorporate a blurring of traditional gender, sexuality, and other identity constructions into their ethos and branding, as well as active promotion of their dance floors as safe and respectful environments for all clubbers. Promoters and performers have made explicit efforts to foster an environment free, for both DJs and audiences, from gender discrimination or violence. Such spaces distinguish themselves wholly from the marketing strategies of night clubs that use standardized corporate "sex sells" tactics to attract potential participants, like clubs that encourage women to dress in revealing clothing in return for free entry as a promotional tactic.[33] Of course, no environment can be entirely free from gender trouble. Even queer spaces with explicit goals of safety, which aim to be queer-only,

---

[33]Stephen Deal, "'Sluttiest Dressed Bird' Promo Causes Outrage," *The Metro* (July 20, 2011), 15.

cannot completely control whether, for example, heterosexual men attend in order to target women or queer people seeking harassment- and abuse-free spaces for dancing. Moreover, perceptions of what constitutes sexual and nonsexual intimacy on dance floors can differ from one participant to the next, as can the expectations or desires for such intimacy.[34] As a result, clashes can erupt between those who seek fleeting experiences of sexual or drug-induced freedom and intimacy, on the one hand, and those dancers approached by them who do not seek such experiences, on the other.

When this research started, the media that I encountered often perpetuated prejudices through their focus on "scandals" or what they saw as "trashy" nature of women's participation in club culture. The fact that Nina Kraviz was interviewed in a bubble bath, or that Paris Hilton was invited to DJ in Las Vegas for exorbitant fees without DJing experience or subcultural capital, were used as justifications for negative attention and commentary on their appearances.[35] (Of course, there are legitimate critiques of the pressures that women DJs continue to be under to stylize themselves in particular ways, but these were not the direction that such reporting took.) Since around 2015, it became more common to come upon articles about sexual harassment in night clubs. This was not because more of it happened, but because there was a greater consciousness that it happened. And alongside these stories came new kinds of reporting: the successes of women, trans, and nonbinary people in club culture.[36] As the

---

[34]Garcia-Mispireta, *Together, Somehow*. Luis-Manuel Garcia, "Can You Feel It, Too?" 97–113.

[35]Matt Medved, "Paris Hilton Reveals Las Vegas DJ Residency, Defends DJ Career," *The Hollywood Reporter*, March 31, 2015, https://www.hollywoodreporter.com/news/music-news/paris-hilton-reveals-las-vegas-785656/.

[36]See, for example Matt McDermott, "Association for Electronic Music Establishes UK Hotline for Sexual Harassment in the Electronic Music Industry," *Resident Advisor*, December 22, 2017, https://ra.co/news/40676; Joe Muggs, "Techno Star Helena Hauff: 'Every Woman Who DJs and is Visible Helps to Make a Change,'" *The Guardian*, July 20, 2018, https://www.theguardian.com/music/2018/jul/20/helena-hauff-techno-woman-dj; Natalie Robehmed, "How Discwoman Is Diversifying Electronic Music," *Forbes*, August 24, 2017, https://www.forbes.com/sites/natalierobehmed/2017/08/24/how-discwoman-is-diversifying-electronic-music/?sh=4eb78e3761a1; Andre Frois, "How Female DJs in Singapore Fought Sexist Stereotyping To Be Judged on Their Sounds, Not Their Looks," *South China Morning Post*, January 30, 2018, https://www.scmp.com/culture/music/article/2130986/how-female-djs-singapore-fought-sexist-stereotyping-be-judged-their; Peter Kirn, "Let's Talk Consent: How to Make Nightlife Safe From Harassment," *CDM*, September 24, 2015, https://cdm.link/2015/09/organization-looks-ways-make-nightlife-safe-harrassment/.

next chapter shows, the dance floors and DJ booths where these positive shifts occur are also spaces of contestation and reaction. Aspirations toward gender equality through formal quotas or informal policies are not always matched by the qualitative dynamics of gender in real life, where beliefs in meritocracy and neoliberalism inform gender politics, and where the insecurity of informal economies mix with archaic understandings of creativity, talent, and skill.

6

"It's Not about Gender": Merit, Talent, and Other Myths

It's not about gender. It's not about gender. It's about being good, or not.
And you're playing because you're a good DJ, not because you're a girl …
I see some bookings, they book because you're a girl as well, but probably
because you are a good girl.[1]

Musikkfest is an annual music festival in Oslo, Norway. In the lead up to the 2016 festival, a DJ and editor of a local arts and entertainment magazine complained that there were few women booked to DJ at the festival—four, to be precise, out of forty-seven.[2] Some of the festival's DJ booking agents responded with a heated defense against what they saw as political correctness. A debate with fans and DJs followed on online social media. In a group interview about this incident, booking agents and DJs expressed their conviction that hard work, skill, and talent are the legitimate means to a successful DJing career.

This chapter is a reworked version of "Forty-Seven DJs, Four Women: Meritocracy, Talent and Postfeminist Politics," *Dancecult* 9, no. 1 (November, 2017): 50–72.
[1]Lars, interview with the author (Oslo), October 31, 2016.
[2]Karima Furuseth, "47 artister, fire kvinner—her er 8 kvinnelige DJs Musikkfest Oslo KUNNE ha booket," *Natt&Dag*, May 24, 2016, https://nattogdag.no/2016/05/musikkfest-oslo-skjev-fordeling/.

They also argued that gender bias is an overstated issue that does not factor into their booking decisions.

The tone of the above debate is an example of art worlds discourses that champion the arts' ability to supersede inequalities or render such inequalities irrelevant in the face of individual merit. It is also an example of the limits of understanding equality with reference to underrepresentation. What both sides of the debate fail to address is the bigger problem of fluid, unregulated work practices and informal social connections that commonly govern workplace hierarchies in so-called creative industries (the label for these art worlds in policy).[3] Workplaces driven by creative entrepreneurialism will always result in imbalances of power against oppressed groups because such groups have tended to fare worse economically. Most music-based workplaces run in part on free or low-paid labor through such activities as networking, internships, self-promotion and marketing, and the music-making itself.[4] The precariousness of most individual workers and bosses means that they have clear material imperatives to compete with each other in order to survive.[5] The problem with the myth of merit is not only that it is a myth but also that it pits people against each other. Where individuals are forced to compete for a limited slice of an extraordinarily small pie, such power, once attained, is very rarely relinquished and the incentive for defending the status quo is strong.

The very same booking agents who believe that the aesthetic qualities of art will triumph over inequality also believe in the neoliberal ideas of postfeminism, meritocracy, and talent. Definitions of postfeminism (or post-feminism) vary. Catherine Malabou's definition points to gender and queer theory's antiessentialist, antidualist stance on gender.[6] However, I use "postfeminism"

---

[3]Bridget Conor, Rosalind Gill, and Stephanie Taylor, "Gender and Creative Labour," *The Sociological Review* 63, no. 1 supp. (May 2015): 1–22; Simon Frith, "Creativity as a Social Fact," in *Musical Imaginations: Multidisciplinary Perspectives on Creativity, Performance and Perception*, ed. David Hargreaves, Dorothy Miell, and Raymond MacDonald (Oxford: Oxford University Press, 2011), 62; Reitsamer "The DIY Careers of Techno and Drum 'n' Bass DJs in Vienna," 30–1.

[4]Gross and Musgrave, *Can Music Make You Sick?*; McRobbie, *Be Creative*; David Hesmondhalgh and Sarah Baker, *Creative Labour: Media Work in Three Cultural Industries* (London: Routledge, 2011), 220–1.

[5]Jo Littler, *Against Meritocracy* (London: Routledge, 2018), 2–3, 8, 31, 90, 101. Chibber, *The Class Matrix*, 55–64.

[6]Catharine Malabou, *Changing Difference: The Feminine and the Question of Philosophy* (Cambridge: Polity Press, 2011), 1.

(one word, no hyphen) as it is used to refer to a kind of antifeminism in media and culture. Postfeminists hold that the work of feminism is complete, and no longer has a purpose. In other words, they espouse the view that we are living in an era in which women have as much agency as men, and feminist concerns are outdated. Scholars have increasingly identified and critiqued this perspective as it has manifested across the West since the 1990s, as well as its prevalence in cultural policy and media.[7] For Rosalind Gill, the link between postfeminism and neoliberal, individualist ideals is exemplified by the bodily self-policing that many women practice, and the packaging of such self-policing as a choice, or expression of empowerment.[8] The pop group the Spice Girls incorporated this postfeminist version of empowerment into their ethos and slogan "Girl Power" in the mid-1990s, which became a means of brand identification and marketing to girls. Through a variety of feminine symbolism and imagery, the Spice Girls provided "identification with an image of personal autonomy but one which is constructed within the forms offered by patriarchal society."[9] As this chapter shows, the *Musikkfest* booking agents have postfeminist attitudes in their opposition to what they see as an overattention—in the media, within musical communities, in political rhetoric, in law—on quantitative gender equality.[10] What is more, when they express their objections to the types of gender equality concerns articulated in the *Natt&Dag* editorial, they feel

---

[7]Ann Brooks, *Postfeminisms: Feminism, Cultural Theory and Cultural Forms* (London: Routledge, 1997); Conor et al., "Gender and Creative Labour," 1–22; Rosalind Gill, "Postfeminist Media Culture: Elements of a Sensibility," *European Journal of Cultural Studies* 10, no. 2 (May 2007): 147–66; Rosalind Gill, "Post-Postfeminism? New Feminist Visibilities in Postfeminist Times," *Feminist Media Studies* 16, no. 4 (2016): 610–30; McRobbie, *The Aftermath of Feminism*; Angela McRobbie, "Post-Feminism and Popular Culture," *Feminist Media Studies* 4, no. 3 (2004): 255–64; Tania Modleski, *Feminism Without Women: Culture and Criticism in a "Postfeminist" Age* (New York: Routledge, 1991).

[8]Gill, "Post-Postfeminism?", 613.

[9]Nicola Dibben, "Representations of Femininity in Popular Music," *Popular Music* 18, no. 3 (1999): 344–50.

[10]Far from being simple, "gender equality" is a set of multifaceted, interrelated ideas. What gender equality means for different communities depends on how these communities define it, and what values they hold. Some ways of understanding gender equality allow it to be measured, whereas others focus on less quantifiable notions such as culture, knowledge, power, opportunity, and individual upward mobility. See Ronald Inglehart and Pippa Norris, *Rising Tide: Gender Equality and Cultural Change Around the World* (Cambridge: Cambridge University Press, 2003); Mari Teigen and Lena Wängnerud, "Tracing Gender Equality Cultures: Elite Perceptions of Gender Equality in Norway and Sweden," *Politics & Gender* 5, no. 1 (March 2009): 21–3.

silenced by their peers. This chapter addresses the above issues using the case study of *Musikkfest* against this backdrop of gender politics and history in Norway.

Gender in Norway

Norway is often cited in media and popular discourse as "one of the best countries in the world to be a woman," together with other countries in the Nordic region with similar social democratic systems of government.[11] Given that binary gender equality has established itself as normal across generations, people in the arts and cultural industries who advocate for "quality" over equality feel that they represent an "underdog" view, speaking up as a minority against the grain of popular culture discourse among a broadly affluent, educated populace. The *Musikkfest* booking agents' postfeminist and neoliberal perspectives reflect those of precarious, arts, and culture environments both in and out of Norway, which means that attitudes toward gender equality policies do not always correspond to their prevalence in state law. This is especially true outside of the shelter of public sector labor. The *Musikkfest* case shows an example of gender politics in dance music cultures that are more entrepreneurial than egalitarian.

Gender equality has been common to social democratic political philosophies underlying many policies in the other Nordic countries (Denmark, Finland, Iceland, Sweden), with the workplace as a key site for action.[12] There is evidence

---

[11]Siobhán Dowling, "Women on Board: Norway's Experience Shows Compulsory Quotas Work," *Spiegel Online*, July 8, 2010, https://www.spiegel.de/international/business/women-on-board-norway-s-experience-shows-compulsory-quotas-work-a-705209.html; The Economist, "The Best—And Worst—Places To Be a Working Woman," May 3, 2016, https://www.economist.com/graphic-detail/2016/03/03/the-best-and-worst-places-to-be-a-working-woman. For analyses that challenge the popular discourses on gender equality in the Nordic countries, see also Mari Teigen, "Gender Quotas on Corporate Boards," in *Gender and Power in the Nordic Countries*, ed. Kirsti Niskanen (Oslo: NIKK, 2011), 87–109; Sigrun Åsebø, "Representation of Gender and/in Visual Culture," Lecture. Sundvolden (Norway): Gender National Research School General Course.

[12]Kirsti Niskanen, "Gender and Power in the Nordic Countries: A Comparative Perspective," in *Gender and Power in the Nordic Countries*, ed. Kirsti Niskanen (Oslo: NIKK, 2011), 11; The Economist, "The Best—And Worst—Places To Be a Working Woman."

of gender equality discourse becoming normalized as early as the 1920s and 1930s in Norway's print media. At this time, women began to participate as equals in civic society through such moves as gaining the right to vote, accessing higher education, and organizing themselves institutionally and politically.[13] The public sphere discussions propelled the strength and momentum of the movements for equality for all citizens.[14] In the late twentieth century, a core policy that anchored a change in work environments was the aforementioned Gender Equality Act, originally instated in the Norwegian parliament in 1978.[15] The Act contains clauses that compel government institutions to employ female and male genders equally on "committees, governing boards, councils, delegations, etc." through strict rules of ratio. It instructs employers to "make active, targeted and systematic efforts" to pursue gender equality, rendering any "discrimination on the basis of gender" illegal. "Direct differential treatment" means that "a person is treated worse than others in the same situation, and that is due to gender", while "indirect differential treatment" means "any apparently neutral provision, condition, practice, act or omission that results in persons being put in a worse position than others, and that occurs on the basis of gender."[16]

Following institutional implementation, the policies that related to the Act underwent a cultural normalization over time. To be expected, they were also met with resistance from some quarters, and not only those that were socially conservative. In the early 2000s, for example, board executives expressed concerns that positive discrimination toward women on corporate

---

[13]Dagbladet, "Ellen Gleditsch hjemme igjen: 500 dollars til stipendier for kvinner som vil arbeide videnskapelig," May 13, 1929, 1–2; Marie (Mais) Fearnley, "Den modern Eva: Borghild Langaard tilbake—hun åpner sangskole til høsten," *Dagbladet*, August 5, 1930; Gunnar (Kollskegg) Larsen, "Oslo Kvinneparti Blev Stiftet Igår," *Dagbladet*, December 7, 1927; Lise Lindbæk, "En ny tids kvinnesak: Inntrykk fra Yrkes kvinners sommerleier på Hundorp," *Urd* 36 (1936): 1126–7; Halldis (Hast) Stenhamar, "Kvinnelige studenter gjennem 50 år—jubileumsboken er ferdig," *Dagbladet*, February 25, 1932: 1, 3.

[14]See Drude Dahlerup, "Women in Nordic Politics—A Continuing Success Story?" in *Gender and Power in the Nordic Countries*, ed. Kirsti Niskanen (Oslo: NIKK, 2011), 59–86; Niskanen, "Gender and Power in the Nordic Countries," 11–58; Teigen, "Gender Quotas on Corporate Boards," 87–109.

[15]See Teigen, "Gender Quotas on Corporate Boards," 88; Gender in Norway, "National Legislation," last accessed November 15, 2016, https://gender.no/Legislation/National_legislation.

[16]Government.no, "The Act Relating to Gender Equality," last updated April 20, 2007, https://www.regjeringen.no/en/dokumenter/the-act-relating-to-gender-equality-the-/id454568/.

boards would result in managers having their freedom of choice compromised during hiring and would lead to employers overlooking better qualified male applicants.[17] Such an objection is ideologically consistent with the corporate board, which exists as a capitalist governing body at the level of the workplace. It is therefore not surprising that older, established conservative institutions such as the Church are superseded in such debates by the concerns of capital.

In the early twenty-first century, measurable gender equality policies have been wholly internalized and integrated into the mainstream. Even Norway's Conservative Party, *Høyre*, was among the parties that have supported such initiatives while it was in power.[18] Another example of the "evolution" of gender policies is the 2016 legislation that allows people the freedom to identify as female or male regardless of their biological or birth designations.[19] Yet some scholars argue that the belief in (and cultural support for) equality is not in popular discourse in the same way for non-white ethnic minorities as it is for marginalized genders. Specifically, people of color and of non-western backgrounds have not been incorporated into a cultural definition of Nordic social democracy.[20] Instead, in an echo of the ideas of far-right populist sentiments in other countries, the gender equality ideal is conflated with white Nordicness and progressive politics, while gender oppression is uncritically associated with non-white or non-Nordic cultures.[21]

---

[17]Teigen, "Gender Quotas on Corporate Boards," 88; Dowling, "Women on Board."

[18]Dowling, "Women on Board"; Høyre, "Høyre's Parliamentary Election Manifesto for 2017–2021," adopted at Høyre's National Convention, March 9–12, 2017: 36–7, 84, 89–90; Teigen, "Gender Quotas on Corporate Boards," 88.

[19]France Rose Hartline, "(Trans)gender Outlaws? A Critical Analysis of Norway's 2016 Gender Self-determination Law," *Tijdschrift Voor Genderstudies* 21, no. 4 (January 2019): 361–80; Ministry of Health and Care Services, "Prop 74L: Proposisjon til Stortinget (forslag til lovvedtak): Lov om endring av juridisk kjønn," March 18, 2016, https://www.regjeringen.no/no/dokumenter/prop.-74-l-20152016/id2479716/; Olemic Thommessen, "Lovvedtak 71 (Første gangs behandling av lovvedtak)," May 30, 2015–2016; Janneke van der Ros, "The Norwegian State and Transgender Citizens: A Complicated Relationship," *World Political Science* 13, no. 1 (June 2017): 123–50.

[20]Stine H. Bang Svendsen, "The Cultural Politics of Sex Education in the Nordics," in *The Palgrave Handbook of Sexuality Education*, ed. Louisa Allen and Mary Lou Rasmussen (London: Palgrave Macmillan, 2017), 137–56.

[21]See also Judith Butler, "Sexual Politics, Torture, and Secular Time," *The British Journal of Sociology* 59, no. 1 (March 2008): 1–23; Paul Mepschen, Jan Willem Duyvendak, and Evelien H. Tonkens, "Sexual Politics, Orientalism and Multicultural Citizenship in the Netherlands," *Sociology* 44, no. 5 (October 2010): 962–79; Bang Svendsen, "The Cultural Politics of Sex Education in the Nordics," 137–56.

While the Norwegian national goal of gender equality has concrete effects in formal organizations, such as strict gender ratios in hiring practice, there is a large disparity between gender ratios in public and private sectors. In 2016, employed women were 70.4 percent of the public sector and 36.6 percent of the private sector.[22] Unlike public sector jobs, nightclub managers, promoters, booking agents, and DJs—as entrepreneurs in the private sector—are often self-employed and contracted to jobs on an ad hoc basis. The night club economy in a social democracy is similar to that of liberal democratic and capitalist countries, which is to say that the protections that public and formal private institutions are compelled to provide are mostly absent. Dance music settings, as art worlds driven by informal networks, are exempt from accountability on implementing policies. This lack of accountability is a characteristic feature of the "flexible" work world of DJs everywhere, and Norway is no exception. People's livelihoods depend on the decisions of others—booking agents, promoters, label owners, and club managers.[23] In contrast to social services departments or public health systems, DJs' working environments are unpredictable, cash-driven, devoid of official paperwork or organized representation, and intertwined with networks that are below the radar of the law.[24] DJs are frequently sole traders, thereby not falling within the category of employment that safeguards the rights of other staff at the same events, such as bartenders. Consequently, if people experience discrimination, there are no systems in place to protect them—they have no formal method of complaint and no one to complain to. Where work is competitive and limited, oppressed groups are particularly susceptible to discrimination.[25] Norwegian cultural commentator Joachim Lund notes that "culture is a self-referential universe ... the rules and mechanisms valid for the rest of the world do not have

---

[22]Stovik in Dowling, "Women on Board"; Statistics Norway, "Gender-Divided Labour Market," December 18, 2017, https://www.ssb.no/en/befolkning/artikler-og-publikasjoner/gender-divided-labour-market.

[23]Reitsamer "The DIY Careers of Techno and Drum 'n' Bass DJs in Vienna," 28–43.

[24]Reitsamer "The DIY Careers of Techno and Drum 'n' Bass DJs in Vienna," 28–43. This is the case for DJs at the local level; international, touring DJs have managers, lawyers, and insurance. Moreover, although some events operate "off the radar," such as in illegal spaces and at unlicensed events, many do take place within publicly regulated spaces such as night clubs and within publicly regulated events that work within legal frameworks.

[25]Conor, Gill, and Taylor, "Gender and Creative Labour," 1–22.

validity here."[26] Again, there is a return to the idea that governs dance music exceptionalism: that culture is supposed to float *above* or *beyond* sociocultural phenomena (in this case, gender and other identity groupings). As such, the idealism of extraordinary culture is also prevalent as a postfeminist sensibility in neoliberal art worlds and industries such as club nights. Unless directly challenged, such an attitude allows discrimination to continue.

Such a conception of culture necessarily affects participants from minority backgrounds. For example, in a 2015 interview, a white booking agent and DJ in Oslo explained that a venue hired her to diversify the genre profile of the club—namely, to steer the music away from hip hop. She linked this to the club's reputation as a hub "where most of the drug dealing Africans hang out." This had previously been used by local authorities as a rationale for closing down other hip hop venues, which had been popular with first- and second-generation young people in the African and other diasporas. When asked why authorities do not also crack down on the primarily white night clubs for parallel drug dealing practices, the booking agent stated that "these people tend to be rude to the staff" and are "a bit touchy." This reasoning—drug dealing, rudeness, and harassment—is not unique to events where black and brown people socialize. White men deal drugs, are rude to staff, and physically harass women of all backgrounds. Such impressions are often formed, on the one hand, by elusive discourse and behavior, and on the other, by the decisions of local authorities to implement policies differently for clubs that primarily host poorer and darker people. It is hard not to see such decisions, together with the subsequent choices of venue managers and booking agents, as indicative of prejudices about class and race. Better-off, white clubbers are allowed to do as they wish. The *Musikkfest* case in this chapter is made up of white DJs and booking agents who perform and book DJs mostly at the latter venues. Given that they benefit from being part of a dominant and majority ethnic group, it is unsurprising that they do not raise ethnic or racial profiling as an issue. This contrasts with the conversation with a Norwegian DJ of Ethiopian heritage, who expressed the benefits and pitfalls of being marked as "ethnic" and "immigrant" such that a large proportion of her gigs are themed along such lines, for example

---

[26]Joachim Lund, "Mer østrogen, takk!" *Aftenposten*, March 24, 2012: 6.

being invited to perform as part of Oslo World, a "world music" festival, even though she is from Stavanger, an oil town in south-west Norway.

Norwegian contemporary media, especially mainstream and local newspapers, cover discussions about gender and music industries in numerous editorials and commentaries that include statistics and debates. Issues in music that they address range from the programming of the Oslo Philharmonic orchestra to the percentage of women on stage at *Øya*, a popular music festival.[27] One article cites international coverage of Norway for how it meets gender quotas in the music festival scene more effectively than in other countries.[28] Nevertheless, the case of the *Musikkfest* editorial shows how people with power in art worlds assume defensive positions when people with less power complain about discrimination.[29] Thus, the fact that gender equality discourse and consciousness has been absorbed into state and corporate media, as well as party politics and policy, is not an indication of the acceptance of such ideas by those in society with power to uphold or undermine them. What is more, most media coverage and public discussion in Norway, reflective of many other western countries, are based on the idea that "equality" means measurable ratios of women to men. Such an approach neither addresses how gender informs behavior nor acknowledges the experiences of gender nonconforming, genderqueer, or transgender people at all. This is despite recent legislation that espouses more open understandings of gender.[30] The promotion of gender equality through numbers is now a

---

[27]Astrid Kvalbein, "Menn jubilerer for full musikk," *Aftenposten*, April 7, 2013: 7; Cecilie Asker, "Balansekunst," *Aftenposten*, August 4, 2010: 9; Joachim Lund, "Her kommer guttemusikken," *Aftenposten*, June 4, 2011: 12.

[28]Nicolay Woldsdal, "Øya får internasjonal oppmerksomhet for sin line-up," *Dagbladet*, July 7, 2015, http://www.dagbladet.no/2015/07/07/kultur/oya/musikk/festival/konsert/40013709/.

[29]See Furuseth, "47 artister, fire kvinner."

[30]Ministry of Health and Care Services, "Prop 74L: Proposisjon til Stortinget"; Stortinget, "Article 98"; Stortinget, "Komiteens tilråding om endring av juridisk kjønn," May 30, 2016, https://www.stortinget.no/ no/Saker-og-publikasjoner/Saker/Sak/Voteringsoversikt/?p=64488&dnid=1#id=7357&view=vote-text; Thommessen, "Lovvedtak 71 (Første gangs behandling av lovvedtak)." Hartline notes that on the one hand, the new legislation has been celebrated as forward thinking, and has been understandably embraced by those who have transitioned from female to male, or male to female. However, it is still a form of discrimination against those who identify as genderqueer or gender nonconforming, who still have to choose between "female" or "male." In addition, there are still deep systemic issues that remain unresolved, such as the tendency to "diagnose" gender nonconformity as a medical condition by public health services. See Hartline "(Trans) gender outlaws?", 365–6, 375–6; van der Ros, "The Norwegian State and Transgender Citizens," 129–30.

prominent, even dominant position to take on gender issues in some of the widely read newspapers and through the main public broadcaster in Norway, the NRK. Yet it is in the meeting of gender equality discourse in media with gender prejudice in everyday life—through popular culture and postfeminist discourse—where an increased gender consciousness causes discontent.

Musikkfest: Gender in Booking Practices

Inspired by the French *Fête de la Musique*, or National Music Day, *Musikkfest*, formerly known as *Musikkensdag*, is a free, multigenre music festival in Oslo. The festival has run since 1992 as a public initiative of the City of Oslo with the cooperation of public venues and spaces.[31] In 2016, DJs performed both within the official *Musikkfest* program and as part of the afterparties in local nightclubs. Of the forty-seven DJs booked for the 2016 event, four were women. Before the festival, DJ and music editor Karima Furuseth commented on this disproportionate male majority in a music magazine, *Natt&Dag*, through her article, *47 artister, fire kvinner* ("47 artists, four women"). Her editorial provoked impassioned reactions from dance music participants of all genders and debates on social media. Some participants proceeded to protest through what could be called an "anti-party" of DJs who were exclusively women. At the same time, booking agents asserted that they felt unfairly accused of sexism.

Some bookers and DJs believe that the *Natt&Dag* article is one-sided, simplistic and disingenuous. These and other specifics are subsumed within two overarching themes: first, that any engagement with the topic of gender balance that does not come down on the side of booking more women leads to (unfair) accusations of political incorrectness; and second, that gender balance moves the focus away from the merit of the performer. The first point is made by a booking agent, Hans:

> H: Last year, 90 percent of the DJ line-up at *Musikkfest* was female, so we've had a lot of the girls already, so it [didn't feel] natural to do it

---

[31]Hilde Bjørhovde, "Musikkfest Oslo: Karnevalsparade og gratis konsertfest hele lørdag," *Aftenposten*, June 5, 2015, http://www.aftenposten.no/osloby/byliv/Musikkfest-Oslo-Karnevalsparade-og-gratis-konsertfest-hele-lordag-38268b.html.

again. I think the programming aspect of the whole thing has been left out. I think it's left out that a lot of our culture's based on community. We felt that the criticism … was wrong, and came from someone who has benefitted from being part of that community. And she also has, of course … her own agenda, and it's a good thing—but we felt that we couldn't speak out because it would be politically incorrect to say something, or criticize or comment on it. I guess this is the core of the problem: that we don't feel like we're either leaving the girls out or not thinking about them or not booking them. We feel like we actually make an effort, booking female DJs throughout the year. But you have to look at the ratio between how many female DJs you have, and you have to compare the guys. You have to consider that these girls aren't always available; that's left out of this discussion … How a DJ plays is left out of the discussion. And … I didn't feel like taking part in this discussion because everything I said would have been conceived as politically incorrect.

TG: In what sense politically incorrect?

H: That if you criticize … it's always going to come back to, "okay, not booking enough girls. You should have had girls … at that event. You should have had more girls at [club] throughout the year." But there's [*sic*] so many people who speak in this discussion who don't know how the booking industry works, which means it's very difficult to discuss this … you always end up discussing it on very different terms.

Here, Hans not only objects to what he perceives as an omission of relevant information from the *Natt&Dag* article but also articulates a frustration with criticisms of gender ratios in DJ bookings—on the basis that they misunderstand the industry. Furthermore, he argues that Furuseth should not critique her "community," where community is implied as a collective description of Oslo's dance music participants. Lastly, he points to "how a DJ plays" as a factor excluded from the article. This thread is taken up later in the interview, when Hans states that he only chooses DJs for their talent (not their gender). The second booking agent, Lars, argues in parallel that hard work such as networking (not gender) leads to gigs. The necessarily gendered nature

of networking is overlooked, and "hard work" and "talent" constitute a strong postfeminist dual narrative throughout the interview.

The politics of the *Natt&Dag* author and the booking agents are subsumed into a longer history of a local dance music community where most people know each other professionally and personally. There is little room for detail in the short article by Furuseth, whose main goal is to address a lack of women invited to DJ in festivals. It is true that some women had turned down *Musikkfest* invitations because of previous commitments, as confirmed by those DJs during the course of the investigation into the incident. It is also reasonable that any journalistic account that critiques the actions of others should be verified and corroborated. In this sense, the booking agents Hans and Lars are fair in their objections. The problem is not so much these specific objections but the overarching contention that merit should take precedence over equality.[32]

Merit and Gender

At first glance, the elevation of merit seems an innocent contestation against positive discrimination. Why, indeed, should an artist be booked "just because she is a woman?" Dani, a prominent Oslo-based DJ with a longstanding career, agrees with this sentiment. She was also one of the four women booked to DJ at *Musikkfest* and takes the criticism of the festival's gender balance as a personal affront to her skills:

> D: For me it was an attack on a lot of us … and I didn't think it was fair …
> If you want to be represented in what you're doing … being a female …
> yes, it is unfair: this is a lot more ratio of men to women; we are not
> listed on "Top 100 DJs," possibly. But my agenda is: "work harder, be
> heard," and that's what it's about. It's not about "man versus female"

---

[32]This is not a view exclusive to this community. The idea that merit is compromised when a gender balance is prioritized is prevalent across the arts in Norway, including the visual arts. See, for example, Åsebø, "Representation of Gender and/in Visual Culture." Additionally, this was the discourse that prevailed in objections to gender equality policies for corporate boards. See Dowling, "Women on Board"; Teigen, "Gender Quotas on Corporate Boards," 87–109.

or "female versus man," and I don't want to be booked just because I'm a girl. And I'm starting to notice that's kind of happening … that I'm being put together with Ellen Allien or Miss Kitten or whoever, not for my merit and what I do, but because I am a woman … I think it's a weird topic, and I feel both sides by being a female, but I also understand, you can't just book women because they're women. And to build a balance about it, you need to actually be a great DJ.

Dani's perspective thus fluctuates between frustration with being branded as a woman when being booked for gigs with women headline acts on the one hand, and being discriminated against for being a woman on the other:[33]

> D: Publications need to talk about what [female musicians] are actually doing, instead of what they're wearing or what they look like or who they're dating … I mean, even look at Nina Kraviz: she still gets every article mention, pretty much, [because] she was together with Ben Klock, you know … Which is probably how she did get where she is.

Dani's views on Nina Kraviz are conflicted. Kraviz is both a target of unfair media representations and a DJ who benefited from her relationship with a prolific male DJ. Thus, on the one hand, Dani identifies with women's struggles and frustrations, and on the other, she believes the meritocratic arguments of Hans and Lars. There are good reasons for Dani to feel frustrated with the gender critiques, on the one hand, and agreement with them, on the other. As one of the only four women chosen for this festival, Dani sought acknowledgement of her deservedness for the role based on her skills alone. It is possible to see her success as the same as that of anyone else—an example of resilience, skill, and good fortune and timing with connections in the right social worlds. But in an aggressively competitive, male-dominated milieu, this is unlikely. The fact that one individual woman can overcome such obstacles does not constitute proof that DJ cultures are equal and fair working environments where all genders can succeed. It is, instead, an uncommon case of success against the odds.

---

[33]The latter occurred most notably when the two male booking agents of the group had departed.

In contrast to perspectives that intersect with postfeminist sensibilities, women are subject to judgements of their merit based on a range of criteria. And while some of these are the same as the criteria used to judge their male counterparts, others are markedly different, such as expectations of how they should look and dress. Scholars have addressed and challenged this along with other disparities on the basis that they are informed by limited, binary conceptions of gender.[34] Nevertheless, the apparently gender-neutral ideal of meritocracy is a neoliberal paradigm that posits that individual hard work is rewarded, no matter what. The fact that scores of people are excluded at the outset due to the setup of the competitive marketplace and to a lack of economic and cultural capital due to sexism, racism, ableism, classism, ageism and more, is glossed over by the positive terms of this ideology ("work hard, succeed"). Lars promotes the neoliberal paradigm through his own personal narrative:

> L: Stand in the door, do decorations, hand out flyers, promote … I did that for five years before I got even a gig. I was … running around with crates of beer for all the party promoters … you have to make a choice, and be poor for several years … before you can make a living out of it … now I'm making money, but the first ten years I didn't make shit. I hustled and I sold clothes and I sold stuff—I was a small-time gangster … And I guess you have to make a few tough choices regarding that, and for a few people they need to bite the apple and take a job instead … in order to survive.[35]

Hans proceeded to observe how such risk-taking may be gendered:

> H: You see people who are really, really thorough—who work, work, work—they succeed. And I'm not saying that girls don't, but … I think there's more guys who dare to take a chance and live off nothing for ten years than girls.

---

[34]Farrugia, *Beyond the Dance Floor*; Gavanas and Reitsamer, "DJ Technologies, Social Networks and Gendered Trajectories in European DJ Cultures," 51–77.

[35]This statement also hinges on gendered assumptions. It disregards the masculine connotations of the "small-time gangster" and the question of whether it is as socially acceptable for women to "hustle" as for men.

Hans acknowledges the disparities of risk between the genders without accounting for them, while Lars focuses on what he calls the relative "interest" of men and women:

> L: There's always been quite a few females on the scene ... I remember going on a national tour with [name] back in '96, and we brought [name] onto national radio in '98, so there's always been talent about ... and even to look up to, I guess. But obviously not enough, but I don't think that has to do with the male DJs, probably ... The lack of female DJs doesn't necessarily have to do with the 80 percent of male DJs ... It might have to do with interest.
>
> TG: In what way, because you've said this "interest" thing a few times?
>
> L: About spending enough time with the craftsmanship and with music.

Here, the explanation for fewer women is a comparable lack of commitment by women to the labor-intensive pursuit of DJing. He continues in this vein when discussing what he implies is an obsessive hobby of record collecting:

> L: When I was a kid, growing up, buying records, starting into this culture, I always saw one or two girls in the record stores.
>
> TG: Out of how many people?
>
> L: Let's say if there were twenty guys digging for the same imports, there were one or two girls there. And they often came too late to get the imports, probably because they didn't have time or they didn't have enough interest. But those who were around ... spent time, and they were good enough and started to DJ. I guess it probably has to do with the nerd factor of it as well, about spending so much time and being so interested in getting that music and being involved in the scene, and spending those hours in order to understand it and dig it. And it takes up all your time when you're a kid. And I guess for a girl who's 15, 16, 17, probably she has other interests, more often than guys, regarding digging deep into a certain type of music style. You can see that when you look at [name], which is like a local band music competition for kids, 80 percent are guys, performing their music, and it's 20 percent girls. And I guess that has to do with how culture is. I don't know. How females want to spend their time, you know?

In this account, women are less likely to be "nerds," and girls of fifteen to seventeen are less likely to be interested in the pursuit of crate digging.[36] Lars suggests, for a moment, that factors beyond motivation and interest play a role, but he subsequently returns to choice: girls do not *want* to spend their time collecting records. Claims about the lack of interest of women in the obsessive pursuit of recorded music have a history across musical genres. Will Straw has identified the fetishization of the material artefact as more than simply a means to playing back recorded sound, but a marker of masculinity—reinforced by understandings of record collecting as a mode of expertise.[37] In Sarah Thornton's terminology, they are also markers of subcultural capital.[38] So-called mastery excludes women due to a process of male homosociality—realms of socialization where men are the sole bearers and sharers of their "nerdish" obsessions.[39] Indeed, the rarer the records are, and the more they cater to the tastes of niche, genre-focused musical communities, the more women are denied access.[40]

The "work hard, be heard" narrative is powerful, not only because it is prevalent in creative workplaces but also because it is the ideology into which everything is integrated. As Hans speculates, such unpredictable work is not possible for everyone. The first people to stop working in such jobs are those with less money and the disadvantages that come with having less money. In countries in the West, Indigenous people, labor migrants (especially from Africa and Asia), refugees, and women are disproportionately affected, as a result of being lower income groups.[41] In nightclub work, as in other music

---

[36]For a compelling analysis of the strong gendering of "nerd" cultures with reference to record collecting, see Will Straw, "Sizing Up Record Collections: Gender and Connoisseurship in Rock Music Culture," in *Sexing the Groove: Popular Music and Gender*, ed. Sheila Whiteley (London: Routledge, 1997), 3–16.

[37]Straw, "Sizing Up Record Collections," 4–5.

[38]Thornton, *Club Cultures*, 60–1.

[39]Straw, "Sizing Up Record Collections," 7–9.

[40]Marion Leonard, *Gender in the Music Industry: Rock, Discourse and Girl Power* (Aldershot: Ashgate, 2007), 46–7; Straw, "Sizing Up Record Collections," 11–12.

[41]Conor et al., "Gender and Creative Labour," 5, 8, 11; see also Australian Institute of Health and Welfare, "Indigenous Income and Finance," September 16, 2021, https://www.aihw.gov.au/reports/australias-welfare/indigenous-income-and-finance; Marie H. Slettebak, "Labour Migration and Increasing Inequality in Norway," *Acta Sociologica* 64, no. 3 (August 2021): 314–30; Statistics Norway, "Facts about Immigration: Earnings," 2021, https://www.ssb.no/en/statbank/table/12525/tableViewLayout1/; Hadas Mandel and Moshe Semyonov, "The Gender-Race Intersection and the 'Sheltering-Effect' of Public-Sector Employment," *Research in Social Stratification and Mobility* 71 (2021): 100581.

work, gender is among the factors that affect the extent to which people can achieve the "ideal" balance of creative artistry and an entrepreneurial drive sufficient to sustain it.[42] To take the most obvious example, women's bodies in a neoliberal, postfeminist lens are policed (by themselves and by others) and closely maintained through "beauty" treatments and other modifications.[43] Hannah's experiences, and the focus on image in the "She Can DJ" competition, typify this phenomenon.

Ageism is also built into such capitalistic gender disciplining—namely, the "expiry date" imposed on women. This is true of DJ communities, where high profile male DJs, producers, promoters, and record label owners continue to be revered as they age, and indeed sometimes acquire a higher (sub)cultural credibility, the older they get. Despite the presence of high-profile women DJs and producers in their forties, fifties, and beyond, older women who DJ are still a long way from the stereotypical cultural figure of the DJ. The youthful woman still dominates neoliberal marketing imagery. Such imagery matters because DJing is performance and people look at DJs when they play. This type of bodily disciplining is integral to the neoliberal female subject's individual "hard work" ethic, evident in dance music communities.[44] The reality of visual foregrounding stands in opposition to the traditional (and often idealized) role of the DJ—to simply play music that people dance to. Along the same lines, purists argue that a DJ's job ought to differ from that of musical performers such as guitarists or singers, as unlike performance that has an overt stage orientation, if the goal is to make people dance by mixing or blending recorded music, it does not matter whether they can see the DJ. Yet in the contemporary dance music setting, such an ideal is rarely realized. DJs sometimes play on the very same elevated stages as instrumental performers and singers, at other times are at the front, but in most cases, are visible in one way or another. There are significant differences between a visible person directing the music and a venue with a sound system where no one is visible.

[42]Reitsamer "The DIY Careers of Techno and Drum 'n' Bass DJs in Vienna," 36–9; Gross and Musgrave, *Can Music Make You Sick*; McRobbie, *Be Creative*.

[43]Gill, "Postfeminist Media Culture," 149.

[44]Farrugia *Beyond the Dance Floor*; Gavanas and Reitsamer, "DJ Technologies, Social Networks and Gendered Trajectories in European DJ Cultures," 51–77.

In the latter, participants assume that there is a sound system playing a pre-programmed playlist or existing DJ mix. The ability to see a person actively making musical choices in response to others and a mood of a setting has a significant social effect. Such a social effect is recognized in law, in that whether there is a DJ or not can differentiate the licensing categories that venues fall into, by which local governments police them. All this means that DJs are, by and large, subject to the same kinds of judgements as other kinds of musical performers in terms of how they look and behave. It also means that women who DJ are subject to judgements on how attractive they are to heterosexual, western, male audiences, and judgements about whether such attractiveness has an inversely proportionate relationship to their skills.

Many interviewees express that networking is more difficult for them, due to what Reitsamer's participants describe as "male networks."[45] After Hans and Lars left the interview about *Musikkfest*, Lill and Dani began to talk more freely about their impression of a "boys' club." This may be symptomatic of fears of alienating booking agents by disagreeing with them, leading to a loss of future DJ work. Whether or not such fears dictated this, it is true that any laborer is at the whim of an employer and those who do the work of recruiting for the employer. The power asymmetry is material, and the effects are that people are, entirely understandably, more likely to protect their interests than they are to protest injustice.[46]

> Lill: Why can't we say this when the guys are here? Why are we holding back on these comments?
>
> Dani: I didn't really think about it till now.
>
> L: When they say: "You need to go down to the club and hang out and get to know people"—that's a boys' club; there's no girls in that club. And you don't get invited ... what they're saying, in between the lines, is basically that "we book on talent," that "we book more guys than girls." And what I'm hearing is that there isn't [*sic*] enough good girls.

---

[45]Reitsamer, "The DIY Careers of Techno and Drum 'n' Bass DJs in Vienna," 33; see also Farrugia, "'Let's Have at It!'" 89.

[46]Techno producer Kate Simko shows a similar pattern in an interview with Rebekah Farrugia. See Farrugia, "'Let's Have at It!'" 90.

D: Yeah, that's what they're saying, yeah.

L: But they would never admit that. But that's what they think. And they think that based on their completely subjective opinion—because they are so geeky about production and technical abilities.

This last passage is indicative of how the enduring paradigm of sound production and reproduction technologies' gendering is internalized by all genders, despite women's active involvement in the development of electronic musics. The sociocultural histories of sound technologies have contributed to their contemporary status as gendered.[47] The conversation continued:

TG: But why didn't you think you could say all this stuff in front of Hans and Lars?

L: Oh, I've had this conversation with Hans so many times.

D: Lars was very dominating in the conversation.

L: Yeah, I got thrown off by that comment. Like, he comes in and he talks about his long experience rather than the actual issue at hand, which, I just thought there was no getting anywhere here, anyway … 'Cause he kept bringing up, you know: "If you want to make it, you have to do this full-time and put your heart and soul into it." And I tried vaguely to say: "But … fair enough, there is [*sic*] loads of full-time DJs in Oslo, but there is [*sic*] also loads of non-full-time DJs. Both guys and girls— and the guys get booked more than the girls." So, if we can look at it from that perspective, and not: "girls aren't putting enough into it."

The ideas of meritocracy that the booking agents articulate are so entrenched that it is easy to overlook the underlying belief that they rest on, which is that inequality is inevitable. If this is the underlying belief, then it is helpful to believe also that meritocracy is the most just system by which to decide who is deserving of a higher place in the unequal order. (At least, it seems better than inheritance, or other old-world determinants.) The "ladder of opportunity" metaphor can then take on the significance of an almost spiritual journey of self-determination and uplift. This normally comes with an

---

[47]Farrugia, *Beyond the Dance Floor*, 8–10, 21–3; Rodgers, *Pink Noises*, 6–8.

additional belief, which is that anyone who works hard enough, and is willing to remain "in a permanent state of competition with each other," can succeed regardless of gender or anything else. It ignores, at best, or denies, at worst, the realities that come with beginning at a lower "rung."[48] In the same way as meritocracy ensnares people into material subordination, it discredits any claims to objective judgment of the work of groups who are disadvantaged. This applies to women in DJ communities that are dominated by men. There is an assumption built into the booking agents' statements that the club milieu is a neutral space, where people curating DJ line-ups for events make their decisions based exclusively on performers' skills, the "quality" of their mixing, and their track choices. Evidence points to a lack of neutrality, as the previous chapters have shown, because the club, like society, is not neutral—just as it is not equal.

Gender asymmetries are among the asymmetries so normalized that they are often invisible to participants. In many dance music communities, it is a common experience for women to have difficulty convincing club security that they are there for DJing work, not to simply "jump the queue" as a clubber. Even once inside clubs, many women are presumed to be in attendance only to assist or support their partners, who are, in turn, presumed to be men. Furthermore, DJs are asked to play on a variety of grounds, including those other than the music that they play: friendship; agreements ("if you book me for a gig at your club night, I'll book you at mine"); loyalty; group musical tastes; sexual relationships; and innumerable other factors. In other words, the whim of booking agents and promoters plays a significant role in DJ bookings.[49]

Talent, Creativity, and Gender

While arguments that selection is an objective process do not stand up as justifications for inequality, there are several sociocultural paradigms that work together with capitalism to contribute to its upkeep. Such paradigms

---

[48]Hickman in Littler, *Against Meritocracy*, 3; Littler, *Against Meritocracy*, 2, 9.
[49]This is rarely acknowledged openly, presumably due to impressions of professionalism, and more specifically that it would contradict their claims to choosing DJs on the basis of skill alone.

include talent, a particularly slippery idea. In music pedagogical and psychological fields, talent appears to be discussed as ability that pre-exists effort or work, also sometimes described through terms such as "innate."[50] In both neuroscience and psychology, analyses of musical talent are further complicated by arguments that claim that genetic and environmental factors combine to affect a person's capacity to realize talent.[51] Similarly, popular neuroscience on musical learning distinguishes between "music instinct," posited as a myth on the one hand, and other types of *actual* "talent," a category that is accepted, on the other.[52]

In the interview with *Musikkfest* booking agents and DJs, the theme of talent emerged interchangeably with merit:

> TG: I asked you [earlier], "in your scene, is it just about talent when
>   people get booked?" and you said "yes." But previously, you said that
>   you have to be "hustling," or … on the door, or be active in the scene.
> L: Well, you have to spend time in the scene, I guess.
> TG: Okay, so that's not just based on talent, then, right?
> L: No, it's based on being interested—showing interest as well, of course,
>   yeah.

Here Lars again raises the element of "interest" that DJs must show in order to secure bookings. This emphasis between two seemingly opposing concepts—hard work and "networking" on the one hand and talent on the other—has an internal logic. They are, after all, constituents of the same narrative: the brilliant and inspired, yet struggling, artist. They are a figure that tirelessly

---

[50]See Norman M. Weinberger, "Musical Talent: Real or a Myth?" *MuSICA Research Notes* 8, no. 2 (2001); Lynn Helding, "Innate Talent: Myth or Reality? Mindful Voice," *Journal of Singing* 67, no. 4 (March/April 2011): 451–8; Michael J. A. Howe, Jane W. Davidson, and John A. Sloboda, "Innate Talents: Reality or Myth?" *Behavioral and Brian Sciences* 21 (June 1998): 399–400.

[51]David Z. Hambrick and Elliot M. Tucker-Drobb, "The Genetics of Music Accomplishment: Evidence for Gene-Environment Correlation and Interaction," *Psychonomic Bulletin and Review* 22 (February 2015): 112–20; Miriam A. Mosing et al., "Practice Does Not Make Perfect: No Causal Effect of Music Practice on Music Ability," *Psychological Science* 25, no. 9 (September 2014): 1800–2. See also Bret Stetka, "What Do Great Musicians Have in Common? DNA," *Scientific American* 5 (August 2014), https://www.scientificamerican.com/article/what-do-great-musicians-have-in-common-dna/.

[52]Gary Marcus, *Guitar Hero: The New Musician and the Science of Learning* (New York: The Penguin Press, 2012), 9.

and obsessively works at their art. Such a depiction fits into a particular, contemporary incarnation of Romanticism that reinforces neoliberal ideals of individual self-determination.[53] In this framework, an individual "with talent" can defy structural barriers such as wealth and class, race, gender, age, sexuality, and ability, if they only work hard enough. Ideas about talent, and of the different, though related, notions of creativity in western musical communities, elevate "a particular sense of selfhood and the valorization of the new."[54]

Given that I was not clear on what they meant, I asked the interviewees to explain how they understood talent. Their responses were as follows:

Dani: Quality of track selection, how you mix that track section ... reading a crowd ...

Hans: Researching the club.

D: That too, yeah. And just having tracks that are new, but also can be combined with old. I hate when DJs play just straight up classics and stuff like that.

Lill: I think it's very difficult to answer, because it's so situational ... Sometimes I appreciate someone who's good technically ... and that a night flows naturally.

D: I know for me it's engagement with the DJ and audience.

H: One thing is what you perform at the club, but if you're a shitty person and just a generally bad guy or girl, you're not going to get booked again. So being professional—from the moment you ... set your foot inside a club, until you leave—is also a big, big aspect of it. Because promoters ... talk to each other, and a lot of ... people also want to come back if they have a good night ... I think Dani summed it up pretty well, because it's about production talent and it's about how you perform at the club. You have to know that playing from 12 'til 3 or 1 'til 3 in Norway is very different from playing 1 'til 3 in Germany.

---

[53]Frith, "Creativity as a Social Fact," 62–3; Gill, "Postfeminist Media Culture," 147–66; Reitsamer "The DIY Careers of Techno and Drum 'n' Bass DJs in Vienna," 28–43.
[54]Frith "Creativity as a Social Fact," 70.

So, it's about research, it's about ... looking who played there the last
weekend—should you have a chat with that person, maybe, just to hear
how it was? What worked, what didn't work? How can you fit your
style into that? Again, because style is ... personal ... but it's still the
interaction with the people—and how you see them moving, how you
actually look them in the eyes, be present when you're there—that's
very important, I think. 'Cause there's [*sic*] so many good DJs with
good track selection. But it's the flow, it's the groove, it's the presence.

L: It's so subjective, music. You have to be able to communicate that with
the dance floor.

Sylvi: It's both about being technically good and building and getting
the floor to dance and ... communicating with people, you know, in a
musical way. I think that's talent.

All the interviewees agree that "flow," "groove," "presence," and "musicality"
are learned skills, even though they are concepts that are difficult to define. The
idea of the "born artist" is a cultural feature of western classical or art music
worlds than of dance music, which could partly explain the interchangeability
of "hard work" with "talent" in the interview. Regardless, these participants
demonstrate how fluid the term "talent" is. For DJs, it can mean: collecting
"quality" music; technical ability on DJ equipment; familiarity with an
audience; responsiveness to clubbers' feedback; the right mix of old with
new music; an understanding of the temporal specificities of club nights;
willingness to receive constructive feedback; showing understanding of genre;
being "weird;" behaving "professionally;" communicating with clubbers; the
capacity to "flow," "groove," and be present; and making people dance. In short,
for these participants, "talent" equates to a DJ being good at their job. Gender,
according to the booking agents, does not factor into how they evaluate talent.

The question of how the Oslo participants define talent also matters because
of the argument that emerges repeatedly throughout the interview: that to
prioritize gender balance is to deprioritize talent. Three implications of this
common claim stand out. On one level, the subtext is that on average, fewer
women than men possess talent in DJing. On another, the argument rests on
a common (mis)understanding of the idea of talent—one that is not specific

to music participation, but that is central to it: namely that it can be evaluated objectively. As the conversation between Oslo participants highlighted, talent is not an objective or measurable variable, and sociologists of the arts and music have made it their business to problematize this and similar notions that elevate art above other types of work.[55] Understandings of talent in DJ cultures are, on the contrary, often based on personal impressions. These can vary dramatically as DJing involves a wide choice of technologies and techniques. Talent is therefore too contingent a concept to be "threatened" by gender equality policies.

Creativity has a similar social role to talent, dictating many contemporary cultural policies in the West. Like talent, creativity has many possible meanings, depending on whether artists (and what kinds of artists), cultural policy makers, or market investors are defining it. Creativity in the business world can equate to productivity or utility, while in music, including in DJ worlds, the idea is still Romantic—it demands newness, novelty and "freedom," while being dependent on the contemporary market economy. This dependence is dysfunctional: music requires the work of many actors to materialize, yet it is referred to in musical worlds in old terms of distinction between expressive capacities of individual artists and the "craft" of performing music for money.[56]

A helpful parallel to the argument about talent is how the artistic "genius" in western musical histories and canons has always been gendered. In one example, philosopher Christine Battersby has accounted for the way that genius across the arts has been framed as the exclusive property of men, all the while possessing "feminine" qualities.[57] Battersby's critique of "genius" is to focus on challenging its gendering:

> The concept of genius is too deeply embedded in our conceptual scheme for us to solve our aesthetic problems by simply amputating all talk of genius, or by refusing to evaluate individual authors and artists. Before we can

---

[55]Howard S. Becker, *Art Worlds* (Berkeley: University of California Press, 1982); Frith, "Creativity as a Social Fact, 62–72"; Frith, *Performing Rites*.

[56]Frith, "Creativity as a Social Fact," 62–3, 68–70; Reitsamer, "The DIY Careers of Techno and Drum 'n' Bass DJs in Vienna," 30–2, 39–40; Becker, *Art Worlds*. See also Conor et al., "Gender and Creative Labour," 3–5.

[57]Christine Battersby, *Gender and Genius: Towards a Feminist Aesthetics* (Bloomington: Indiana University Press, 1989), 3–11.

fundamentally revalue the old aesthetic values, the concept of genius has to be appropriated by feminists, and made to work for us.[58]

Genius is a historically specific paradigm. To critique it is far from "amputating all talk" of it. However the gendering of genius *is* partly a problem precisely because it employs the very concept of genius in the first place—a politically questionable social construct.[59]

Overall, talent, creativity, and genius are concepts that reflect Romantic values of artistry. Although the Romantic artist—the DJ, in this chapter—seems in some ways to be at odds with the discipline that is required of the neoliberal female subject, the primacy of the individual is not only common, but also central to Romanticism *and* neoliberalism. As the group interview shows, DJs are embodiments of this blend, with expectations of being both "entrepreneurial" and "free" at once. What is more, in articulating a "grammar of individualism,"[60] the above participants deny, and thus contribute to, the realities and effects of systematic gender discrimination.

In sum, when it comes to gender equality, Norway is a nation with relative advantage. This is most visible in its legal frameworks, where gender parity—albeit on problematic, binary models of gender—is a key goal. Governments formalized equality as a goal through such measures as women's rights to vote, access to university education and unionization in the early twentieth century, the Gender Equality Act in 1978, affirmative action to hire more women on corporate boards in the early 2000s, and the gender self-determination law in 2016. However, there is a substantial difference between the equality achieved in public and private sectors, respectively, and further, between established institutions and the casual workforce that makes up DJ and other musicians' work. It is very difficult to keep track of inclusive practices in such fluid and unpredictable environments. Consequently, victims of discrimination in these settings are unsurprisingly the same people for whom the equality policies have been necessary in the first place.

Moreover, while various media have facilitated marginalized people's issues, the counterreactions coming from cultural intermediaries such as Hans

---

[58]Battersby, *Gender and Genius*, 15.
[59]I take my cue here from Frith's aforementioned approach to creativity (2011).
[60]Gill, "Postfeminist Media Culture," 153.

and Lars have been at least as audible. Specifically, Hans and Lars argue that they are misunderstood: that they do not discriminate against anyone, but that women tend to be less interested in the "craftsmanship" of DJing, less involved with the "nerding out" cultures of record collecting, and less active at informal networking than men. This is often coupled with the assertion that intuitive understandings of dance floor dynamics and other markers of quality have nothing to do with gender. The implication is that imbalances are coincidental by-products of the demographics of the people who happen to be performing well. Yet as this chapter shows, these criteria are all profoundly gendered. Indeed, as Gill observes, "the notion that all our practices are freely chosen is central to postfeminist discourses, which present women as autonomous agents no longer constrained by any inequalities or power imbalances whatsoever."[61] Together, these counterreactions make up the widespread paradigm of individualism, of which postfeminist and meritocratic philosophies are a part.

The popular discourses on utopianism in dance music culture leave little room for addressing problematic gender dynamics in such communities. Specifically, celebratory perspectives overlook the many spaces that reiterate the same types of discrimination that occur off the dance floor. Moreover, the idea that the extraordinary, original dance floors from which dance music culture sprung forth were free from discrimination or prejudice indirectly affirms postfeminist ideas that gender inequality is a problem of the past. Although the two political positions are contrasting, both utopian and postfeminist perspectives of dance music cultures ultimately avoid and deny the hostility and violence that takes place because of gender—behind DJ booths, on dance floors, and between events.

Finally, the *Musikkfest* case shows DJ and dance music culture to be an art world where artistic value is idealized to the point that it nullifies the value of social problems. In this case, the music, through the skill of the DJ, is more important than the effects of inequality. This is an unsettling demonstration of what postfeminism, in its omnipresence, actually embodies: a collection of defenses used by those in decision-making or power positions—and internalized by those who are not—in industries where women are significant, active, and audible, but where they nevertheless remain unequal participants.

---

[61]Gill, "Postfeminist Media Culture," 153.

Conclusion: Dance Music
Is Ordinary

Dance music is where some people seek solace, difference, and escape. It is also where people simply go to have fun. It is a global culture fragmented into multiple, local, micro-cultures. It provides people with escape from the grind of contemporary life, from danger, and from struggle, while embracing the spirit of entrepreneurialism; it rejects the standardized temporalities of daytime work, conformity, and propriety in favor of 24-hour hyperactivity, insomnia, and speed. The escape itself embodies the experience that people are escaping. Such tensions, though not unique to dance music, are at its core. Fans and clubbers, DJs, promoters, booking agents, bartenders, security staff, sound engineers, and drug dealers are part of dance music culture. Dance floors are hubs for all kinds of experiences, regardless of music genre orientation. The music does not float freely above or beneath worldly matters or matter, but can nevertheless provide some lucky people with a transcendent experience. It can help to foster community, trust, and belonging. Dance music is a space of "emergent democratic possibilities."[1] However, this music can also reproduce social asymmetries, exclusionary attitudes, violent encounters, and beliefs in meritocracy as a sorting mechanism for who is in and who is out. Dance music

---

[1]Sophie Watson, "Cultures of Democracy: Spaces of Democratic Possibility," in *Spaces of Democracy: Geographical Perspectives on Citizenship, Participation and Representation*, ed. Clive Barnett and Murray Low (London: Sage, 2004), 216–7.

studies is an undisciplined field that addresses such themes, founded on an intellectual history that ranges from anthropology to music psychology. With a few exceptions, dance music studies advocates what dance music can do, including politically, for individuals in a collective context. Theories support the transformative aspects of dance music spaces, especially those that belong to particular genres. Nonnormative modes of participation are synonymous with political action.

The origin stories of extraordinary places have received more attention than the forms of club culture that most people encounter when they go out to dance to music played by DJs. Initially, this would have served an important purpose. Documenting the contributions of exceptional dance music communities disrupted the existing popular music canon, which focused mostly on genres like rock. Dance music studies sought to teach people about exciting subcultures (that were not rock or punk) with oppositional politics and a different set of aesthetics. They also drew attention to the dance music that was enormously popular, yet obstinately ignored by mainstream commercial music industries. Where it was not ignored in mainstream, mass culture, it was frequently only known with reference to the negative press it received in tabloid media.[2] Thus, the first accounts were correctives, explaining to readers that dance music cultures have as much to offer aesthetically as rock, and as much to offer politically as punk.

What has happened since, however, is that such interventions have become the accepted stories of dance music culture.[3] As such, they no longer serve their original function, and their politics are no longer radical. In emphasizing the transformative (or transcendent) experiences of individuals dancing to the right combination of elements—space, sounds, light, drugs—they continue the same underlying belief of subcultural theory: that there is resistance in the ritual. Where they differ from subcultural theory is in the move toward the idea that dancing is a mode of consumption or an expression of individual identity. In doing so, they reject the structural conceptual part of subcultural

---

[2]See Thornton, *Club Cultures*, 130–4.
[3]For example, Lawrence, *Life and Death on the New York Dance Floor*, 103–4; Rietveld, "Disco's Revenge", 7–8; Graham St. John, "Aliens Are Us: Cosmic Liminality, Remixticism, and Alienation in Psytrance," *The Journal of Religion and Popular Culture* 25, no. 2 (Summer 2013): 188–9.

studies, where subversive behaviors are about mobilizing political, collective action. Instead, the politics are squarely located in the individual's transcendent experiences. Whether the politics are articulated overtly or implicitly, whether the definitions of it are rigid or fluid, the potential is enough by itself, and the power lies in the individual to actualize it.

Many people want to use dance music to escape from the challenges that they face day-to-day. The infrastructures that allow them to escape are part of the same material and value systems that cause these challenges, but this does not make escape any less necessary. Dancing to music played by a DJ is an activity with no obvious productive end goal or utility beyond the dancing itself, the drug-taking, and the social connection to other people. It is possible to see this as fulfilling the same need as the cinema (or watching movies at home), football matches, or going to the pub. There are parallels in such activities of reaching transcendence of the everyday. Sports fans, for example, have deep connections to their favorite teams and express it collectively. In any case, the dance floor, like other spaces of leisure, provides people with something that they do not receive in their daily lives. In a paradoxical sense, then, what is ordinary about dance music is precisely what it has in common with ordinary activities such as spectator sport—its transcendence of the everyday.[4]

Today there is no more disco demolition, from which authors such as Dyer needed to defend disco. Dance music's value is well-known to fans, to journalists and music critics, to DJs and producers, to audio technology corporations, to alcohol and energy drink brands that sponsor events, to bars, clubs and festival venues, to event organizers, booking agents, social media, fanzines, and record retailers, to ticket sellers, and to cities who gain tourists from it, to drug dealers, and to innumerable others. Thus, this book has approached the topic with the degree of skepticism, sometimes antipathy, fit for what I witnessed. As Elizabeth A. Wilson puts it, "[a]gainst the idea that the negative can be made valuable (productive, valorized, connected) … we need to pay more attention to the destructive and damaging aspects of politics that cannot be repurposed to good ends."[5]

---

[4]There is a conceptual link here to the exclusionary taste-based politics that Sarah Thornton has shown is present in club cultures.

[5]Elizabeth A. Wilson, *Gut Feminism* (Durham and London: Duke University Press, 2015), 6, 176–9.

It is worth asking, then, what function dance music writing whose main goal is advocacy or defense serves now that there is no longer an orthodoxy to challenge. Who is it that needs convincing? From a feminist, anticapitalist perspective, the political significance or radicality of experiences stops at the edge of the dance floor and the afterglow of a big night out. It is not only that there are too many realities that inhibit full and meaningful participation in dance music. It is also that when observing and asking people from all walks of life about their motivations for partying and their experiences of doing so, their responses muddy the waters about the bolder claims to dance music's special political status. And when asking women from all around the world about their experiences of DJing, many of their responses illustrate a reality that is firmly at odds with utopian claims. In the spirit of ambitious political goals, it is important to admit when falling short of them.

It is also important to reexamine the goals themselves. Experiences of the "higher," transcendent kind—the kind emphasized most by committed fans and fan-scholars, and the kind that the counterculture in the 1960s aimed for—may not unequivocally be the best goal. To begin with, if there is an assumption that reaching this kind of state is what it is all about, and by extension, this is the baseline from which all other analytical moves emanate, many stories (perhaps even most stories) will remain untold. Furthermore, there are structural obstacles to those who have internalized the mythos and *expect* such experiences, in much the same way as there are structural obstacles to those who aspire to have a successful life under late capitalism. The most meaningful and enjoyable dance floor encounter is inhibited when a person is singled out as an outsider before they make it through the door, to the bar, or to the dance floor. Common human abuses and oppressions, even internalized prejudices, all of which manifest on as much as off dance floors, undermine potential routes to a good dance floor experience. Perhaps not having a "higher" dance floor experience is more common than having one. Perhaps having regular transcendent experiences on most dance floors is more likely to be a marker of a person who experiences fewer barriers overall. But beyond this, underlying the belief in the Good dance floor is not only the belief in the dance floor as a cultural-political space in and of itself, but of a particular idea of what it means to be radical. The philosophy underpinning such aspirations is the same: if

you work (it) hard enough and focus your energies in the right ways, which includes harnessing subversive symbolism, nonnormative behavior, and even unlawful practices, you can transform, you will belong to a life affirming, culturally radical collective. You may take such experiences with you off the dance floor in a psychic sense, but not in a material sense. The politics start and end on the dance floor.

It is inevitable that my personal experiences colored the considerations presented in this book. The goal going into it emerged from a personal obsession with dance music's effects and the assumption that it worked in the same way for others. My question was "what makes people dance?" The assumptions underlying this question are manifold, and the perspective, one of a person incorporated into the world I was trying to understand. The unquestionable Good of dance music was my conclusion before the research started. Yet where I remained open to other people's perspectives and new experiences, there were immediately counterexamples that brought forth new questions: where things went wrong, how dance music was "contaminated" by society's problems, and so on. It soon became clear that, once more, the question was clouded by the inability to see beyond what I took for granted. Dance music was not contaminated, because it was never separate, different, or exceptional, and as such, alternative, radical, or oppositional ideas could not have failed, or been failed by, people doing it wrong. The ideals in themselves were built of, and nested in, the world as it was.[6]

The question, then, is what, if anything, is being transcended, transformed, overcome? Even where the collective encounter of a group of people dancing is experienced as part of the special affective qualities of dance music, a route to something vaguely better is the end game, where "better" is about self-discovery, individual transformation, and communal/in-group belonging that is bracketed off from the world off the dance floor. It is compartmentalized, temporary and elusive. Transcendence occurs in individuals' consciousness. In some spaces it occurs in a greater openness to nonnormative behavior than off the dance floor.

---

[6]The idea that dance music was being tainted by, say, neoliberal entrepreneurialism was brought to a real reckoning in Angela McRobbie's argument that club culture itself has played a role in shaping the wider culture of entrepreneurialism and creative utility. See McRobbie, "Clubs to Companies," 519–21.

In others, transcendence occurs for western ravers escaping from themselves, through rituals and objects from cultures that are closer than they are to Nature. Contemporary dance music cultures have embraced 1960s-inspired reconstitutions of paganism and medievalism, already reinterpreted in the nineteenth century, through the ideas of connection to nature and transformation of the inner self, with the help of technologies. Parties since the 1980s that have taken place on beaches, in forests, in deserts, or on farms, have been the most overtly influenced by such aesthetics, but corporate festivals have also taken many of them on, as have commercial club cultures. Beyond this, the aspirational "better" remains in the abstract, or at best, symbolic. What is being transcended is the psychic state of individuals on a dance floor for an event that will end. On Sunday morning, the dancer, the DJ, and the organizers go home. On Monday, they return to their ordinary lives. Will their transcendent experiences propel them into making the world around them more just? Perhaps.

The argument—that for all its aesthetic and cultural particularities, dance music is ordinary—comes from having been there, done that, and talked to people about it. Some dance floors, genres, club nights, or cities might do something to subvert the ordinary, but as already illustrated, other authors have done the work of writing about this.[7] At the same time, even the most exceptional spaces can be host to ordinary experiences. The sociocultural or political power of dance music is as contingent as any other form of culture. It is both as important and as limited in its transformative political capacities as those other transcendent experiences: sport, opera, fashion, literature, painting. All such activities are a necessary part of human flourishing and within limits, they can also be potent sites for political provocation, statement-making, and awareness-raising. Affect, aesthetic, or rhetoric, uses of sound effects, names of events or tracks, or statements by DJs or record labels can all articulate politics. Such politics can be made material when people fundraise, boycott, occupy, or strike. But even the more "direct action" forms

---

[7]For example, Melville, *It's a London Thing*, 14–21. In addition, see Graham St. John, "Seasoned Exodus: The Exile Mosaic of Psyculture," *Dancecult* 4, no. 1 (May, 2012); Dave Haslam, *Life After Dark: A History of British Nightclubs and Music Venues* (London: Simon & Schuster, 2015); Salkind, *Do You Remember House?*

of dance music event do nothing to inaugurate the large-scale overhaul that is currently required for society to reset and humanity to survive. That does not preclude imagining what dance music in a post-capitalist, post-military-industrial society might look, sound, and feel like. It does, though, require acknowledging that the dance music culture addressed in this book emerged from the late twentieth century accompanied by the deregulation of the world financial markets, the shift of responsibility for wellbeing onto individuals, the increased bureaucratization and militarization of all forms of corporate and state governance, and the increase of state power through technocratic surveillance—forces more powerful than ever at the time that this book is being finalized. It is true that dance music is both a reaction against some of the worst effects of these forces—such as unemployment, repression, racism, class stratification, and alienation—and an outcome of them. It is not a coincidence that the freewheeling, entrepreneurial neoliberalism, supported by the very same forces, and unleashed in their extreme forms under Reagan and Thatcher from the late 1970s, coincided with the emergence of disco and the DJ-led dance floors we know today. Thornton's bold critique of subcultural capital, and even Gilbert and Pearson's ambivalent but largely optimistic analysis, both published in the 1990s, are remarkably farsighted in their observations of such contradictions before they were obvious for many people to see.[8] Indeed, the tensions that Dyer articulates "In Defence of Disco"—of a subversive culture that simultaneously foregrounds, celebrates, *and* acts in defiance of its source (capitalism)—are relevant in the 2020s.[9]

Whether dance music would remain the same, transform, reincarnate, or cease to exist in a world that is politically and materially, maybe violently transformed, remains to be seen. Maybe dance music could find a unique place within this transformed world, along with other forms of meaningful, creative, and leisurely cultural activity.

But for that to be possible, dance music fans, or at least, those of us who are politically inclined, concerned, and engaged, would need to do something

---

[8]Jeremy Gilbert and Ewan Pearson, *Discographies: Dance Music, Culture and the Politics of Sound* (London: Routledge, 1999), 179–84. See also Thornton, *Club Cultures*, 98–105.
[9]Dyer, "In Defence of Disco," 20.

other than pin our hopes on dance floors as sites for such a transformation. We would need to mobilize a utopian vision in mass, organized, direct action. If we set aside music-specific allegiances, tastes, scene loyalties and identities in the service of a multigenre coalition that enforces the potent collectivism that we have rehearsed on dance floors, then perhaps another world—one that is safe and just for everyone, on or off dance floors—will be possible.

Acknowledgments

My first debt of gratitude is to the *Alternate Takes* series editors Matt Brennan and Simon Frith, and Leah Babb-Rosenfeld at Bloomsbury, for their unending patience with me while I wrote this book.

My colleagues at RMIT, Cath Strong, Shelley Brunt, Ian Rogers, and Seb Diaz-Gasca, cheered me on persistently, including while we were locked in our houses for the better part of two years. My colleagues at the University of Oslo helped me get this off the ground to begin with. Stan Hawkins and Georgina Born provided me with vital mentorship and opportunities to start publishing on gender in particular.

The extended Alison House community at the University of Edinburgh, which includes too many people to list, were formative for this book. They were a source of weekly comradery, coffee, and commentary. The weekly seminars taught me how to listen. Nick Prior, Patrick Valiquet, and Klaus Nathaus, all gave me incisive, critical feedback at the earliest brainstorming stages of this book, as well as leading by example on how to think and learn.

Irene Noy, from whom I learned about the history of sound art for the first time, continues to be one of my favorite intellectual conversationalists, who challenges my convictions (in the best possible sense) and helps to stoke my feminist fire.

Various Edinburgh dance music communities gambled on me by welcoming me into their DJ world with open arms. They were gracious and willing in their involvement in the early stages of this project and were my first interviewees. I want to particularly note that many of the interview excerpts from these communities that are present in this book are from approximately ten years ago and I am cognizant of the extent to which their perspectives on the world

and on their own communities have evolved since then. I hope that they can see what is included here as a snapshot in time, a historical record.

The scholarly work of Luis Manuel Garcia-Mispireta and Mark J. Butler gave me impetus to undertake my own research on dance music. Both Luis and Mark provided me with early leads and contacts and have always been generous with me. I am particularly thankful to Luis for being the editor willing to give me my earliest opportunity to write and publish.

I owe a debt of gratitude to co-authors and colleagues in Sweden, Ann Werner and Sam de Boise for their expansion of my scholarly frames of reference for gender issues in music.

Maria Witek, my sister-in-dance music studies showed me how important critically-informed science is and opened my mind to what it can contribute to dance music research—I only wish we had met earlier.

Most academics remember "that paper" they heard at a conference that spurred on a memorable shift in perspective or radical rethink of their own limitations. Mine was Jared Mackley-Crump and Kirsten Zemke's presentation at IASPM-ANZ in 2015 on the FAFSWAG ball.[1] Their account of "queerness and Pacific bodies" at the New York balls-inspired events was detailed, but my personal takeaway was basic: I had to start expanding my thought beyond the English-speaking, European, and US-culture-dominated public sphere that formed my intellectual frame of reference so far. This book falls short of the goal, but we have to start somewhere. On that note, Stefanie Alisch, Noriko Nakahama, and Leandro Brouschert's translation work, together with Astrid Kvalbein's language assistance, were all critical to starting the goal of working outside the Anglosphere. Thank you also to Miranda Moen (and to Luis for putting us in touch) for guiding me to Norwegian sources of interest for the project. Thanks also to Tejaswinee Kelkar for putting me in touch with one of my interviewees, "Veena," and for helping me with the names of Indian cities and states mentioned in our interview.

---

[1] See Jared Mackley-Crump and Kirsten Zemke, "The FAFSWAG Ball: Event Spaces, Counter-Marginal Narratives and Walking Queer Bodies into the Centre," in *Marginalisation and Events*, ed. Trudie Walters and Allan Stewart Jepson (London: Routledge, 2019), 95–109.

My lifelong friend Natasha has been a source of big-hearted support, which I also receive daily from my extended, anonymous family in Melbourne, New York, Oslo, and so on.

My former partner Jake Poole spent years convincing me that I had something worthwhile to contribute as a musician, as a DJ, and as an academic. He moved to the other side of the world with me to help me do that. I have this and his overarching support to thank him for.

My fellow adventurer and best friend Kyle Devine has been a formidable professional role model, in the best possible sense, and enormous support for me. I am exceptionally grateful.

Lastly, the unconditional love and intellectual weight of my family, Raya, Simon, and Jonathan, is equaled only by their uncompromising belief in my abilities. When it comes to ideas, they question everything and agree on nothing. They are at the root of my skeptical propensities and commitment to critical thought. This book is dedicated to them.

Bibliography

Adams, R. A. *The Social Dance*. Kansas, 1921.

Adorno, Theodore W. "On Jazz," translated by Jamie Owen Daniel. *Discourse* 12, no. 1. (Fall–Winter, 1989–90): 45–69.

Adorno, Theodore W. *Prisms*, translated by Samuel and Shierry Weber. Cambridge, MA: MIT Press, 1967.

Ahmad, Jaleel, M. E. Khan, Arupendra Mozumdar, and Deepthi S. Varna. "Gender-Based Violence in Rural Uttar Pradesh, India: Prevalence and Association with Reproductive Health Behaviors." *Journal of Interpersonal Violence* 31, no. 19 (2015): 3111–28.

Alwakeel, Ramzy. "The Aesthetics of Protest in UK Rave." *Dancecult: Journal of Electronic Dance Music Culture* 1, no. 2 (July 2010): 50–62.

Antisocial Behaviour etc. (Scotland) Act. 2004. "Part 5: Noise Nuisance: Summary Procedure for Dealing with Noise from Certain Places." https://www.legislation.gov.uk/asp/2004/8/part/5.

Applegate, Celia. "How German Is It? Nationalism and the Idea of Serious Music in the Early Nineteenth Century." *19th-Century Music* 21, no. 3 (Spring 1998): 274–96.

Armstrong, Victoria. *Technology and the Gendering of Music Education*. Farnham: Ashgate, 2011.

Åsebø, Sigrun. "Representation of Gender and/in Visual Culture." Lecture. Sundvolden (Norway): Gender National Research School General Course.

Asker, Cecilie. "Balansekunst." *Aftenposten*, August 4, 2010, 9.

Athanasopoulos, George, Vasilis Sarafidis, Don Weatherburn, and Rohan Miller. "Longer-Term Impacts of Trading Restrictions on Alcohol-Related Violence: Insights from New South Wales, Australia." *Addiction* 117, no. 5 (May 2022): 1304–11.

Auslander, Philip. *Liveness: Performance in a Mediatized Culture*. London: Routledge, 2008.

Australian Institute of Health and Welfare. "Indigenous Income and Finance." September 16, 2021. https://www.aihw.gov.au/reports/australias-welfare/indigenous-income-and-finance.

Bain, Katie. "Datsik Breaks His Silence in Lengthy Video Statement After Sexual Assault Allegations." Billboard, May 5, 2019. https://www.billboard.com/music/music-news/datsik-video-statement-sexual-assault-allegations-8542801/.

Baldassari, Erin. "Former Ghost Ship Residents Struggle with Trauma, Finding Permanent Housing." *East Bay Times*, April 30, 2017, https://www.eastbaytimes.com/2017/04/30/

former-ghost-ship-residents-still-struggling-with-trauma-finding-permanent-housing/.

Bang Svendsen, Stine H. "The Cultural Politics of Sex Education in the Nordics." In *Palgrave Handbook of Sexuality Education*, edited by Louisa Allen and Mary Lou Rasmussen, 137–56. London: Palgrave Macmillan, 2017.

Barnes, Marcus. "Maceo Plex on Nina Kraviz, the Return of Maetrik and Juggling Fame with Family Life." *Independent*, April 25, 2013. http://blogs.independent. co.uk/2013/04/18/maceo-plex-on-nina-kraviz-the-return-of-maetrik-and-juggling-fame-with-family-life/.

Barrie, Matt. "Would the Last Person in Sydney Please Turn the Lights Out?" LinkedIn, February 3, 2016. https://www.linkedin.com/pulse/would-last-person-sydney-please-turn-lights-out-matt-barrie/.

Battersby, Christine. *Gender and Genius: Towards a Feminist Aesthetics*. Bloomington: Indiana University Press, 1989.

Beck Kehoe, Alice. "Primal Gaia: Primitivists and Plastic Medicine Men." In *The Invented Indian: Cultural Fictions and Government Policies*, edited by James A. Clifton, 193–209. New York: Routledge, 1990.

Beck, Jerome, and Marsha Rosenbaum. *Pursuit of Ecstasy: The MDMA Experience*. Albany: State University of New York Press, 1994.

Becker, Howard S. *Art Worlds*. Berkeley: University of California Press, 1982.

Becker, Howard S. "Becoming a Marijuana User." *American Journal of Sociology* 59, no. 3 (November 1953): 235–42.

Becker, Howard. "The Professional Dance Musician and His Audience." *American Journal of Sociology* 57, no. 2 (September 1951): 136–44.

Becker, Judith. "Music and Trance." *Leonardo Music Journal* 4 (1994): 41.

Bennett, Andy. "Paganism and the Counterculture." In *Pop Pagans: Paganism and Popular Music*, edited by Donna Weston and Andy Bennett, 13–23. London and New York: Routledge, 2013.

Bennett, Andy. "Consolidating the Music Scenes Perspective." *Poetics* 32, no. 3–4 (June–August 2004): 223–34.

Bennett, Andy. *Popular Music and Youth Culture: Music, Identity and Place*. London: Macmillan, 2000.

Bennett, Andy. "Subcultures or Neo-Tribes? Rethinking the Relationship Between Youth, Style and Musical Taste." *Sociology* 33, no. 3 (August 1999): 599–617.

BFH v. Senate. *Judgment of the 23rd of July, 2020* V R 17/17. "Reduced Tax Rate for the Organization of Techno and House Concerts." https://www.bundesfinanzhof.de/en/entscheidungen/entscheidungen-online/decision-detail/STRE202010223.

Bjørhovde, Hilde. "Musikkfest Oslo: Karnevalsparade og gratis konsertfest hele lørdag." *Aftenposten*, June 5, 2015. https://www.aftenposten.no/oslo/byliv/i/2lLR/musikkfest-oslo-karnevalsparade-og-gratis-konsertfest-hele-loerdag.

Blackstock, Gordon. "Revenge Porn Victim Says Police Scotland Fobbed Off Complaint So They Could 'Solve Murders'." *Daily Record*, May 19, 2019. https://www.dailyrecord.co.uk/news/scottish-news/revenge-porn-victim-says-police-16166386.amp?__twitter_impression=true.

Boiler Room, 2022, www.boilerroom.tv/about.

Born, Georgina, and Kyle Devine. "Music Technology, Gender, and Class: Digitization, Educational and Social Change in Britain." *Twentieth-Century Music* 12, no. 2 (September 2015): 135–72.

Bourdieu, Pierre. *Sociology in Question*, translated by Richard Nice. London: Sage, 1993.

Bourdieu, Pierre. "The Practice of Reflexive Sociology (The Paris Workshop)." In *An Invitation to Reflexive Sociology*, edited by Pierre Bourdieu and Loïc J. D. Wacquant, 217–60. Chicago: The University of Chicago Press, 1992.

Brewster, Bill. "Interview with Terry Noel." *DJhistory.com*, October 30, 1998. http://www.djhistory.com/interviews/terry-noel. Accessed February 16, 2011.

Brewster, Bill, and Frank Broughton. *Last Night a DJ Saved My Life: The History of the Disc Jockey*. London: Headline, 2006.

Breyley, Gay Jennifer. "Raving Iran (Review)." *Dancecult: Journal of Electronic Dance Music Culture* 11, no. 1 (November 2019): 97–100.

Brooks, Ann. *Postfeminisms: Feminism, Cultural Theory and Cultural Forms*. London: Routledge, 1997.

Buchowski, Michał. "Against Nationalism and the Idea of Auxiliary Anthropologies." *American Anthropologist* 121, no. 4 (December 2019): 932–3.

Burke, Tarana. *Unbound: My Story of Liberation and the Birth of the Me Too Movement*. New York: Flatiron Books, 2021.

Business Sale Report, "G1 Group Acquires Several Edinburgh Pubs." July 27, 2011. https://www.business-sale.com/news/business-sale/g1-group-acquires-several-edinburgh-pubs-176681.

Bustamante, Carlos D., and Brenna M. Henn. "Shadows of Early Migrations." *Nature* 486 (December 2010): 1044–5.

Butler, Judith. "Sexual Politics, Torture, and Secular Time." *British Journal of Sociology* 59, no. 1 (March 2008): 1–23.

Butler, Judith. "Performative Acts and Gender Constitution: An Essay in Phenomenology and Feminist Theory." *Theatre Journal* 40, no. 4 (December 1988): 519–31.

Butler, Mark J. *Playing with Something that Runs: Technology, Improvisation, and Composition in DJ and Laptop Performance*. Oxford: Oxford University Press, 2014.

Butler, Mark J. *Unlocking the Groove: Rhythm, Meter, and Musical Design in Electronic Dance Music*. Bloomington: Indiana University Press, 2006.

Cangelosi, Ilenia. "The DJ Sex Battle: Maceo Plex Speaks Out on Nina Kraviz' RA Video." *Less Than 3* (blog), April 9, 2013. http://blog.lessthan3.com/2013/04/the-dj-sex-battle-maceo-plex-speaksout-on-nina-kraviz-ra-video/.

Caprice87. "Dance! New Dance Show 1990: Recorded in November 1990 at Key Wat TV Studios, Detroit, MI" (video). https://www.youtube.com/watch?v=DVBE4mcBiSo&ab_channel=Caprice87.

Cheng, William. *Just Vibrations: The Purpose of Sounding Good*. Ann Arbor: University of Michigan Press, 2016.

Chibber, Vivek. *The Class Matrix: Social Theory After the Cultural Turn*, Cambridge, MA: Harvard University Press, 2022.

Child, Hayley. "Collectively Tackling Sexual Violence After Dark." *Global Cities After Dark Outcomes Paper*, November 2018.

Christodoulou, Chris. "Rumble in the Jungle: City, Place and Uncanny Bass." *Dancecult: Journal of Electronic Dance Music Culture* 3, no. 1 (June 2011): 44–63.

City of Oslo. "Salutt Course." https://www.oslo.kommune.no/english/licence-to-serve-food-and-alcohol/salutt-course/#gref. Accessed May 18, 2022.

Clarke, John, Stuart Hall, Tony Jefferson, and Brian Roberts. "Subcultures, Cultures and Class." In *Resistance Through Rituals: Youth Subcultures in Post-War Britain*, edited by Stuart Hall and Tony Jefferson, 9–74. Birmingham: The Centre for Contemporary Cultural Studies, 1976.

Conor, Bridget, Rosalind Gill, and Stephanie Taylor. "Gender and Creative Labour." *Sociological Review* 63, no. 1 supp. (May 2015): 1–22.

Cressey, Paul G. *The Taxi-Dance Hall: A Sociological Study of Commercialized Recreation and City Life*. New York: Greenwood Press, 1968/Chicago: University of Chicago Press, 1932.

Csikszentmihalyi, Mihalyi. *Beyond Boredom and Anxiety*. San Francisco: Jossey-Bass, 1985.

Cultures of Resistance Films. *Modulations*. Directed by Iara Lee, produced by George Gund, Jan 18, 2020 (original film released 2000), https://youtu.be/icpDt6aQDww.

Dagbladet. "Ellen Gleditsch hjemme igjen: 500 dollars til stipendier for kvinner som vil arbeide videnskapelig." May 13, 1929, 1–2.

Dahlerup, Drude. "Women in Nordic Politics—A Continuing Success Story?" In *Gender and Power in the Nordic Countries*, edited by Kirsti Niskanen, 59–86. Oslo: NIKK, 2011.

Dass, Ram, and Ralph Metzner. *Birth of a Psychedelic Culture: Conversations About Leary, the Harvard Experiments, Millbrook and the Sixties*. Santa Fe, NM: Synergetic Press, 2010.

De Koven Bowen, Louise. *The Public Dance Halls of Chicago*. The Juvenile Protective Association of Chicago, 2000.

Deal, Stephen. "'Sluttiest Dressed Bird' Promo Causes Outrage." *Metro*, July 20, 2011.

DeNora, Tia. *Music in Everyday Life*. Cambridge: Cambridge University Press, 2000.

Dibben, Nicola. "Representations of Femininity in Popular Music." *Popular Music* 18, no. 3 (1999): 331–55.

Doubleday, Veronica. "Sounds of Power: An Overview of Musical Instruments and Gender." *Ethnomusicology Forum* 17, no. 1 (June 2008): 15–18.

Dowling, Siobhán. "Women on Board: Norway's Experience Shows Compulsory Quotas Work." *Spiegel Online*, July 8, 2010. https://www.spiegel.de/international/business/women-on-board-norway-s-experience-shows-compulsory-quotas-work-a-705209.html.

Du Mont, Janice, Karen-Lee Miller, and Terri L. Myhr. "The Role of 'Real Rape' and 'Real Victim' Stereotypes in the Police Reporting Practices of Sexually Assaulted Women." *Violence Against Women* 9, no. 4 (April 2003): 466–86.

Dyer, Richard. "In Defence of Disco." *Gay Left*, no. 8 (Summer, 1979): 20–3.

Economist. "The Best—And Worst—Places to be a Working Woman." May 3, 2016. https://www.economist.com/graphic-detail/2016/03/03/the-best-and-worst-places-to-be-a-working-woman.

Edinburgh Literary Pub Tour. "What You Need to Know." 2019. http://www.edinburghliterarypubtour.co.uk/the-tour/what-you-need-know.

Edward Clowes. YouTube Comment on Nina Kraviz, 2015, https://www.youtube.com/watch?v=YIcbIIHcx44&ab_channel=BoilerRoom.

Eggesvik, Olav, and Erlend Tro Klette. "Forskere: Har ikke lykkes med å redusere utelivsvold i Oslo sentrum." *Aftenposten*, March 9, 2017. https://www.aftenposten.no/oslo/i/epkdR/forskere-har-ikke-lykkes-med-aa-redusere-utelivsvold-i-oslo-sentrum.

Eichner, Barbara. "Richard Wagner's Medieval Visions." In *Oxford Handbook of Music and Medievalism*, edited by Kirsten Yri and Stephen C. Meyer, 174–202. New York: Oxford University Press, 2020.

Elliott, Luther. "Goa Is a State of Mind: On the Ephemerality of Psychedelic Social Emplacements." In *The Local Scenes and Global Cultures of Psytrance*, edited by Graham St. John, 21–39. New York: Routledge, 2010.

Eshun, Kodwo. "House: The Reinvention of House." In *Modulations: A History of Electronic Music: Throbbing Words on Sound*, edited by Peter Shapiro, 72–87. New York: Capirinha Productions, 2000.

Eversham, Emma. "G1 Group Launches New Company to Increase Edinburgh Presence." Big Hospitality, July 25, 2011. https://www.bighospitality.co.uk/Article/2011/07/26/G1-Group-launches-new-company-to-increase-Edinburgh-presence.

Ezzy, Douglas. "Dancing Paganism: Music, Dance and Pagan Identity." In *Pop Pagans: Paganism and Popular Music*, edited by Donna Weston and Andy Bennett, 110–25. London and New York: Routledge, 2013.

Fachner, Jörg. "Drugs, Altered States, and Musical Consciousness: Reframing Time and Space." In *Music and Consciousness*, edited by Eric Clarke and David Clarke, 263–80. Oxford: Oxford University Press, 2011.

Factmag. "Russian DJ Nina Kraviz Addresses *that* Bath Scene after Greg Wilson and Maceo Plex Have Their Say." *Fact*, April 9, 2013. https://www.factmag.com/2013/04/09/russian-dj-nina-kraviz-addresses-that-bath-scene-after-greg-wilson-and-maceo-plex-have-their-say/.

Farrugia, Rebekah. *Beyond the Dance Floor: Female DJs, Technology and Electronic Dance Music Culture*. Bristol: Intellect, 2012.

Farrugia, Rebekah. "'Let's Have at It!': Conversations with EDM Producers Kate Simko and DJ Denise." *Dancecult: Journal of Electronic Dance Music Culture* 1, no. 2 (July 2010): 87–93.

Farrugia, Rebekah, and Magdalena Olszanowski. "Introduction to Women and Electronic Dance Music Culture." *Dancecult: Journal of Electronic Dance Music Culture* 9, no. 1 (November 2017): 1–8.

Faulkner, T. A. *The Lure of the Dance*. Los Angeles, 1916.

Faulkner, T. A. *From the Ball-Room to Hell*. Chicago: The Henry Publishing Co., 1892.

Fearnley, Marie (Mais). "Den modern Eva: Borghild Langaard tilbake—hun åpner sangskole til høsten." *Dagbladet*, August 5, 1930.

Fig Les. YouTube Comment on Nina Kraviz, 2015. https://www.youtube.com/watch?v=YIcbIIHcx44&ab_channel=BoilerRoom.

Fikentscher, Kai. *You Better Work! A Study of Underground Dance Music in New York City*. Hanover: Wesleyan University Press, 2000.

Fitzsimmons, Caitlin. "Violence Spread Across City by Lockout Laws Could Hurt Sydney's Nightlife Revival." *Sydney Morning Herald*, January 23, 2022. https://www.smh.com.au/national/nsw/violence-spread-across-city-by-lockout-laws-could-hurt-sydney-s-nightlife-revival-20220111-p59nfv.html.

Free To Be. "Free To Be Archive Map." *Plan International.* https://crowdspot.carto.
com/builder/ca6d8917-579c-463c-a918-8ac8d6402500/embed?state=%7B%22ma
p%22%3A%7B%22ne%22%3A%5B-37.86624854400498%2C144.9191951751709
3%5D%2C%22sw%22%3A%5B-37.74669320259962%2C145.01051902771%5D%
2C%22center%22%3A%5B-37.80649506738787%2C144.96485710144046%5D%2C%2
2zoom%22%3A14%7D%7D.

Friedman, P. Kerim. "Who Owns a Language?" *American Anthropologist* 122, no. 1
(March 2020): 175–6.

Frith, Simon. "Remembrance of Things Past: Marxism and the Study of Popular Music."
Twentieth-Century Music 16, no. 1 (February 2019): 141–55.

Frith, Simon. "Creativity as a Social Fact." In *Musical Imaginations: Multidisciplinary
Perspectives on Creativity, Performance and Perception*, edited by David Hargreaves,
Dorothy Miell, and Raymond MacDonald, 62–72. Oxford: Oxford University Press, 2011.

Frith, Simon. "The Popular Music Industry." In *The Cambridge Companion to Pop
and Rock*, edited by Simon Frith, Will Straw, and John Street, 26–52. Cambridge:
Cambridge University Press, 2001.

Frith, Simon. *Performing Rites: On the Value of Popular Music.* Cambridge, MA: Harvard
University Press, 1996.

Frith, Simon. "The Good, the Bad, and the Indifferent: Defending Popular Culture from
the Populists." *Diacritics* 21, no. 4 (Winter, 1991): 101–15.

Frith, Simon, and Angela McRobbie. "Rock and Sexuality." In *On Record: Rock, Pop, and
the Written Word*, edited by Simon Frith and Andrew Goodwin, 371–89. New York:
Pantheon Books, 1990.

Frois, Andre. "How Female DJs in Singapore Fought Sexist Stereotyping to be Judged on
their Sounds, Not Their Looks." *South China Morning Post*, January 30, 2018, https://
www.scmp.com/culture/music/article/2130986/how-female-djs-singapore-fought-
sexist-stereotyping-be-judged-their.

Furuseth, Karima. "47 artister, fire kvinner—her er 8 kvinnelige DJs Musikkfest Oslo
KUNNE ha booket." *Natt&Dag*, May 24, 2016. https://nattogdag.no/2016/05/
musikkfest-oslo-skjev-fordeling/.

G1 Group. 2020. https://www.holyroodpr.co.uk/client-hub/g1-group/.

Gadir, Tami. "Understanding Agency from the Decks to the Dance Floor." *Music
Theory Online* 24, no. 3 (September 2018), https://mtosmt.org/issues/mto.18.24.3/
mto.18.24.3.gadir.html.

Gadir, Tami. "'I Don't Play Girly House Music': Women, Sonic Stereotyping, and the
Dancing DJ." In *Routledge Research Companion to Popular Music and Gender*, edited by
Stan Hawkins, 196–210. London: Routledge, 2017.

Gadir, Tami. "Forty-Seven DJs, Four Women: Meritocracy, Talent and Postfeminist
Politics." *Dancecult: Journal of Electronic Dance Music Culture* 9, no. 1 (November,
2017): 50–72.

Gadir, Tami. "Resistance or Reiteration?: Rethinking Gender in DJ Culture." *Contemporary
Music Review* 35, no. 1 (February 2016): 115–29.

Gadir, Tami. "Musical Meaning and Social Significance: Techno Triggers for Dancing."
PhD diss., University of Edinburgh, 2014.

Garcia-Mispireta, Luis Manuel. *Together, Somehow: Music, Affect, and Intimacy on the
Dancefloor.* Durham, NC: Duke University Press, 2023.

Garcia, Luis-Manuel. "Whose Refuge, This House? The Estrangement of Queers of Color in Electronic Dance Music." In *The Oxford Handbook of Music and Queerness*, edited by Fred Everett Maus and Sheila Whiteley, 35–61. Oxford: Oxford University Press, 2022.

Garcia, Luis-Manuel. "Agnostic Festivities: Urban Nightlife Scenes and the Sociability of Anti-Social Fun." *Annals of Leisure Research* 21, no. 4 (2018): 462–79.

Garcia, Luis-Manuel. "Techno-Tourism and Post-Industrial Neo-Romanticism in Berlin's Electronic Music Scenes." *Tourist Studies* 16, no. 3 (September 2016): 276–95.

Garcia, Luis-Manuel. "Beats, Flesh, and Grain: Sonic Tactility and Affect in Electronic Dance Music." *Sound Studies* 1, no. 1 (2015): 59–76.

Garcia, Luis-Manuel. "At Home, I'm a Tourist: Musical Migration and Affective Citizenship in Berlin." *Journal of Urban Cultural Studies* 2, no. 1–2 (June 2015): 121–34.

Garcia, Luis-Manuel. "Richard Dyer, 'In Defence of Disco.'" In *History of Emotions— Insights into Research*, November 2014.

Garcia, Luis-Manuel. "An Alternate History of Sexuality in Club Culture." Resident Advisor, January 28, 2014, http://www.residentadvisor.net/feature.aspx?1927.

Garcia, Luis-Manuel. "Doing Nightlife and EDMC Fieldwork." *Dancecult: Journal of Electronic Dance Music Culture* 5, no. 1 (May 2013): 3–17.

Garcia, Luis-Manuel. "Can You Feel It, Too?: Intimacy and Affect at Electronic Dance Music Events in Paris, Chicago, and Berlin." PhD diss., University of Chicago, 2011.

Garcia, Luis-Manuel. "On and On: Repetition as Process and Pleasure in Electronic Dance Music." *Music Theory Online* 11, no. 4 (October 2005), https://www.mtosmt.org/issues/mto.05.11.4/mto.05.11.4.garcia.html.

Gartrell, Nate. "Ghost Ship Criminal Case Ends with Restitution Order: Victims' Families Ordered to Receive $5,800 each, but are doubtful they'll ever see the money." *East Bay Times*, July 23, 2021. https://www.eastbaytimes.com/2021/07/23/ghost-ship-criminal-case-ends-with-restitution-order-victims-families-ordered-to-receive-5800-each-but-are-doubtful-theyll-ever-see-the-money/.

Gavanas, Anna, and Rosa Reitsamer. "DJ Technologies, Social Networks and Gendered Trajectories in European DJ Cultures." In *DJ Culture in the Mix: Power, Technology, and Social Change in Electronic Dance Music*, edited by Bernardo Alexander Attias, Anna Gavanas, and Hillegonda C. Rietveld, 51–77. New York: Bloomsbury, 2013.

Gender in Norway. "National Legislation." https://gender.no/Legislation/National_legislation. Accessed November 15, 2016.

Gilbert, Jeremy and Ewan Pearson. *Discographies: Dance Music, Culture and the Politics of Sound*. London: Routledge, 1999.

Gill, Rosalind. "Post-Postfeminism? New Feminist Visibilities in Postfeminist Times." *Feminist Media Studies* 16, no. 4 (2016): 610–30.

Gill, Rosalind. "Postfeminist Media Culture: Elements of a Sensibility." *European Journal of Cultural Studies* 10, no. 2 (May 2007): 147–66.

Glasgow Indicators Project: Understanding Glasgow. "Post-War Housing Changes." *Glasgow Centre for Population Health*. https://www.understandingglasgow.com/indicators/environment/housing/post_war_housing.

Global Cities After Dark. 2022, https://www.globalcitiesafterdark.com/.

Gomez, Shyamala Y. M. "A Measure of Justice: Alternatives to Pursuing Criminal Accountability in Conflict-Related Sexual Violence in Sri Lanka." *Violence Against Women* 28, no. 8 (June 2022): 1824–41.

Goodman, Steve. *Sonic Warfare: Sound, Affect, and the Ecology of Fear.* Cambridge, MA: MIT Press, 2010.

Government.no. "The Act Relating to Gender Equality." last updated April 20, 2007. https://www.regjeringen.no/en/dokumenter/the-act-relating-to-gender-equality-the-/ id454568/.

Great Cities Institute, "Abandoned in their Neighborhoods: Youth Joblessness Amidst the Flight of Industry and Opportunity." *Great Cities Institute*, University of Illinois at Chicago, January 2017.

Grewe, Oliver, Reinhard Kopiez, and Eckart Altenmüller. "The Chill Parameter: Goosebumps and Shivers as Promising Measures in Emotion Research." *Music Perception* 27, no. 1 (September 2009): 61–74.

Gross, Sally Anne and George Musgrave. *Can Music Make You Sick? Measuring the Price of Musical Ambition.* London: University of Westminster Press, 2020.

Guardian. "Yoko Ono's Meltdown: Patti Smith, Boy George and Siouxsie Sioux Sign Up." April 4, 2013. https://www.theguardian.com/music/2013/apr/04/yoko-one-meltdown-patti-smith-siouxsie-sioux.

Guggenheim. "Richie Hawtin aka Plastikman to Perform at the Guggenheim on November 6." September 17, 2013, https://www.guggenheim.org/press-release/gig-2013.

Hall, Joanna. "Heterocorporealities: Popular Dance and Cultural Hybridity in UK Drum 'n' Bass Culture." PhD diss., University of Surrey, 2009.

Hambrick, David Z. and Elliot M. Tucker-Drobb, "The Genetics of Music Accomplishment: Evidence for Gene-Environment Correlation and Interaction." *Psychonomic Bulletin and Review* 22 (February 2015): 112–20.

Haraway, Donna. *Simians, Cyborgs, and Women: The Reinvention of Nature.* London: Free Association Books, 1991.

Harkins, Paul. *Digital Sampling: The Decline and Use of Music Technologies.* New York: Routledge, 2020.

Harkins, Paul and Nick Prior, "Dislocating Democratization: Music Technologies in Practice." *Popular Music and Society* 45, no. 1 (2022): 84–103.

Hartline, France Rose. "(Trans)gender outlaws? A critical analysis of Norway's 2016 gender self-determination law." *Tijdschrift Voor Genderstudies* 21, no. 4 (January 2019): 361–80.

Hartogsohn, Ido. *American Trip: Set, Setting, and the Psychedelic Experience in the Twentieth Century.* Cambridge, MA: MIT Press, 2020.

Harvati, Katerina, Carolin Röding, Abel M. Bosman, Fotios A. Karakostis, Rainer Grün, Chris Stringer, Panagiotis Karkanas, Nicholas C. Thompson, Vassilis Koutoulidis, Lia A. Moulopolous, Vassilis G. Gorgoulis, and Mirsini Kouloukoussa. "Apidima Cave Fossils Provide Earliest Evidence of *Homo Sapiens* in Eurasia." *Nature* 571 (July 2019): 500–4.

Haslam, Dave. *Life After Dark: A History of British Nightclubs and Music Venues.* London: Simon & Schuster, 2015.

Hawkins, Stan. *The British Pop Dandy*. Farnham: Ashgate, 2009.

Hebdige, Dick. *Subculture: The Meaning of Style*. London: Routledge, 1979.

Helding, Lynn. "Innate Talent: Myth or Reality? Mindful Voice." *Journal of Singing* 67, no. 4 (March/April 2011): 451–8.

Hendy, David. "The Birth of TV: Opening Night: November 1936." BBC 100. https://www.bbc.com/historyofthebbc/100-voices/birth-of-tv/opening-night/. Accessed May 20, 2022.

Henriques, Julian. *Sonic Bodies: Reggae Sound Systems, Performance Techniques, and Ways of Knowing*. New York: Continuum, 2011.

Hesmondhalgh, David, and Sarah Baker. *Creative Labour: Media Work in Three Cultural Industries*. London: Routledge, 2011.

Heuguet, Guillaume. "When Club Cultures Goes Online: The Case of Boiler Room," translated by Luis Manuel Garcia-Mispireta. *Dancecult* 8, no. 1 (November, 2016): 73–87.

Holiday, Billie. "Don't Explain [dZihan and Kamien Remix]." *Verve Remixed*, Verve Records, 2002.

Holt, Fabian. *Everyone Loves Live Music: A Theory of Performance Institutions*. Chicago: University of Chicago Press, 2020.

Holt, Fabian. "The Evolution of Sponsorship in Sensitive Cultural Spheres in the Early 21st Century: Lessons from a Culture-Producing Marketing Unit." In *Prekäre Genres: Zur Ästhetik peripherer, apokrypher und liminaler Gattungen*, edited by Hanno Berger, Frédéric Döhl, and Thomas Morsch, 101–33. Bielefeld: Transcript Verlag, 2015.

Homan, Shane. "'Lockout Laws' or 'Rock Out' Laws?: Governing Sydney's Night-Time Economy and Implications for the 'Music City.'" *International Journal of Cultural Policy* 25, no. 4 (2019): 500–14.

Host, Vivian. "Don't Stop Now: Revisiting the New Dance Show of Detroit." *Red Bull Music Academy*, May 24, 2019. https://daily.redbullmusicacademy.com/2019/05/rj-watkins-lawanda-new-dance-show.

Howe, Michael J. A., Jane W. Davidson, and John A. Sloboda. "Innate Talents: Reality or Myth?" *Behavioral and Brian Sciences* 21 (June 1998): 399–442.

Høyre. "Høyre's Parliamentary Election Manifesto for 2017–2021." Adopted at Høyre's National Convention, March 9–12, 2017.

Hubbell, Diana. "Meet Nakadia, the DJ from Rural Thailand Who Is Underground Techno's Rising Star." *Vice*, February 4, 2016. https://www.vice.com/en/article/8q7xv5/nakadia-mungphanklang-interview-thailand-dj-sven-vath.

Hulme, Kyle. "How Thailand's Full Moon Parties Became an International Phenomenon." *Culture Trip*, March 19, 2019. https://theculturetrip.com/asia/thailand/articles/how-thailands-full-moon-party-went-from-small-gathering-to-international-phenomenon/.

Human Traffic. Directed by Justin Kerrigan (Cardiff: Irish Screen & Fruit Salad Films, 1999; In2Film & Metrodome Distribution, 2007), DVD.

Hutton, Fiona. *Risky Pleasures? Club Cultures and Feminine Identities*. Aldershot: Ashgate, 2006.

Iadarola, Alexander. "Berghain Officially Given High Culture Status and Lower Tax Rate." *Vice*, September 13, 2016. https://www.vice.com/en/article/8q7vd3/berghain-high-culture-german-court.

Ighoubah, Farid. "Forsvarer for Gaute Drevdal reagerer på demonstrasjon mot voldtektsom." *Nettavisen*, February 2, 2022. https://www.nettavisen.no/nyheter/ forsvarer-for-gaute-drevdal-reagerer-pa-demonstrasjon-mot-voldtektsdom /s/12-95-3424240661.

Ighoubah, Farid. "Kulturprofil Gaute Drevdal frikjent for åtte av ni voldtektsanklager." Nettavisen, January 29, 2022. https://www.nettavisen.no/nyheter/kulturprofil-gaute-drevdal-frikjent-for-atte-av-ni-voldtektsanklager/s/12-95-3424237555.

Inglehart, Ronald, and Pippa Norris. *Rising Tide: Gender Equality and Cultural Change Around the World*. Cambridge: Cambridge University Press, 2003.

Jasen, Paul. *Low End Theory: Bass, Bodies and the Materiality of Sonic Experience*. New York: Bloomsbury, 2016.

Jazbinsek, Dietmar, Bernward Joerges, and Ralf Thies. *The Berlin "Großstadt-Dokumente": A Forgotten Precursor of the Chicago School of Sociology*. Berlin: Wissenschaftszentrum Berlin für Sozialforschung, 2001.

Johnstone, Henry. "Maceo Plex Calls Out Nina Kraviz Over 'That' RA Video." *Pulse*, April 9, 2013. http://pulseradio.net/articles/2013/04/maceo-plex-calls-out-nina-kraviz-over-that-ra-video-feature.

Kalms, Nicole, Gill Matthewson, and Pamela Salen. "Safe in the City? Girls Tell It Like It Is." *The Conversation*, March 27, 2017. https://theconversation.com/safe-in-the-city-girls-tell-it-like-it-is-72975.

Kassabian, Anahid. *Ubiquitous Listening: Affect, Attention, and Distributed Subjectivity*. Berkeley: University of California Press, 2013.

Katz, Mark. *Capturing Sound: How Technology Has Changed Music*. Berkeley: University of California Press, 2010.

Kelly, Brian C. "Mediating MDMA-Related Harm: Preloading and Post-Loading Among Ecstasy-Using Youth." *Journal of Psychoactive Drugs* 41–1 (March 2009): 19–26.

Kerr, P. Personal communication with author, November 14, 2012.

Kessler, Kim Andreas. "Anthropology at the University of the South Pacific: From Past Dynamics to Present Perceptions." *The Australian Journal of Anthropology* 32, no. 1 (April 2021): 33–53.

Kirn, Peter. "Let's Talk Consent: How to Make Nightlife Safe from Harassment." *CDM*, September 24, 2015. https://cdm.link/2015/09/organization-looks-ways-make-nightlife-safe-harrassment/.

Knudsen, Marianne. "Vakten dro meg ut av utestedet og la meg på hodet ned i trappa." *Adresseavisen*, May 14, 2018, 38.

Kohn, Marek. "Cocaine Girls." In *The Clubcultures Reader: Readings in Popular Cultural Studies*, edited by Steve Redhead, 119–29. Oxford: Blackwell, 1997.

Kolioulis, Alessio. "Borderlands: Dub Techno's Hauntological Politics of Acoustic Ecology." *Dancecult: Journal of Electronic Dance Music Culture* 7, no. 2 (November 2015): 64–85.

Kosofsky Sedgwick, Eve. "Paranoid Reading and Reparative Reading; or, You're So Paranoid, You Probably Think This Introduction Is About You." In *Novel Gazing: Queer Readings in Fiction*, edited by Eve Kosofsky Sedgwick, 1–37. Durham: Duke University Press, 1997.

Kraviz, Nina. (@NinaKraviz) "I'm praying for peace! #mir #мир." *Twitter*, February 27, 2022, 7:41 a.m. https://twitter.com/NinaKraviz/status/1497673257771745281?s=20&t=ColMvbqEspi1o4iY_zihBw.

Kraviz, Nina. "Greg Wilson Wrote an Article About Me." *Facebook*, April 8, 2013. https://www.facebook.com/permalink.php?story_fbid=556948164349995&id=192110944137172.

Kvalbein, Astrid. "Menn jubilerer for full musikk." *Aftenposten*, April 7, 2013, 7.

Lal, Kish. "Meet the Djs Challenging Melbourne's Blokey Club Scene." *Inthemix*. https://inthemix.junkee.com/meet-the-new-djs-challenging-melbournes-blokey-club-scene/. Accessed July 6, 2016.

Larsen, Gunnar (Kollskegg). "Oslo Kvinneparti Blev Stiftet Igår." *Dagbladet*, December 7, 1927.

Lawrence, Tim. *Life and Death on the New York Dance Floor 1980–1983*. Durham: Duke University Press, 2016.

Lawrence, Tim. "Life and Death on the Pulse Dance Floor: Transglocal Politics and the Erasure of the Latinx in the History of Queer Dance." *Dancecult: Journal of Electronic Dance Music Culture* 8, no. 1 (November 2016): 1–25.

Lawrence, Tim. *Love Saves the Day: A History of American Dance Music Culture, 1970–70*. Durham and London: Duke University Press, 2003.

Leight, Elias. "The Essential Mix at 25: Pete Tong on Creating One of Dance Music's Most Important Mix Shows." *Rolling Stone*, October 26, 2018. https://www.rollingstone.com/music/music-news/pete-tong-essential-mix-dance-music-bbc-radio1-745904/.

Leneghan, Sean. "The Varieties of Ecstasy Experience: An Exploration of Body, Mind and Person in Sydney's Club Culture." PhD diss., University of Sydney, 2010.

Leonard, Marion. *Gender in the Music Industry: Rock, Discourse and Girl Power*. Aldershot: Ashgate, 2007.

Lindbæk, Lise. "En ny tids kvinnesak: Inntrykk fra Yrkes kvinners sommerleier på Hundorp." *Urd* 36 (1936): 1126–7.

Lins Ribeiro, Gustavo. "Outsiders and Insiders in the Making of Anthropological Knowledge." *American Anthropologist* 118, no. 3 (September 2016): 628–9.

Littler, Jo. *Against Meritocracy*. London: Routledge, 2018.

Liu, Wu, Chang-Zhu Jin, and Ying-Qi Zhang. "Human Remains from Zhirendong, South China, and Modern Human Emergence in East Asia." *Proceedings of the National Academy of Sciences of the United States of America* 107, no. 45 (November 2010): 19201–6.

Loben, Carl. "Who Are the Women Pioneers of Dance Music?" Huffpost Entertainment UK, April 28, 2016. https://www.huffingtonpost.co.uk/carl-loben/women-pioneers-of-dance-music_b_9794186.html.

Lochhead, Judy. "Theorizing Gender, Culture, and Music: The Sublime, the Ineffable, and Other Dangerous Aesthetics." *Women and Music: A Journal of Gender and Culture* 12 (2008): 63–124.

Luengo, María. "Gender Violence: The Media, Civil Society, and the Struggle for Human Rights in Argentina." *Media, Culture and Society* 40, no. 3 (2018): 397–414.

Lund, Joachim. "Mer østrogen, takk!" *Aftenposten*, March 24, 2012, 6.

Lund, Joachim. "Her kommer guttemusikken." *Aftenposten*, June 4, 2011, 12.

Mackley-Crump, Jared, and Kirsten Zemke. "The FAFSWAG Ball: Event Spaces, Counter-Marginal Narratives and Walking Queer Bodies into the Centre." In *Marginalisation and Events*, edited by Trudie Walters and Allan Stewart Jepson, 95–109. London: Routledge, 2019.

Maffesoli, Michel. *The Time of the Tribes: The Decline of Individualism in Mass Society*, translated by Rob Shields. London: Save, 1996.

Magubane, Zine. "Science, Reform, and the 'Science of Reform': Booker T. Washington, Robert Park, and the Making of a 'Science of Society.'" *Current Sociology* 62, no. 4 (July 2014): 568–83.

Malabou, Catharine. *Changing Difference: The Feminine and the Question of Philosophy*. Cambridge: Polity Press, 2011.

Malbon, Ben. *Clubbing: Dancing, Ecstasy and Vitality*. London: Routledge, 1999.

Malnig, Julie, ed. *Ballroom, Boogie, Shimmy Sham, Shake: A Social and Popular Dance Reader*. Chicago: University of Illinois Press, 2009.

Mandel, Hadas, and Moshe Semyonov. "The Gender-Race Intersection and the 'Sheltering-Effect' of Public-Sector Employment." *Research in Social Stratification and Mobility* 71 (2021): 100581.

Marcus, Gary. *Guitar Hero: The New Musician and the Science of Learning*. New York: Penguin Press, 2012.

Marx, Karl, and Friedrich Engels. *The Communist Manifesto*. Milton Keynes: Penguin Random House UK, 2015.

Matos, Michelangelo. *The Underground Is Massive: How Electronic Music Conquered America*. New York: Dey St., 2015.

Matos, Michelangelo. "Nightclubbing: Your Sisters' House." Red Bull Music Academy Daily, February 17, 2015. http://daily.redbullmusicacademy.com/2015/02/nightclubbing-your-sisters-house Mitchell 2016.

Matos, Michelangelo. "The Techno Feminists Next Door." NPR Music, November 6, 2015. https://www.npr.org/sections/therecord/2015/11/06/454946162/the-techno-feminists-next-door.

Matthews, Tomas E., Maria A. G. Witek, Torben Lund, Peter Vuust, and Virginia B. Penhume. "The Sensation of Groove Engages Motor and Reward Networks." *NeuroImage* 214 (July 2020). PMID: 32217163

McAllister, Jeremiah. Interview by Jason Myles, Pascal Robert, and Marcus of the Left Flank Vets. *This Is Revolution Podcast*, March 31, 2022. https://youtu.be/HGWSYIzyjTM?t=1539.

McClary, Susan. *Feminine Endings: Music, Gender, and Sexuality*. Minneapolis: University of Minnesota Press, 1991.

McDermott, Matt. "Association for Electronic Music Establishes UK Hotline for Sexual Harassment in the Electronic Music Industry." Resident Advisor, December 22, 2017. https://ra.co/news/40676.

McElrath, Karen, and Kieran McEvoy. "Negative Experiences on Ecstasy: The Role of Drug, Set, and Setting." *Journal of Psychoactive Drugs* 34, no. 2 (April–June 2002): 199–208.

McRobbie, Angela. *Be Creative: Making a Living in the New Culture Industries*. Cambridge: Polity Press, 2016.

McRobbie, Angela. *The Aftermath of Feminism: Gender, Culture and Social Change*. London: Sage, 2009.

McRobbie, Angela. "Post-Feminism and Popular Culture." *Feminist Media Studies* 4, no. 3 (2004): 255–64.

McRobbie, Angela. "Clubs to Companies: Notes on the Decline of Political Culture in Speeded Up Worlds." *Cultural Studies* 16, no. 4 (2002): 516–31.

McRobbie, Angela. *Postmodernism and Popular Culture*. London: Routledge, 1994.

Medved, Matt. "Paris Hilton Reveals Las Vegas DJ Residency, Defends DJ Career." Hollywood Reporter, March 31, 2015. https://www.hollywoodreporter.com/news/music-news/paris-hilton-reveals-las-vegas-785656/.

Melville, Caspar. *It's a London Thing: How Rare Groove, Acid House and Jungle Remapped the City*. Manchester: Manchester University Press, 2020.

Mepschen, Paul, Jan Willem Duyvendak, and Evelien H. Tonkens. "Sexual Politics, Orientalism and Multicultural Citizenship in the Netherlands." *Sociology* 44, no. 5 (October 2010): 962–79.

microglitch. YouTube Comment on Nina Kraviz, 2015. https://www.youtube.com/watch?v=YIcbIIHcx44&ab_channel=BoilerRoom.

Middleton, Richard. *Studying Popular Music*. Milton Keynes: Open University Press, 1990.

Ministry of Health and Care Services. "Prop 74L: Proposisjon til Stortinget (forslag til lovvedtak): Lov om endring av juridisk kjønn." March 18, 2016. https://www.regjeringen.no/no/dokumenter/prop.-74-l-20152016/id2479716/.

Mixmag. "Nina Kraviz: Biography." https://mixmag.net/artist/nina-kraviz. Accessed May 8, 2022.

Mjaaland, Ola, Kirsti Haga Honningsøy, Eirin Tjoflot, and Emily Louisa Millan Eide. "Gaute Drevdal får stor reduksjon i straff—anker erstatningskrav." NRK, January 29, 2022. https://www.nrk.no/norge/gaute-drevdal-far-stor-reduksjon-i-straff-_-anker-erstatningskrav-1.15827803.

Mjaaland, Ola. "Voldtektsdømte Gaute Drevdal med nye forsvarere og ny strategi før ankesaken." NRK, October 14, 2021. https://www.nrk.no/norge/voldtektsdomte-gaute-drevdal-med-nye-forsvarere-og-ny-strategi-for-ankesaken-1.15685321.

Modleski, Tania. *Feminism Without Women: Culture and Criticism in a "Postfeminist" Age*. New York: Routledge, 1991.

Montague, Eugene. "Entrainment and Embodiment in Musical Performance." In *The Oxford Handbook of Music and the Body*, edited by Youn Kim and Sander L. Gilman, 177–92. Oxford: Oxford University Press, 2019.

Montague, Eugene. "Moving to Music: A Theory of Sound and Physical Action." PhD diss., University of Pennsylvania, 2001.

Montano, Ed. "DJ Culture in the Commercial Sydney Dance Music Scene." *Dancecult* 1, no. 1 (September 2009): 81–93.

Mosing, Miriam A., Guy Madison, Nancy L. Pedersen, Ralf Kuja-Halkola, and Fredrik Ullén. "Practice Does Not Make Perfect: No Causal Effect of Music Practice on Music Ability." *Psychological Science* 25, no. 9 (September 2014): 1800–2.

Muggs, Joe. "Techno Star Helena Hauff: 'Every Woman Who DJs and Is Visible Helps to Make a Change.'" *The Guardian*, July 20, 2018. https://www.theguardian.com/music/2018/jul/20/helena-hauff-techno-woman-dj.

Muñoz, José Esteban. *Cruising Utopia: The Then and There of Queer Futurity*. New York: New York University Press, 2009.

Napier-Raman, Kishor. "Sydney Finally Scraps Lockout Laws—Was It Worth It?" Crikey, February 11, 2021. https://www.crikey.com.au/2021/02/11/sydney-lockout-laws/.

Nathaus, Klaus. "Why 'Pop' Changed and Why It Mattered (Part I): Sociological Perspectives on Twentieth-Century Popular Culture in the West." *Soziopolis*, August 1, 2018, https://www.soziopolis.de/why-pop-changed-and-how-it-mattered-part-i.html#_ftn6.

Natteravene. "Hi, Join the Night Ravens! Helping to Keep the Streets Safe Since 1990." 2018–2021. http://www.natteravnene.no/resources/infobrosjyrer/Natteravn-brosjyre_Engelsk.pdf.

Nelson, Peter. "Where Have All the Anthros Gone? The Shift in California Indian Studies from Research 'on' to Research 'with, for, and by' Indigenous Peoples." *American Anthropologist* 123, no. 3 (September 2021): 469–73.

Nemola, Guido. "Come Out." *Freakin' EP*, Recycle Records, 2012.

Nien-hwa Cheng, Marietta. "Women Conductors: Has the Train Left the Station?" *Harmony: Forum of the Symphony Orchestra Institute* 6 (April 1998): 81–90.

Niskanen, Kirsti. "Gender and Power in the Nordic Countries: A Comparative Perspective." In *Gender and Power in the Nordic Countries*, edited by Kirsti Niskanen, 11–58. Oslo: NIKK, 2011.

Nott, James. "Getting Together to 'Get Down:' Social Dancing from Dance Hall to Rave." In *Musicking in Twentieth-Century Europe: A Handbook*, edited by Klaus Nathaus and Martin Rempe, 257–79. Oldenburgh: De Gruyter, 2020.

Nott, James. *Going to the Palais: A Social and Cultural History of Dancing and Dance Halls in Britain, 1918–1960*. Oxford: Oxford University Press, 2015.

NPR. "Watch Four-Tet's Sumptuous Live Performance in Sydney." August 18, 2016. https://www.npr.org/sections/allsongs/2016/08/18/490487910/watch-four-tets-sumptuous-live-performance-in-sydney.

NSW Government. "Lockout Laws Lifted for Kings Cross." February 9, 2021. https://www.nsw.gov.au/media-releases/lockout-laws-lifted-for-kings-cross.

"Oakland Fire Victims Remembered." *BBC*, January 4, 2017. https://www.bbc.com/news/world-us-canada-38218022.

O'Grady, Alice. "Dancing Outdoors: DIY Ethics and Democratised Practices of Well-Being on the UK Alternative Festival Circuit." *Dancecult: Journal of Electronic Dance Music Culture* 7, no. 1 (June 2015): 76–96.

O'Grady, Alice. "Interrupting Flow: Researching Play, Performance and Immersion in Festival Scenes." *Dancecult* 5, no. 1 (May 2013): 18–38.

O'Grady, Alice, and Anna Madill. "Being and Performing 'Older' Woman in Electronic Dance Movement Culture." *Dancecult: Journal of Electronic Dance Music Culture* 11, no. 1 (November 2019): 7–29.

Oltermann, Philip. "High Culture Club: Berghain Secures Same Tax Status as Berlin Concert Venues." *The Guardian*, September 12, 2016. https://www.theguardian.com/music/2016/sep/12/berlins-berghain-nightclub-classed-as-culturally-significant-venue.

Park, Robert E. "The City: Suggestions for the Investigation of Human Behavior in the City Environment." *The American Journal of Sociology* 20, no. 2 (March 1915): 577–612.

Passalacqua, Nicholas V., and Marin A. Pilloud. "The Importance of Professional Organizations as Disciplinary Leaders and the Need for Meaningful Ethical Codes in Anthropology." *American Anthropologist* 124, no. 1 (January 2022): 198–203.

Paul, Newly. "When Love Wins, Framing Analysis of the Indian Media's Coverage of Section 377, Decriminalization of Same Sex Relationships." *Newspaper Research Journal* 43, no. 1 (March 2022): 7–28.

Pawel, Katherina. "Black Feminism and the Violence of Disco." *Dancecult: Journal of Electronic Dance Music Culture* 13, no. 1 (December 2021): 22–35.

Peacock, Dean. "Moving Beyond a Reliance on Criminal Legal Strategies to Address the Root Causes of Domestic and Sexual Violence." *Violence Against Women* 28, no. 8 (June 2022): 1890–907.

Pedersen, Willy, Torbjørn Skardhamar, and Silje Bringsrud Fekjær. "Utelivsvolden og overskjenkingen i Oslo bare fortsetter." *Aftenposten*, March 9, 2017. https://www. aftenposten.no/meninger/debatt/i/4aRkG/utelivsvolden-og-overskjenkingen-i-oslo-bare-fortsetter-willy-pedersen-torbjoern-skardhamar-og-silje-bringsrud-fekjaer.

Pentney, Alana R. "Exploration of the History and Controversies Surrounding MDMA and MDA." *Journal of Psychoactive Drugs* 33, no. 3 (2001): 213–21.

Phillips, Matthew T. "Dancing with Dumont: Individualism at an Early Morning Melbourne Rave." *Dancecult: Journal of Electronic Dance Music Culture* 13, no. 1 (December 2021): 88–100.

Pinch, Trevor, and Frank Trocco. *Analog Days: The Invention and Impact of the Moog Synthesizer.* Cambridge, MA: Harvard University Press, 2002.

Pini, Maria. *Club Cultures and Female Subjectivity: The Move from Home to House.* Basingstoke: Palgrave, 2001.

Pini, Maria. "Cyborgs, Nomads, and the Raving Feminine." In *Dance in the City*, edited by Helen Thomas, 111–29. London: Palgrave Macmillan, 1997.

Plan International. "Unsafe in the City: The Everyday Experiences of Girls and Young Women." *The State of the World's Girls Report*, July 8, 2018 (Monash University), https://www.plan.org.au/publications/unsafe-in-the-city-the-everyday-experiences-of-girls-and-young-women/.

Pope, Richard. "Hooked on Affect: Detroit Techno and Dystopian Digital Culture." *Dancecult: Journal of Electronic Dance Music Culture* 2, no. 1 (March 2011): 38.

Press Services of the Federal Fiscal Court. "Reduced VAT Rate for Techno and House Concerts: Judgment of 10 June 2020V R 16/17." Press release, no. 049/20, October 29, 2020. https://www.bundesfinanzhof.de/en/press/press-releases/detail/ermaessigter-umsatzsteuersatz-fuer-techno-und-house-konzerte.

Prior, Nick. "On Vocal Assemblages: From Edison to Miku." *Contemporary Music Review* 37, no. 5–6 (2018): 488–506.

Prior, Nick. "Software Sequencers and Cyborg Singers: Popular Music in the Digital Hypermodern." *New Formations* 66 (March 2009): 81–99.

Prodis Sulek, Julia. "Oakland Fire: The Last Hours of the Ghost Ship Warehouse." *East Bay Times*, December 11, 2016. https://www.eastbaytimes.com/2016/12/11/oakland-fire-ghost-ship-last-hours/.

Push, and Mirelle Silcott. *The Book of E: All About Ecstasy.* London: Omnibus Press, 2000.

Rapp, Tobias. *Lost and Sound: Berlin, Techno and the Easyjet Set*, translated by Paul Sabin. Frankfurt: Inversions, 2010.

Reamer, Jacob. "Nina Kraviz Video Scandal Explained." *TickPick: Where Smart Fans Buy Tickets*, April 12, 2013. https://www.tickpick.com/blog/nina-kraviz-video-scandal-explained/.

Reitsamer, Rosa. "The DIY Careers of Techno and Drum 'n' Bass DJs in Vienna." *Dancecult: Journal of Electronic Dance Music Culture* 3, no. 1 (June, 2011): 28–43.

Resident Advisor. "Between the Beats: The Black Madonna." August 11, 2016, https://ra.co/features/2793.

Resident Advisor. "Kraftwerk Bring 3D Concerts to Oslo." October 20, 2015, https://ra.co/news/31863.

Reynolds, Simon. *Energy Flash: A Journey Through Dance Music and Rave Culture.* London: Picador, 2008.

Reynolds, Simon. "Kosmik Dance: Krautrock and Its Legacy." in *Modulations: A History of Electronic Music: Throbbing Words on Sound*, edited by Peter Shapiro, 24–37. New York: Capirinha Productions, 2000.

Rietveld, Hillegonda C. "Disco's Revenge: House Music's Nomadic Memory." *Dancecult: Journal of Electronic Dance Music Culture* 2, no. 1 (March, 2011): 4–23.

Rietveld, Hillegonda C. "Infinite Noise Spirals: The Musical Cosmopolitanism of Psytrance." In *The Local and Global Cultures of Psytrance*, edited by Graham St. John, 69–88. New York: Routledge, 2010.

Rietveld, Hillegonda C. *This Is Our House: House Music, Cultural Spaces and Technologies.* London: Ashgate, 1998.

Robehmed, Natalie. "How Discwoman Is Diversifying Electronic Music." *Forbes*, August 24, 2017. https://www.forbes.com/sites/natalierobehmed/2017/08/24/how-discwoman-is-diversifying-electronic-music/?sh=4eb78e3761a1.

Robertson, Carol E. "Power and Gender in the Musical Experiences of Women." In *Women and Music in Cross-Cultural Perspective*, edited by Ellen Koskoff, 225–44. Champaign: University of Illinois Press, 1987.

Rodgers, Tara. *Pink Noises: Women on Electronic Music and Sound.* Durham: Duke University Press, 2010.

Romano, Tricia. "Women Edging their Way into the DJ Booth." *New York Times*, November 1, 2013. https://www.nytimes.com/2013/11/03/arts/music/women-edging-their-way-into-the-dj-booth.html.

Room 4 Resistance, https://room4resistance.net/.

Rouget, Gilbert. *Music and Trance: A Theory of the Relations Between Music and Possession*, translated by Brunhilde Biebuyck and Gilbert Rouget. Chicago: University of Chicago Press, 1985.

Saldanha, Arun. "The Ghost of Goa Trance: A Retrospective." In *The Local Scenes and Global Cultures of Psytrance*, edited by Graham St. John, 55–65. New York: Routledge, 2010.

Saldanha, Arun. *Psychedelic White: Goa Trance and the Viscosity of Race*. Minneapolis: University of Minnesota Press, 2007.

Salimpoor, Valorie N., Mitchel Benovoy, Kevin Larcher, Alain Dagher, and Robert J. Zatorre. "Anatomically Distinct Dopamine Release During Anticipation and

Experience of Peak Emotion to Music." *Nature Neuroscience* 14, no. 2 (February 2011): 257–62.

Salkind, Micah E. *Do You Remember House?: Chicago's Queer of Color Undergrounds.* Oxford: Oxford University Press, 2019.

Schmidt, Bryan. "Boutiquing at the Raindance Campout: Relational Aesthetics as Festival Technology." *Dancecult: Journal of Electronic Dance Music Culture* 7, no. 1 (June 2015): 35–54.

Schmidt, Joshua I. "(En)Countering the Beat: Paradox in Israeli Psytrance." In *The Local and Global Cultures of Psytrance*, edited by Graham St. John, 131–48. New York: Routledge, 2010.

Schwencke, Morten, and Harald Stolt-Nielsen. "Derfor frikjennes Gaute Drevdal for åtte voldtekter." *Aftenposten*, January 28, 2022. https://www.aftenposten.no/norge/i/lVL6v9/derfor-frikjennes-gaute-drevdal-for-aatte-voldtekter.

Sellers, Rod. "Chicago's Southeast Side Industrial History." *Southeast Historical Society*, March 2006.

Shapiro, Harry. *Waiting for the Man: The Story of Drugs and Popular Music.* London: Helter Skelter Publishing, 2006.

Shapiro, Peter, ed., *Modulations: A History of Electronic Music: Throbbing Words on Sound.* New York: Capirinha Productions, 2000.

Shaw, Robert. *The Nocturnal City.* London: Routledge, 2018.

Sicko, Dan. *Techno Rebels: The Renegades of Electronic Funk.* New York: Billboard, 1999.

Slettebak, Marie H. "Labour Migration and Increasing Inequality in Norway." *Acta Sociologica* 64, no. 3 (August 2021): 314–30.

Smith, Alexandra. "Sydney's Final Lockout Laws Axed to Revive CBD." *Sydney Morning Herald*, February 9, 2021. https://www.smh.com.au/politics/nsw/sydney-s-final-lockout-laws-axed-to-revive-cbd 20210208-p570nf.html.

Smith, Kevin. "Kevin Smith Response to David Trigger." *The Australian Journal of Anthropology* 31, no. 1 (April 2020): 31–3.

Sound Diplomacy. "About Us." 2022. https://www.sounddiplomacy.com/about.

Sound Diplomacy and Andreina Seijas. "A Guide to Managing Your Night Time Economy." London: Sound Diplomacy, 2017.

St. John, Graham. "Civilised Tribalism: Burning Man, Event-Tribes and Maker Culture." *Cultural Sociology* 12, no. 1 (March 2018): 1–19.

St. John, Graham. "Liminal Being: Electronic Dance Music Cultures, Ritualization and the Case of Psytrance." In *The Sage Handbook of Popular Music*, edited by Andy Bennett and Steve Waksman, 253–60. London: Sage, 2015.

St. John, Graham. "Total Solar Eclipse Festivals, Cosmic Pilgrims and Planetary Culture." In *Pop Pagans: Paganism and Popular Music*, edited by Donna Weston and Andy Bennett, 126–44. London and New York: Routledge, 2013.

St. John, Graham. "The Vibe of the Exiles: Aliens, Afropsychedelia and Psyculture." *Dancecult: Journal of Electronic Dance Music Culture* 5, no. 2 (November 2013): 56–87.

St. John, Graham. "Aliens Are Us: Cosmic Liminality, Remixticism, and Alienation in Psytrance." *Journal of Religion and Popular Culture* 25, no. 2 (Summer 2013): 186–204.

St. John, Graham. "Seasoned Exodus: The Exile Mosaic of Psyculture." *Dancecult: Journal of Electronic Dance Music Culture* 4, no. 1 (May, 2012): 4–37.

St. John, Graham. *Global Tribe: Technology, Spirituality and Psytrance*. Sheffield: Equinox, 2012.

St. John, Graham. *Technomad: Global Raving Countercultures*. London: Equinox, 2009.

Statistics Norway. "Gender-Divided Labour Market." December 18, 2017. https://www.ssb.no/en/befolkning/artikler-og-publikasjoner/gender-divided-labour-market.

Statistics Norway, "Facts About Immigration: Earnings." 2021. https://www.ssb.no/en/statbank/table/12525/tableViewLayout1/.

Stenhamar, Halldis (Hast). "Kvinnelige studenter gjennem 50 år—jubileumsboken er ferdig." *Dagbladet*, February 25, 1932, 1, 3.

Stetka, Bret. "What Do Great Musicians Have in Common? DNA." *Scientific American* 5 (August 2014). https://www.scientificamerican.com/article/what-do-great-musicians-have-in-common-dna/.

Stirling, Christabel. "Gendered Publics and Creative Practices in Electronic Dance Music." *Contemporary Music Review* 35, no. 1 (July 2016): 130–49.

Stortinget. "Article 98." *The Constitution*, as Laid Down on 17 May 1814 by the Constituent Assembly at Eidsvoll and Subsequently Amended, Most Recently in May 2016. https://www.stortinget.no/globalassets/pdf/english/constitutionenglish.pdf.

Stortinget. "Komiteens tilråding om endring av juridisk kjønn." May 30, 2016. https://www.stortinget.no/no/Saker-og-publikasjoner/Saker/Sak/Voteringsoversikt/?p=64488&dnid=1#id=7357&view=vote-text.

Strauss, Matthew. "Berlin Declared High Culture Venue by Berlin Court." *Pitchfork*, September 12, 2016. https://pitchfork.com/news/68211-berghain-declared-high-culture-venue-by-berlin-court/.

Straw, Will. "Media and the Urban Night." *Articulo: Journal of Urban Research* 11 (2015). https://journals.openedition.org/articulo/3098.

Straw, Will. "Sizing Up Record Collections: Gender and Connoisseurship in Rock Music Culture." In *Sexing the Groove: Popular Music and Gender* edited by Sheila Whiteley, 3–16. London: Routledge, 1997.

Straw, Will. "Systems of Articulation, Logics of Change: Communities and Scenes in Popular Music." *Cultural Studies* 5, no. 3 (1991): 368–88.

Straw, Will, and Collaborators. *The Urban Night: An Interdisciplinary Research Project on Cities and the Night*. Last updated May 13, 2022. https://theurbannight.com/night-studies-publications-by-will-straw/.

Strong, Catherine. "Towards a Feminist History of Popular Music: Re-Examining Writing on Musicians and Domestic Violence in the Wake of #MeToo." In *Remembering Popular Music's Past: Memory-Heritage-History*, edited by Lauren Istvandity, Sarah Baker, and Zelmarie Cantillon, 156–65. London: Anthem Press, 2019.

Strong, Catherine, Shane Homan, Seamus O'Hanlon, and John Tebbutt. "Uneasy Alliances: Popular Music and Cultural Policy in the 'Music City.'" In *Routledge Handbook of Global Cultural Policy*, edited by Victoria Durrer, Toby Miller, and Dave O'Brien, 468–81. London: Routledge, 2018.

Suarez-Villa, Luis. *Technocapitalism: A Critical Perspective on Technological Innovation and Corporatism*. Philadelphia: Temple University Press, 2009.

Teigen, Mari. "Gender Quotas on Corporate Boards." In *Gender and Power in the Nordic Countries*, edited by Kirsti Niskanen, 87–109. Oslo: NIKK, 2011.

Teigen, Mari, and Lena Wängnerud. "Tracing Gender Equality Cultures: Elite Perceptions of Gender Equality in Norway and Sweden." *Politics & Gender* 5, no. 1 (March 2009): 21–44.

Théberge, Paul. "'Plugged In': Technology and Popular Music." In *Cambridge Companion to Pop and Rock*, edited by Simon Frith, Will Straw, and John Street, 3–25. Cambridge: Cambridge University Press, 2001.

Thommessen, Olemic. "Lovvedtak 71 (Første gangs behandling av lovvedtak)." May 30, 2015-6.

Thornton, Sarah. *Club Cultures: Music, Media and Subcultural Capital*. Cambridge: Polity Press, 1995.

Till, Rupert. "Paganism, Popular Music and Stonehenge." In *Pop Pagans: Paganism and Popular Music*, edited by Donna Weston and Andy Bennett, 24–42. London and New York: Routledge, 2013.

Times of India. "Honour Killings: More than 300 Cases in Last Three Years." September 22, 2018. https://timesofindia.indiatimes.com/india/honour-killings-more-than-300-cases-in-last-three-years/articleshow/65908947.cms.

Torvanger Solberg, Ragnhild. "Waiting for the Bass to Drop: Correlations Between Intense Emotional Experiences and Production Techniques in Build-Up and Drop Sections of Electronic Dance Music." *Dancecult: Journal of Electronic Dance Music Culture* 6, no. 1 (June 2016): 61–82.

Torvanger Solberg, Ragnhild, and Nicola Dibben. "Peak Experiences with Electronic Dance Music: Subjective Experiences, Physiological Responses, and Musical Characteristics of the Break Routine." *Music Perception* 36, no. 4 (April 2019): 371–89.

Trevarthen, Colwyn, Jonathan Delafield-Butt, and Benjamin Schögler. "Psychobiology of Musical Gesture: Innate Rhythm, Harmony and Melody in Movements of Narration." In *Music and Gesture II*, edited by Anthony Gritten and Elaine King, 11–43. Aldershot: Ashgate, 2011.

Tucker, Sherrie. *Dance Floor Democracy: The Social Geography of Memory at the Hollywood Canteen*. Durham and London: Duke University Press, 2014.

Turner, Fred. *From Counterculture to Cyberculture: Stewart Brand, The Whole Earth Network, and the Rise of Digital Utopianism*. Chicago: The University of Chicago Press, 2006.

Unicomb, Matt. "German Court Deems Berghain 'Cultural' Space Along with Theatres and Museums." Resident Advisor, September 13, 2016. https://ra.co/news/36363.

Vágnerová, Lucie. "Nimble Fingers in Electronic Music: Rethinking Sound Through Neo-Colonial Labour." *Organised Sound* 22, no. 2 (July 2017): 250–8.

van der Ros, Janneke. "The Norwegian State and Transgender Citizens: A Complicated Relationship." *World Political Science* 13, no. 1 (June 2017): 123–50.

van Veen, tobias c. "Vessels of Transfer: Allegories of Afrofuturism in Jeff Mills and Janelle Monae." *Dancecult: Journal of Electronic Dance Music Culture* 5, no. 2 (November 2013): 7–41.

van Veen, tobias c. "Technics, Precarity and Exodus in Rave Culture." *Dancecult: Journal of Electronic Dance Music Culture*, 1, no. 2 (2010): 29–49.

Watson, Sophie. "Cultures of Democracy: Spaces of Democratic Possibility." In *Spaces of Democracy: Geographical Perspectives on Citizenship, Participation and Representation*, edited by Clive Barnett and Murray Low, 207–22. London: Sage, 2004.

Weber, Max. *The Protestant Ethic and the Spirit of Capitalism*. New York: Charles Scribner's Sons, 1958.

Weber, William. "Mass Culture and the Reshaping of European Musical Taste, 1770–1870." *International Review of the Aesthetics and Sociology of Music* 8, no. 1 (June 1977): 5–22.

Weinberger, Norman M. "Musical Talent: Real or a Myth?" *MuSICA Research Notes* 8, no. 2: (2001).

Weiner, Sophie. "Can Teaching Young Women to DJ and Produce Solve Gender Equality in Electronic Music?" *Vice*, February 26, 2016. https://www.vice.com/en/article/bmajww/can-teaching-young-women-to-dj-and-produce-solve-gender-inequality-in-electronic-music.

Weisethaunet, Hans, and Ulf Lindberg. "Authenticity Revisited: The Rock Critic and the Changing Real." *Popular Music and Society* 33, no. 4 (August 2010): 465–85.

Weiss, Margot. "The Interlocutor Slot: Citing, Crediting, Cotheorizing, and the Problem of Ethnographic Expertise." *American Anthropologist* 123, no. 4 (December 2021): 948–53.

Westerhausen, Klaus. *Beyond the Beach: An Ethnography of Modern Travellers in Asia*. Bangkok: White Lotus Press, 2002.

Weston, Donna and Andy Bennett. "Towards a Definition of Pagan Music." In *Pop Pagans: Paganism and Popular Music*, edited by Donna Weston and Andy Bennett, 1–12. London and New York: Routledge, 2013.

Wilkinson, W. C. *The Dance of Modern Society*. New York: Oakley, Mason & Co., 1869).

Williams, Raymond. "Culture is Ordinary [1958]." In *Everyday Life Reader*, edited by Ben Highmore, 91–100. London: Routledge, 2002.

Williams, Sean. "Letter: Owner, City Also at Fault in Ghost Ship Tragedy." *East Bay Times*, December 13, 2017. https://www.eastbaytimes.com/2017/12/13/letter-owner-city-also-at-fault-in-ghost-ship-tragedy/.

Wilson, Elizabeth A. *Gut Feminism*. Durham and London: Duke University Press, 2015.

Wilson, Greg. "Nina Kraviz: The Mistress of Her Own Myth." *Greg Wilson: Being a DJ* (blog), April 8, 2013. https://blog.gregwilson.co.uk/2013/04/nina-kraviz-the-mistress-of-her-own-myth/.

Witek, Maria A. G. "Feeling at One: Socio-Affective Distribution, Vibe, and Dance-Music Consciousness." In *Music and Consciousness 2: Worlds, Practices, Modalities*, edited by Ruth Herbert, David Clarke, and Eric Clarke, 93–112. Oxford: Oxford University Press, 2019.

Witek, Maria A. G. "Filling In: Syncopation, Pleasure and Distributed Embodiment in Groove." *Music Analysis* 36, no. 1 (March 2017): 138–60.

Witek, Maria A. G., Tudor Popescu, Eric F. Clarke, Mads Hansen, Ivana Konvalinka, Morten L. Kringelbach, and Peter Vuust. "Syncopation Affects Free Body-Movement in Groove." *Experimental Brain Research* 235 (April 2017): 995–1005.

Woldsdal, Nicolay. "Øya får internasjonal oppmerksomhet for sin line-up." *Dagbladet*, July 7, 2015. http://www.dagbladet.no/2015/07/07/kultur/oya/musikk/festival/konsert/40013709/.

Yri, Kristin and Stephen C. Meyer, "Introduction." In *Oxford Handbook of Music and Medievalism*, edited by Kirsten Yri and Stephen C. Meyer, 1–13. New York: Oxford University Press, 2020.

"Berlin 2018." *Red Bull Music Academy*, 2019. https://www.redbullmusicacademy.com/about/projects/berlin-2018.

"Company: Giving Wings to People and Ideas." *Red Bull*, 2022. https://www.redbull.com/au-en/energydrink/company-profile.

"Full Moon Party Ko Phangan." Phanganist, 2018. Last updated 2022. https://phanganist.com/full-moon-party-koh-phangan.

"Red Bull Music Academy Lectures." *Red Bull Music Academy*, 2019. https://www.redbullmusicacademy.com.

"The History of the Full Moon Party with Manop." Phanganist, November 30, 2017. https://phanganist.com/somewhere-phangan-full-moon-party-culture-article/history-full-moon-party-manop.

"The Original Full Moon Party, Thailand." Full Moon Party. Last updated 2021. https://fullmoonparty-thailand.com/.

"We Run the World Female DJ Agency™." 2022. https://femaledjagency.co.uk/about-us/.

Index

Dance Music